Learning and Teaching Creative Cognition

Learning and Teaching Creative Cognition

The Interactive Book Report

Marjorie S. Schiering

ROWMAN & LITTLEFIELD
Lanham • Boulder • New York • London

Published by Rowman & Littlefield
A wholly owned subsidiary of The Rowman & Littlefield Publishing Group, Inc.
4501 Forbes Boulevard, Suite 200, Lanham, Maryland 20706
www.rowman.com

Unit A, Whitacre Mews, 26-34 Stannary Street, London SE11 4AB, United Kingdom

British Library Cataloguing in Publication Information Available

Library of Congress Cataloging-in-Publication Data Is Available

Schiering, Marjorie S., 1943–
Learning and teaching creative cognition : the interactive book report / Marjorie S. Schiering.
pages cm
Includes bibliographical references.
ISBN 978-1-4758-0778-3 (cloth : alk. paper) — ISBN 978-1-4758-0779-0 (pbk. : alk. paper) — ISBN 978-1-4758-0780-6 (electronic)
1. Creative teaching. 2. Creative ability—Study and teaching. 3. Creative thinking—Study and teaching. 4. Active learning. 5. Student-centered learning. I. Title.
LB1025.3.S298 2015
371.1—dc23
2015013041

∞ ™ The paper used in this publication meets the minimum requirements of American National Standard for Information Sciences Permanence of Paper for Printed Library Materials, ANSI/NISO Z39.48-1992.

Printed in the United States of America

I am not a teacher of how to be creative, but I am one who may lead you to discover your own creativity. I do this by sharing thoughts and ideas, presenting techniques, inspiring and motivating, expressing opinions, and collaborating. I do this without my own self or another having fear of repercussions. This is because, each of us, as we are, is enough.

—(Schiering, 1976)

Contents

Preface ix
Acknowledgments xiii
Introduction xvii

I: Part One **1**

1 Learning, Teaching, Thinking, and Creative Cognition 3
2 Linear and Reciprocal Processes of Creativity 11
3 Personal Perspectives on Creative Cognition 19
4 An Introduction: Creative Cognition's Interactive Methodology and Book Report 31
5 An Overview: IM and IBR 41
6 Advantage Points of the IBR and Leadership Building 51
7 A Guide to Learning and Teaching Creative Cognition 59
8 Creative Cognition with Special Needs Children: Linking Learning Styles, the IM, and the IBR 75
9 Learning and Teaching Creative Cognition: The IBR's Cognitive Collective: Thinking and Feeling 89
10 Learning and Teaching Creative Cognition: The IBR's Reciprocal Thinking Phases 97
11 Learning and Teaching Creative Cognition: The IBR's Reciprocal Feelings Phases 111
12 Using the IM and IBR: A Psychologist's Perspective 121
Audra Cerruto, PhD

II: Part Two **127**

13 Creative Cognition, Neuroplasticity, and IBR: A Scientist's Perspective | Mindfulness and Creativity 129
Harvey Sasken, MD | Michael Russo, PhD
14 IBR Pages and IBR Use as an Assessment Instrument 139
15 Differentiated Instruction and Activities for the IBR Pages 149
16 Differentiated Instruction with More Activities 167
17 Three Topics Including Effects and Affects of IM and IBR 183

III: Part Three **197**

18 The Proof of the Pudding: IM and IBR in Action 199
Patricia Mason, PhD | Lucia Sapienza

19 The Proof of the Pudding: Continued 207
Jennifer Botte | Amanda Lockwood | Audra Cerruto, PhD | Rickey Moroney

20 The Summation: A Research Study Involving the IM and IBR: Ecosystems and Sustainability 217

Afterword 231

Bibliography 233

About the Author 239

Preface

Whenever, whatever, and wherever we are, regardless of being alone or with a partner or group of people, learning is happening, reciprocally and simultaneously for those involved. One could say that learning is always taking place. If you *think* back to your childhood it took place most frequently when you were playing.

Back then as now, when formalized education began, decisions were made "for" instead of "by" the learner. This happened for teachers as well. That's because educational systems became more stringent and analytical. When something was to be done, how, and why with instructions was established as the mainstay.

So, what happened to *learning-through-play* was its replacement with structure and control; a very traditional instruction teaching methodology. This book goes back before that time and invites the reader to once again have learning be imaginative, creative, engaging, interactive, and exciting. This book's methodology and accompanying Interactive Book Report involves the learner teaching him or herself, or others through play.

Being a reflective practitioner you're asked, "What exactly did you play?" Answers may include: Let's play house, cars, shop, teacher, computer, and etc. You may feel free to put in the "etc." part by recalling what you played. Anyway, these play or role-play activities were also preparing and equipping each individual for future life experiences. Interestingly, looking at what we played there was only "one word" to the game. And yet, everyone knew the rules.

Those involved knew what was to be expected. An example might be how "cars" would be done and how long it would take to complete the playing; in time for lunch, dinner, someone's gymnastics class, or going shopping, or predetermined time to be at home. This even applied to video games as technological advances came along, or varied apps, iPad, or iPhone. Regardless, we played using our imaginations, and developed our creativity. The Interactive Method (IM) and Interactive Book Report (IBR) are definite imagination users and *creativity creators*.

What was once done by chance and happenstance during those preschool years of learning through play is presently, in this book, organized and synthesized. This IM "way-to-learn is effective for participants regardless of the setting, age, gender, ethnicity, cultural mores, or ability level" (Schiering, 2000).

When you create a self-corrective IBR, using the IM, you take ownership of what you have learned because you've created the learning and assessment device. This makes the learning more authentic and an experience that the learner remembers and incorporates into their existence going forward. The method and book are at the cutting edge of project- and performance-based teaching and learning to promote thinking and overall creative cognition. These are the major considerations of state and national learning standards.

What is most unique about *The Interactive Method of learning and teaching is that it has the power to remain in someone's thoughts and, while staying there, capture their imagination. Also, it's a natural experience.*

Another consideration of the thoroughness of this book's methodology is that it addresses all learners and those practicing it that either need to "*think to talk*" or "*talk to think*." And for those who require both of these, the methodology addresses that, as does the IBR. In a practical manner, it is a compilation and consolidation of interactive instructional resources on a specific topic which have been developed by the learners themselves.

The central idea of this book is similar to the concept of the book *What Do You Do With An Idea?* by Kobi Yamada. The theme is that a character gets an idea and that idea follows him or her around and soon the character takes ownership of the idea albeit reluctantly. The idea grows and when asking friends about it, the character finds the idea rejected, but continues on nonetheless. The idea is cared for and nurtured as it becomes bigger. The end of the book states the question about what one does with an idea and the answer refers to changing things.

The idea of the *Learning and Teaching Creative Cognition* . . . is to change or at least impact, for the betterment of learning, the educational world. This could also be at home and in places of formal academia, as well as places where social learning occurs. The idea of this book is to enhance imagination leading to creativity, and to know what thinking is involved to accomplish that. The summative idea of this book relates that "*Direct experience through play on a particular topic not only enhances memory and the cognitive functions associated with memory, but also can be considered empowering. And, this happens independently of the condition of the learner, whether they are impaired or not impaired, from one country or another*" (Schiering, 2014, pp. 56–59).

BOOK'S AUDIENCE

This book is for you! And, it's for all those students who wrote to relate, as years went by, how the learning-through-play experience impacted their lives in a positive manner. It's also for all those who didn't write, but expressed, verbally, about how the creativity involved in the IM and

IBR was being part of "who one is" as naturally as awakening in the morning. And, it's for all those who want to develop learning situations that engage the individual, as well as whole groups, in appreciating the wonderment of discovery, the mind's ability to imagine, to create, and to think effectively and identify thinking skills "in-play." Doing thus equates this book's contents with being of primary benefit to best practice when teaching and learning at any grade level: elementary, middle, high school, or college and beyond.

AUTHOR'S PHILOSOPHY AND BOOK INFORMATION

Teaching and learning are reciprocal processes. What we learn becomes who we are and influences how we conduct ourselves and think about ourselves. Learning-through-play/interactive and collaborative means of instruction are the most engaging and enjoyable ways to learn. This Interactive Method (IM) assures retention of information, because of personal involvement, while enhancing thinking skills and stimulating individuals' imagination for creativity implementation.

This book is written as if its author is having a conversation with you, the reader. The reasoning for this style of delivery is incumbent in the author's philosophy that being what we think and feel becomes what we say and do. Subsequently, our lives are very large conversations, in general.

Questions are asked and you're invited to share answers with others to expand your knowledge about how others think and feel, which influences your learning regularly. Sometimes you're asked to just form ideas or respond silently to ones put forth, or to try them for yourself, before moving forward and sharing or creating. Nonetheless, the book is written to engage you in knowing about your thinking and to grow and go with that awareness.

Acknowledgments

I would like to give recognition to those learners and teachers who have been part of my career and who have been involved in creative cognition. It is these persons, nearly 3,000 in total, who asked me over the past forty-plus years to write a book about the learning and teaching method I refer to as IM (Interactive Method), which involves, primarily, creative cognition. Then there were those who asked me, over the past twenty-plus years, to write about the IM's accompanying Interactive Book Report (IBR) involving educational gaming. The reason I think they asked me to do this was because the classes we shared at the elementary, middle school, and college levels were ones where there was acceptance of one another. This acceptance was regardless of so many different ways we were classified by society regarding learning processes or behaviorism.

From 2002 the IM and IBR, along with the principles of building a positive classroom community, have been presented in Hull and Surrey England; at the divisions of education at the Universities of Oslo, Bergen, and Telemark in Norway; at the teacher centers of Asker, Nessodden, and Skien in Norway; at Queen's College in Belfast, Ireland; at the universities of Antwerp and Vlerick Leuven Management School in Ghent, Belgium; as well as at colleges or universities in Buffalo, New York; Tbilisi in the Republic of Georgia; Billund, Denmark; Molloy College on Long Island, New York; and the New York City region; at the Senior Citizen Complex in Columbus, Ohio; and at the Columbus School in Medellin, Colombia, South America. The success of these presentations gives credence to the concept that there is a wide audience for this book, both internationally and within the United States.

Acknowledgment is given with special attention to Dr. Allen Rauch. He was a colleague for ten years at Molloy and we traveled to some of the aforementioned places to do conference presentations. We presented on the topics of cognition and metacognition and the link to scientific discrepant events, creative cognition, and character development. Allen was a continual inspiration for me because of his positivity and belief in life lessons focused on "living-in-the-moment," but also looking to the future. He was always present to lend a helping "organizational" hand, be a friend, and care most deeply about the education of others, such that it was found engaging and worthwhile.

Dr. Rita Dunn who gave me verification of my teaching methodology with the Dunn and Dunn Learning Style Model is acknowledged. Her writing and constant encouragement shaped my desire to be published. Her support was steadfast. She jokingly or perhaps not-so-jokingly referred to me as a late bloomer and one who practiced learning styles before she invented it. Both Allen and Rita are missed.

Applying for a sabbatical to have the time to write this book steadfastly and continually requires my appreciation to Nikki Ceo, acting Associate Dean of Academic Affairs, who helped me with my original book proposal; Maureen Walsh, Dean of the Division of Education at Molloy College, who spent time reading the proposal and editing it for its submission to the Sabbatical Committee. Then there's Valerie Collins, vice president of Molloy, and the Sabbatical Committee who approved my having this time away from my classes to write.

Those who wrote extensive narratives or made personal statements are sincerely thanked. One such person is a lifetime friend, Joan Byrne; she's mentioned, as a trip to her Colorado home found us collaborating on the linear process of creativity. Then there are the fifth graders from PS 188 in Queens, student learners of Jennifer Botte. There are many hundreds, perhaps at this point, thousands of other student learners who made IBRs and/or involved themselves in the methodology of this book. They did this by practicing creative cognition from the start of my career to the present time. Additionally, there are the fourteen persons who wrote or spoke about their creative process in chapter 4.

A large thank you is given to all those teacher candidates and student learners who gave permission to be videotaped presenting their IBRs and who agreed to be on the Creative Cognition IBR Website. Also acknowledged are three additional persons who were assistive in the writing of this book. They are Drew Bogner, James Million, and Anthony Marino. The first of these aforementioned persons is president of Molloy College and is acknowledged for contributions regarding the "voice" of a book, and suggesting the asking of questions within the text to stimulate conversations among the readers. The second person is acknowledged for his support and initial outlining of this manuscript. His dedication to phone conversations about the book's content, as well as arranging and rearranging the organization of chapters proved to be very exacting. He willingly gave of his time and exceptional expertise as a researcher on thinking and feelings.

Anthony Marino, EdD, is acknowledged as a 2000 teacher candidate who was continually interested in the IM and the IBR. As he furthered his research on learning and teaching and stayed in touch over these past fifteen years, he contributed to portions of this book. In so doing, he became a colleague. I have had the privilege of presenting in Europe with him on the core message of this book. Anthony not only contributed to *Creative Cognition* but deserves a special appreciation for his assistance in several portions of this book including the graphic design of *The Reciprocal Creative Cognition Process*, and for his technical savvy, which was applied freely and for numerous hours. His continual interest became an invaluable asset to the book's being written.

Robert Kinpoitner, PhD, is appreciated for reading the original manuscript and being a superlative grammarian. Joining in a first reading of the book or portions thereof were Drs. Joanne O'Brien and Barbara Hayes. Those recognized for reading the entire manuscript for scope and sequence and offering their edification suggestions, shortly before the manuscript going to the publisher are: Drs. Robert Kinpoitner, Eve Dieringer, Barbara Hayes, Vicky Giouroukakis, and Audra Cerruto. Others joining in this endeavor were Joan Byrne and Jan Tacoronti, former teacher of the gifted in Colorado, and New York State mental health care specialist, respectively.

Over the years of my career I spent a good portion of my teaching in the North Rockland Central School District. My last ten years there were at the Stony Point Elementary School. When there the principals were Ted Lindenberg and then Diane Bane. The third through fifth grades who participated in student council and also those in Schiering's fifth grade class practiced the interactive method of learning and teaching others, as well as one's self. In 1998 and 1999 the student learners in my fifth grade class made IBRs and entered them in the NYS Earth Day Competition. They came in second and first place respectively, and contributed to the furtherance of the IM and IBR during my college teaching career. The cooperation of teachers and students alike from Stony Point Elementary School is sincerely acknowledged. Their contribution to the overall philosophy of this book was encouraged by their participation in learning-through-play. The support of the two aforementioned principals who were present at that time is noted.

ADDITIONAL ACKNOWLEDGMENTS

Heartfelt appreciation is extended to my husband, George, who has listened to and commented on my thoughts, ideas, opinions, and feelings regarding this book endeavor over the past year. And, as one is his or her experiential past that affects the present and future, the following persons are also given credit with respect to the writing of this book: my children and their significant others, Matthew and Maddy; Alyssha and Paul; Joshua and fiancée Katie; Jolie; Mara and Dave; and Seth and Carolina; my brother, Ed After and his wife Joan; my nephew Jon Borkum; and my parents, Mollie and Red After.

Daisy Schneider is acknowledged as she served as my mom's helper from the time I was three years old into my teens. She was steadfastly an encouraging person. Mr. Bailent, principal of the first inner-city elementary school in which I taught in Columbus, Ohio, is acknowledged and so are all the students who, during my career, showed me we never stop learning and teaching, simultaneously. Then there is appreciation for my tenth grade social studies teacher, Miss Charragher, who taught me that telling someone "I believe in you" may well serve as the catalyst for respecting oneself and having the courage to go forward in one's studies.

Diane Fornieri is given acknowledgment for her help with the *Teaching and Learning: A Model for Academic and Social Cognition* book from 2011.

Special Acknowledgment: The author of this book offers a special acknowledgment, gratitude, and appreciation to Mrs. Eileen Chapman, assistant to the associate dean. The transcribing of the book's content—addressing photocopying, corrections to text structure, formatting, and a myriad of other activities involved in compiling this manuscript over an extensive time period—would not have been a reality without her dedication to the overall endeavor. A thank you hardly seems adequate considering Eileen's expertise-applications, as well as her attention and allegiance to this project.

Introduction

Does anything "new" exist in teaching or learning? In 2015 it would seem doubtful. What with the stringency of state mandated tests at most grade levels, oftentimes the "how" of presenting curriculum gets lost in the mille of assessments. Fundamentally, this book deals with a means for presenting material that is, for the learner and teacher, exciting, enthralling, cognitively stimulating, and engaging. This is because of the emphasis on "creativity" development and application through the use of the Interactive Method (IM) and Interactive Book Report (IBR) for increasing one's basic awareness, critical thinking, and metacognitive processes.

This book is not just for new teachers, or teacher candidates, but tenured educators, parents, and student learners as well. It's a *melding* of techniques. These are designed to address project-, evidence-, and performance-based instruction that fully engages the learner and teacher. This is instruction that establishes retention of presented material for later recalling and reflecting that may be used to create yet another and another set of thoughts, opinions, or ideas. The method may be used daily or at different times during the year. The IM may be used at any time and the IBR may be used to learn and/or have one teach him or herself a thematic unit in the curriculum or to review literature, to name just two applications.

Each of us, regardless of the title "teacher," is part of teaching and learning through daily experiences. As this process occurs each of us becomes the present and future caretakers of those we encounter. It matters not whether you are four or ten, twenty, thirty, forty, or more years beyond that. Each of us is always involved in learning and teaching ourselves or others through examples and experiences.

Robert Frost in the poem "The Road Not Taken" references two roads diverging in a yellow wooded area. He explains that making a decision about which road to take was particularly difficult. One may wonder why? It would be because one road had been lesser traveled by others while the other was worn and obviously traversed. At poem's end, the first road, for this sojourner, was "kept for another day." Reflection causes one to project that the return to this forested place and choosing differently was doubtful. It is questioned, "How many of us actually go back to the beginning and travel a different path?"

So it is with educators, or all of us; the paths or roads chosen often appear the same or similar. Any differences are probably minute. If you've not incorporated creative interactive instruction into your learning and/or teaching methodology, this book challenges you to do that. If you have, you're asked to hone that skill. Implement the IM and IBR for providing learners the chance to teach themselves, build a sharing community, increase cognition and creative cognition, simultaneously, and hold conversations to increase everyone's knowledge base. This learning/teaching path is open to you. And, you are encouraged to travel it.

I

Part One

ONE

Learning, Teaching, Thinking, and Creative Cognition

CHAPTER OVERVIEW

Have you ever wondered what it means to be creative? Is there an exact definition for everyone being creative or having creative cognition? What about learning and teaching? Are they exclusive from one another? What about the effectiveness of these two? This chapter explores the answer to each of those questions. It also addresses the beginning of creativity with an example and commentary from two persons. Then, Journal and/or Discussion Questions are provided. As you think creativity and creatively, read on . . .

DEFINING TEACHING

This is a pretty broad topic to address, because it's not just for those titled "teacher" by going to college and getting that "education" degree. There's teaching through example, such as in a job you do that another observes and learns from that observation. There's formalized teaching that relies on a curriculum mandated by the state or nation, possibly a school district.

Teaching is the act of passing on information for learning and this may be accomplished in a variety of ways. It may be exemplified by the style of delivery and attention to learners' needs that one uses on a regular basis. These include the interactions of students and teacher with respect to methods used and techniques employed for learning. Defining formalized teaching is not a one-step explanation, but a set of circumstances that employ the wholeness of social and academic literacy with one person, the one titled "educator" being the guide.

So, there is not just one way to teach, any more than teaching is exclusive to the classroom. Often in a classroom there is a particular method favored by educators, schools, or entire systems. This method becomes the one predominately used and therefore it seems that it is "the only one." However, as we process information differently, so too there may be more than one method used to instruct.

You're asked to take a moment now and have a discussion with another about what you found memorable or satisfying during a day you recently experienced. If there's no one around, you're asked to make a list of these memories, and save the conversation for another time. Here are some starting questions to help you address the things you found worth noting during a recent learning or teaching happenstance. Why do you suppose it stands out in your thoughts? Was it experienced with the use of a textbook, through example, or demonstration? Which method was most interesting? Why do you suppose that was the case? What do you recall learning? Was it the same as what was being taught? Was there a subliminal message to the teaching/learning experience? If so, what was it?

DEFINING LEARNING

Overall, learning is the process of linking comprehension or understanding of what's to be taken into cognitive/thinking processes. This is done by developing skills that are genuinely transferable to everyday situations. "Learning is connected to reflective intelligence and affected by self-awareness, beliefs about one's abilities, clarity and strength of learning goals, personal expectations, and motivation to know about things" (Abbott, 1994).

TEACHING AND LEARNING: EXCLUSIVITY AND EFFECTIVENESS

In the introduction to this book, it was stated that teaching and learning are not exclusive to those who are formalized educators. "Teaching is a facilitation of learning," as Haugsbakk and Nordkvelle (2007) stated. By that standard, anyone may be a teacher and/or recipient of information that's taken in through life experiences.

What makes teaching effective for learning is teacher *modeling*. Modeling refers to the demonstration or setting of an example by the teacher. When the students emulate the modeling, there's an ongoing reciprocity between students and teachers. This book presents an Interactive Methodology (IM) for effective learning and teaching. Knowing you have a large cache of creative methods, one sees the IM and IBRs as a wonderful extension to this arsenal.

DEFINING THINKING

Thinking is surely part of learning and teaching, and these definitions have been provided prior to this section. What you think will affect what is learned and vice versa. Thinking is cognition and comes in three forms. "First is basic awareness, then critical and creative thinking is connected to higher-order thinking, which is called metacognition" (Schiering, 1999). Several years ago Schiering and Bogner (2007) examined the definition of thinking by categorizing it into four common areas. These are provided now with a simplified explanation of each one. In chapter 9 each definition is expanded and given with an example. Feelings are also given attention. The four categories of thinking are:

1. Thoughts: Immediate conscious responses to reflection, which involve memory.
2. Ideas: A prediction of future responses or speculation based on one's perspective as a result of reflection.
3. Opinions: A combination of thoughts and ideas in that a formulated concept results.
4. Judgments: Concretized thoughts, ideas, and opinions which are impacted by memory, while being based on reflection concerning past experiences.

EXPLAINING AND DEFINING CREATIVITY: CREATIVE COGNITION

Synonyms for the word "creative" explode from the computer's thesaurus with words like "original, imaginative, inspired, artistic, inventive, resourceful, ingenious, innovative, and productive" listed. These are cognitive or thinking skills that one needs to convey the simple definition of just one word! Confusion may follow, as each word does have a meaning of its own. However, cognition/thinking-development, in terms of one's being "creative," revolves around using imagination and being inventive in varied ways.

This process of creativity, in turn, requires reflecting on what one is thinking—metacognition. Creativity may be looked at as an aspect of personality that is characterized by novel and appropriate ideas and processes. The idea of teaching through the use of applying interactive instructional techniques, a system of teaching referred to in this book as an Interactive Methodology (IM) and the product addressed as the Interactive Book Report (IBR), allows for this application of inventive differentiated thinking in abundance. Linda Neiman (2012), founder of Creativity at Work, a consulting, coaching, and training alliance, says that creativity is the act of turning new and imaginative ideas into reality and involves thinking and producing. "If you have ideas and don't act on them, then you are imaginative, but not creative," she states.

Creativity involves all individuals, whether teachers or students, at any age or grade level. It applies to most fields of work or play. It may be located in one's home, in a group setting, or pretty much anywhere at any time. Creativity is "A defining force in the shaping of identity as there's a person's drive to be different and special. Psychologists define this facet of personality as the need for uniqueness. Levels of creativity or such areas help to establish one's identity through this uniqueness" (*Scientific American Mind*, March/April 2014). In one way or another, we are all unique, and so let's examine this uniqueness in a general context and then move to specifics. In order to do this examination, one must know that creative cognition is thinking that's creative, as cognition is a synonym for thinking.

"Creative Cognition is Creative Thinking" (Schiering, 2012)

CREATIVE COGNITION

Creative cognition is exhibited by an individual's thinking resulting in a new idea—the ability to manipulate humor to design a joke, artistic or literary work, painting or technological innovation—which has been accomplished in an original manner. You may question if this new thing must have the components of an actual object . . . something materialistic that has been produced? The answer I would think is that creativity is represented by an idea as much as something to manipulate. The key factor is that what has been created has not been present anywhere, previously.

> One is actively, mentally, and/or physically involved in cognitive processes that include all varieties of cognitive and metacognitive/higher-order thinking skills. It's when one actually does what he/she has imagined and designed, or uses this creation for physically or mentally designing something that hasn't been presented that creativity is exhibited. The going forth and "doing" the creation is the highest metacognitive process (Schiering, 1999).

> *"The ideas may come from varied media formats or be displayed that way. Nonetheless, this new thing that has been realized is just that, new. Not just new to you, but new in general. One's imagination made it possible to exist in the empirical, heuristic, experience-based realm"* (Schiering, 2011).

CREATIVE METACOGNITION IS HIGHER-ORDER CREATIVE THINKING

Creative metacognition is higher-order thinking that is original, inventive, resourceful, and rather ingenious. And it involves some of these metacognitive skills: organization, evaluation, advanced decision-making and problem-solving, reflection, and self-actualization. These skills are evidenced when designing and making interactive instructional resources for an IBR.

THE BEGINNING OF CREATIVITY

When do you suppose one begins being imaginative? Did this start in school or at home before formal education commenced? In all likelihood, the imagination that led to creativity began when you were very young. "The first way we learn as babies and children is through 'play' (gaming), which can be and often is creative and imaginative" (Schiering, 2000).

Do you remember what you played as a child? Do you remember inviting someone over to your house or being invited for a play-date and what would be "played"? Make a list and share this with someone. When discussing this topic, here's what a few colleagues, elementary school children, and college students recently recalled about "playing" before and shortly after formalized education began: "I remember playing dolls, cars, store, school, teacher, detective, dance, hide-and-go-seek, tag, video games, cell phone apps, raceway, storytelling, telephone, and house."

Looking at this short list, one can readily observe the introduction of technology and yet even many of those "newer" ways of playing involved interaction and innovation. Basically, the invitation to come-over-and-play involved only "one" word to describe the activity. Example: "How about coming over and playing 'house' tomorrow?" Anyone invited to play "house" instantly knew what that entailed, what it looked like, the order it'd be in, probable feelings one would have while playing, the general amount of time it'd take to play that, and the sequence of events one could anticipate, as well as the actions to be taken in order to "create" the play. Interesting, isn't it?

"The beginning learning-through-play involves exploration while it takes place. This is the reality of a small child's putting an object in his/her mouth to study, scrutinize, or inspect it. The exploration is investigating the process where one determines if this experience feels good or isn't quite right. A marshmallow certainly tastes and feels different from a toy car on the floor that's picked up and placed in the mouth. And yet, these early trial and error experiences serve as the forerunner for creativity, as memories formed and were brought into imagining for later creation or 'play'" (Schiering, 2000, EDU.506A).

These beginning explorations were followed by "play" or "role-play" activities, which prepared and equipped each of us involved for future life experiences! They did, as they influenced recollections to be used later for more pretend time or, better yet, a real-life situation. "Most importantly, keep in mind that everyone is creative" (Schiering, 2000).

Anthony Romano (2013), a graduate teacher-candidate at Molloy College, writes, "When I was younger, after reading a book or seeing a movie I would immediately want to act out the characters and the plot. I think a lot of children engage in imaginative play this way. They use the medium given to them as a guide to 'create' their own adventures."

As R. Moroney (2013) relates, "Remember that when one creates (produces, performs, or presents) he/she takes possession of what has been learned. This makes one's learning more authentic and an experience that is taken for future reference and sometimes incorporated into new projects."

ONE EXAMPLE: THE PROCESS OF CREATIVITY

Is there a process of creativity? Businessman by day and guitarist, lyricist, and composer during his "spare" time, Matthew Schiering reflected when asked about how he began creating tunes with rhyming poetry-fashioned stanzas. He offered this explanation: "I was taking guitar lessons for a few years starting at age nine. My first song was written when I was twelve. I thought of the music—a melody; that's what came to mind. This was followed by, if there is a solid progression, notes that complemented each other, then mood, and tempo. I started playing with it, musically, trying grouping of chords and notes and then another set of these: experimenting, deciding, movement within and between ideas; a back and forth.

A mental image formed with addressing of bridges between sections and a chorus. The music led the refrains/lyrics. Real events inspired my first song, which was about the death of John Lennon. The words that came to mind were:

> He was a man of peace. He enlightened us with song.
> Although he may be gone, John's spirit still lives on
> And if we all pull together we may achieve his dream
> Of all men living together unified and free. (M. R. Schiering, 1981)

Interestingly, Matt didn't share his songwriting for nearly a year and did so, he explained, "only to show my mom that the money spent on guitar lessons paid off." When asked what he thought about his talent, he responded with, "It's okay. I compare myself to others more talented. My family thinks I'm fantastic and should go forth with my music and have it published, but the real thing for me is the creating of it, playing it for friends and family, bringing it to those who I know will enjoy it without any question of whether it's good or not. Inside I know my music will be extraordinary to them."

Thinking about what Matt shared and in statements by Anthony a few paragraphs earlier, one sees that there is this period of "reflection," which easily leads one to believe that being creative stems from mental images. These images are stimulated by real events or just happenstance mixed in with that. And that word "image" is part of imagination. So, one cognizing/thinking about an image or images possibly allows for memories to be brought forth through visualizations. This process of image-making leads to more imaginations, by supposing that image one way and then another.

JOURNAL AND/OR DISCUSSION QUESTIONS

1. What's your definition of learning?
2. How would you categorize teaching?
3. What are four forms of thinking and the explanation of each of these?
4. What was explained as the beginning of creativity?
5. What was your reaction to the creative process expressed about Matt's songwriting?

TWO

Linear and Reciprocal Processes of Creativity

CHAPTER OVERVIEW

This chapter presents two new concepts illustrated in graphic organizers addressing linear and reciprocal processes of creativity. Each illustration is explained in a narrative. Sixteen Creativity Viewpoints are presented in bulleted format and this is followed by a section titled: Essential Creative Dispositions with four explained. The chapter closes with journaling and/or discussion questions for review of material presented.

LINEAR AND RECIPROCAL PROCESSES OF CREATIVITY

Think about, for example, the creative drawing of a tree. How do you imagine this image or how-it-looks idea? Is it tall and lean, short and/or broken, with leaves or without, does it have needles, where is it located, is it resting against others that look similar/dissimilar, or is it standing alone? In my mind, I create that image and then, when I go to do the drawing, I have made decisions as to how this object will look on paper. When I have actually done the drawing, I have completed the process of creativity, because I fabricated or produced the drawing.

With this explanation about the tree drawing, it's observable that the process of creativity may be done in a linear fashion. In that case the thinking is sequential and progressively orderly. There is no going back and forth, but a movement from one component to another. The following figure 2.1 shows the terms or cognitive functions associated with creative processes/stages as follows: 1) image(s) and/or ideas/conceptualizations lead to 2) imagining(s), 3) bringing forth memories; 4) visualizing and discerning these impact on 5) a sensory response or trigger which would lead to 6) inventions, and 7) decision-making/critiquing the creative idea, which leads to 8) problem-solving that culminates with 9) creating as the "final" stage. This creative way of thinking is called *The Linear Creative Cognition Process*. This process moves in a steady flow from beginning to end of creating. Subsequently, the Linear Process moves sequentially from one thought to another, going from the initial image or idea to the follow-through of creating" (Schiering & Byrne, 2013).

Images/Ideas➔ Imaginations➔ Bringing-forth Memories➔

Visualizations ➔ and discernment ➔ Sensory responses➔

Inventions ➔ Decision-making and➔ Critiquing➔

Modifications➔ Problem Solving ➔ Creating

Figure 2.1. The Creative Process: Linear Design (Schiering & Byrne, 2013)

When reviewing the flow of the Linear Creative Cognition Process, as seen in figure 2.1, and reflecting on the creating of a tree drawing, it's conceivable that the actual drawing may or may not go along with how it was originally planned or envisioned. Therefore, when creativity is occurring it may be subject to change and may not be sequential, as shown in figure 2.1.

Then again there may be a back-and-forth between each of the numbered Linear Creative Cognition Process stages. Subsequently, as with most things we experience, there is "reciprocity" within and between these ways of thinking creatively, or otherwise. Furthermore, there may be additional thinking skills, such as persistence and modifications being made as one is involved in creating. When modifications are addressed, this is usually for verifying one's creation and then possibly changing it from the original idea. The main point is that there is no specific order for the creativity, other than beginning with one's ideas. Schiering, explaining the back and forth of creative processes, resulted in Marino designing figure 2.2: The Reciprocal Creative Cognition Process.

You are asked to observe the give-and-take on the inside and outside of the figure 2.2, represented by double-sided arrows. It is observable that there is no specific order, but a random movement back and forth.

CREATIVITY VIEWPOINTS

- Rollo May, an influential existential psychologist, defines creativity in his book, *Courage to Create* (1975), as a process of bringing something new into being; creativity requires passion and commitment.

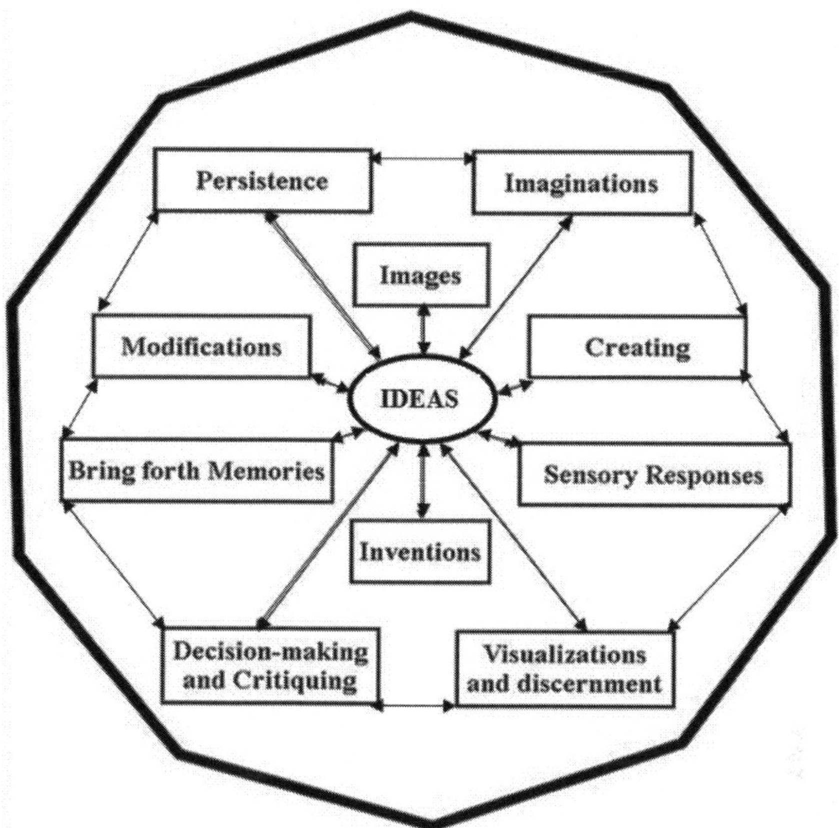

Figure 2.2. The Reciprocal Creative Cognition Process

- James Million (2010), psychosocial drama cocreator, addressed creativity in a *Brain World* magazine article as "the ability to jump from one thought/feeling pool to the other, 'freely,' unencumbered by doctrine or ideas of others, but yet influenced by what has been read, observed, and/or experienced."
- In the early 2000s, Daniel Pink, at the International Center for Studies in Creativity at Buffalo State University, wrote in *A Whole New Mind* that creativity involves artistry, empathy, and emotion.
- Most simply stated "creativity" involves the use of one's imagination, which involves one's "thinking," in order to establish something new through design and then implementation.
- In 2010, in an article on the anatomy of the creative brain, in livestrong.com, Tracey R. explains that the anatomy of creativity is that a pattern of activation and suppression of communication pathways within the brain allows for the emergence of novel thought.

Subsequently, allowing for memory to interface with creating or not allowing it both play a part in being creative.

- "Creativity requires anticipation and commitment," with the former focused on "envisioning something for the future." The latter refers to "the belief that keeps one working to realize the vision despite doubt and discouragement" (Galvin, 1997, in *Creativity: Flow and the Psychology of Discovery and Intention*).
- Creativity is not determined by brain lateralization alone, explains Dr. Harvey Sasken (2014). During creative thought, the neurotransmitter norepinephrine is greatly reduced. Because it's associated with long-term memory retrieval, its reduction during creative thinking helps the brain make connections for ideas being discovered, as new pathways are developed.
- Ingredients for "creative" innovation include "divergent thinking"—the ability to see things differently in a way that improves upon conventional thought.
- "Creativity is any act, idea, or product that changes an existing domain (examples: music, engineering, business, math, social studies, humanities) or that transforms an existing domain into a new one. Subsequently, a creative person is one whose thoughts or actions change a domain, or establish a new domain" (Csikszentmihalyi, 1996). [Such an example would be *The Interactive Book Report* (Schiering, 1995).]
- Csikszentmihalyi (1998), in his book on *Finding Flow*, refers to the period of creativity as being titled "Flow" or "White Time." As poet Mark Strand explains in the aforementioned book, "Well, you're right in the work, you lose your sense of time, you're completely enraptured, you're completely caught up in what you're doing, and you're sort of swayed by the possibilities you see in this work."
- Schiering (2014) refers to this "flow" as "being a time when one is in suspended animation. You're there and not there simultaneously . . . in the moment and separate from it." Also, Schiering and Byrne and Schiering and Marino relate two creative processes of Linear and Reciprocal Creativity. The former is sequential and the latter shows a back-and-forth pattern.
- "Creativity consists largely of rearranging what we know in order to find out what we do not know . . . Hence, to think creatively we must be able to look afresh at what we normally take for granted" (Kneller, 1965).
- Remembering that creative cognition is the same as creative thinking, the idea of thought suppression during creative times, and/or limiting communication pathways to permit new thoughts posits that one is not thinking so much when being creative. If this is true, then the concept of whether cognition develops creativity or crea-

tivity develops cognition comes down to these concepts being interchangeable when referring to the impact of one on the other.

- Creative ideas may come as a result of conversations with others and not simply appear suddenly or, then again, they might, as in isolation from any thought about a topic being discussed. "A creative idea is based upon having knowledge, with plenty of context (and a lot of this context is acquired by interacting with others), and then adding one or more pieces of context that no one else is able to see" (Hargadon, 2003, in *How Breakthroughs Happen: The Surprising Truth about How Companies Innovate*).
- "Creativity is not the exclusive domain of a few fortunate souls. Every person is creative, because creativity is one trait that makes us human. To be creative is to be able to perceive and recognize the world around us, to understand what we need or wish to do in response to it, and to set about changing it. To be creative is to find a way, a thought, an expression, a human manifestation no one has found and to make newly discovered possibilities reality" (Thompson, 2007).
- "To be creative is nothing more than to be fully human, totally alive. It means expressing your latent potential for self-discovery and self-revelation. And we are convinced that this is something that just about any serious person can achieve given the right conditions (proper motivation and supportive, nurturing environment) and sufficient opportunities" (Kline, 2011).

ESSENTIAL CREATIVE DISPOSITIONS

Yet other ideas concerning viewpoints on being creative come from *The Creative Self*. Dr. Michael Russo, philosophy professor at Molloy College, paraphrases the viewpoints in the aforementioned book (Kline, 2011) as follows:

> Many children grow up in households where creative activity, far from being supported, is actually subtly discouraged. In the United States, oftentimes the work ethic maintains a psychological hold over many American families and activities such as writing poetry, painting, or doing photography simply for pleasure can be perceived as frivolous activities. In this sort of environment, creative expression of any kind is typically viewed as an acceptable use of time only when it can be shown to lead directly to financial or career success.
>
> Since the vast majority of creative acts don't fall within this fairly restrictive paradigm, . . . [creative] activity in our society is often seen as the province of so-called experts—those who have shown that they have demonstrated a sufficiently high enough level of talent that they can successfully "monetize" their creative passions. Those who are deemed to lack such expertise, on the other hand, are discouraged—

either subtly or more overtly—from spending time developing their creative potentials and instead are directed towards more pragmatic pursuits.

To counteract this societal bias, Kline recommends the development of four essential creative dispositions that can inspire both children and adults to continue creating throughout the course of their lives, despite the discouragement that they might face at home or in the larger society (pp. 30–34). Such dispositions should be reinforced continually by educators so that children develop a sense that creative expression is a natural part of the lives of well-developed human beings. These essential dispositions include:

1. Nurturing a Sense of Creative Self-Entitlement. In his article, "Creativity is Your Birthright," David Storer (2005, p. 12) argues that we need to develop a sense that, whatever our circumstances may be in life, we have a right to express ourselves creatively. Permission to create cannot be granted by others, because the desire to create—or not to create—always remains our own choice. To break the self-defeating idea that one doesn't have a right to be creative, Kline—somewhat facetiously, I think—recommends the frequent use of the mantra: "I have the right to be creative | I have the ability to be creative | I will be creative no matter what anyone else says."
2. Jumping Right In. Each of us, Kline maintains, probably has some facility or interest in at least one creative medium. Verbally oriented individuals might lean towards writing poetry or fiction; visually oriented people might be more interested in photography, being a videographer, or painting. The medium one chooses for self-expression really doesn't matter. What does matter is the willingness to go beyond the intellectual exploration of a creative activity and jump headlong into the activity of creating something . . . or anything.
3. Embracing Imperfections. In our society, as we've seen, creative activity is frequently linked with the kind of perfectionism that often discourages individuals from attempting to be creative at all. We've all encountered people who maintain that they're just not good enough to try painting or creative writing, for example. (How many of us, in fact, feel that way even as adults?) To counteract these sorts of perfectionist tendencies, Kline recommends giving oneself complete and total license to not do well and to cultivate, in other words, the joy of imperfection, as much as the joy of creating.
4. Cultivating Wildness. As Eric Maisel argues in *Fearless Creating*, there can be no true creativity without the cultivation of a sense of wildness—"an amalgam," he maintains, "of passion, vitality, re-

belliousness, nonconformity, freedom from inhibitions" (1995, p. 12).

JOURNAL AND/OR DISCUSSION QUESTIONS

1. How would you explain the Linear Creative Process?
2. How would you explain the Reciprocal Creative Process?
3. What are four "Creative Viewpoints" that resonated with you?
4. What four dispositions are addressed in the section on Essential Creative Dispositions?

THREE

Personal Perspectives on Creative Cognition

CHAPTER OVERVIEW

Beginning with multiage and international perspectives from an individual's personal experiences regarding creative cognition or one's being creative are given. These are then briefly compared to the Creativity Viewpoints in chapter 1. Creativity as cleverness is examined and an experiment on evaluating one's creativity follows. Two examples of creativity as "entertainment" are provided and analyzed. An opportunity for self-reflection regarding one's creativity is specified as an assignment for applied creative thinking. Sharing with others through storytelling, an anecdotal accounting, or project is suggested. The chapter culminates with Journal and/or Discussion Questions that address your personal perspectives on creative processes.

ELEVEN PERSONAL PERSPECTIVES ON CREATIVE COGNITION

These stories in the form of reflections containing thoughts on being creative are from many different persons. Some were teachers, and several never were in this profession. One is teaching now, and others are in business or retired. One contributor is a child and two are teenagers. All are in different geographical locations in the United States or Europe. The youngest contributor is nine and recalled when he was three years old. Then, there's a seventy-two-year-old who contributed and shows that creativity doesn't stop at sixty-five, although societal norms may stereotype capabilities by one's years. Creativity has been part of each person's life either as a hobby or part of a career. Their personal perspectives do not align with every one of those stated in the section on Creativity Viewpoints, but some of them do.

It was thought that it'd be interesting to have these examples and then examine your own creativity through comparison and contrast using reflection and recall. Give it a try. As you read each one of these creativity descriptions, gathered in the spring of 2014, decide if their process of creativity is similar to your own or, perhaps, opposite from it.

These creativity processes represent persons' viewpoints in different fields. Any idea expressed in these twelve examples could be modified to be part of interactive learning using creative thinking.

1. *Maritza Garcia,* a beautician and part-time artist, related in a 2010 conversation and later (2012) magazine article, "What happens to me when painting is much like what Strand related in *Creative Viewpoints*. We'd never had this discussion before, and, when I read through the remarks from different authors, I found this poet's comments to resonate with me. When I'm being creative, my mind stops. Well, it doesn't really stop, as it is concentrating solely on the painting I'm doing, and nothing else matters or is present for me. That is how it has always been and I've been painting for years and years."

2. *David Bunting,* a veteran teacher from Skien, Norway, explains: "When teaching, I think of ways to make the project interesting so students may explore their imaginations in inventing. I do that when I'm being creative. I'm thinking about a different way to do something, and I use my memory to do that, to create. The students then use their brains to develop ideas and thoughts upon which they'll take action when doing a project or sharing opinions on a selected topic."

3. *Jay Skalaban,* a nine-year-old elementary school student, referred to me by his grandmother, because "he's a storyteller and a creative one at that!" agreed to be interviewed. Sitting in a chair, at first tolerant of a grand-mom taking his time away from friends, became animated and fully engaged in recalling his stories from age two. His favorite was that he loved turtles and took the laundry basket, turned it upside-down and crawled along the floor with this on his back, as ill-fitting as it might have been, pretending to be a turtle.

"Making up stories comes from what you love," Jay explained and then went into telling me about Minecraft on the computer and iPhone games. "I learn by listening and can't sit still much in school, but I listen as I'm moving around. I know I'm creative and ideas just come to me . . . they always have. Everyone tells me I am creative. Know what, the ideas, they have shape and form to them like you asked me about images and that's what I see; images of stories, games I want to play that are made-up/creative."

A few minutes more and Jay is off and running to be with his cousins; animated and delightfully clever, as well as polite, his creativity seems to have a focal point and one in which he's deeply engrossed.

4. *Anthony Romano*, a teacher who resumed this line of work after years of traveling the world, relates: "When I think about creativity and try to define how it happens in the expressive arts that I choose, I am tempted to say that it just occurs. However, I know that's untrue. To try and explain it, I can relate it to writing. If I need to write about a specific topic, my mind will spin out all of the possible different ways to approach the subject. It will wrap around different scenarios, words, sentence structures, similes, metaphors. I will think about everything as much as possible. All of this will happen before I am even close to a keyboard to type my words.

"Sometimes I even choose to walk for a long distance or do some sort of physical activity, to let my mind muster up ideas. Soon all of these ideas are now fully formed in my head, but in no particular order. *It is like the car is in neutral while I am hitting the gas.*

"When I feel good and ready I'll start to write. The direction I write is sometimes undetermined and often unpredictable, but because of the prior thinking phase, that reflective period, I am confident that the words will eventually *flow*, sometimes it is easier than others but they will flow. When I get stuck, I usually take a break and let the thoughts formulate until a solution is found."

5. *Dominick Toscano*, a special education teacher of nearly ten years, believes: "Creativity is born out of my imagination. I recall that, when I was young and playing baseball with my friends, I would think about and conjure up the thought that it was the ninth inning of the World Series, with two outs and a runner on each base, and my being up-at-bat meant I needed to get a 'hit' to win the game. Maybe this was the same thought that anyone who has ever played the game before has, which is regardless of if they had just started playing or were coming to an ending time with this sport; they would all pretend.

"Overall, I think imagination drives us to succeed and our creativity is the tool we use to accomplish it." As a Division II student athlete at Molloy College, Dominick relied on his imagination to help him create new ways to be successful on the lacrosse field.

He further stated that "it was not only in practice or team meetings where we would work together to create and design plays that would make us successful against our opponents, but also during the game itself in the midst of the action where you may have to try a new move or play without ever having practiced it before."

Dominick agrees with Maritza's statement that when she is creative "her mind stops." When playing a sport, Dominick would get in a zone, as athletes call it, where nothing else around has any impact on what you do and your only restraint is how imaginative you can be in that period of time.

As a first-year teacher, Dominick commented on how he witnessed the relationship between imagination and creativity every day in his classroom. "As teachers, we are always planning. Our imagination lays the foundation for how we hope a certain lesson may go with children being engaged and enjoying their learning experience.

"We then depend on our creativity to take over with what activities can one plan for and develop to make his/her imagination a reality? For most of us, no matter how much we plan and create ahead of time, our lessons can end up going in a different direction than originally intended for various reasons such as having to reteach the previous day's lessons, handling a classroom behavior, once again causing us to depend on our creativity to make the proper adjustments on the fly, just as I had to when on the lacrosse field."

6. *Lucia Sapienza,* a teacher in Maspeth Elementary School writes: "I am presently a second-grade teacher at PS 153 in Maspeth, Queens. Being a creative person has its ups and downs. Being creative was one of the reasons why I became a teacher. I thought, what better way for students to learn than by learning creatively instead of constantly following textbooks? Being a teacher for ten years now, I try my best to incorporate art interactive assignments in all subject areas by using the IM and the IBR. I have always been a creative person, but as I got older I felt that my creativity was being restricted by outside sources . . . having so many rules on how to do something that I didn't have to think on my own. Actually, I was encouraged not to imagine and invent.

"As a teacher, you are told to follow curriculum and assess students' knowledge. Of course, I do that, but what I have noticed is that students rarely know how to use their imagination. What might seem easy to me, such as, creating a story, is difficult for students nowadays. I get responses like, 'I don't know what to write.' It's disconcerting to see that kids have somehow lost their sense of imagination. Even when students color or draw, I hear, 'I'm not good at art.' It's like they are in 'put-down' land.

"My response is to relate that 'Art is whatever you make it. Everyone is good at it.' Even when I taught fourth and fifth grade, those students strived to use their creative skills as well, but they seemed unsure of themselves. I believe in interactive learning, the IM, as it gives students the chance to use their imaginations openly. It's an approach that provides success for all students."

7. *Amanda Lockwood* explains: "I'm an ESL (English Second Language) teacher. As a child I was very creative, or I always tried to be. I could not

draw beautiful pictures, as I was not born with that natural talent. However, I have honed it and always appreciated others' artistic abilities, and sometimes felt jealous of people who were born with I-can-draw-anything-easily. I think that with some things I may be a perfectionist, which I now think hinders my creativity by thinking my work or I [myself] am not good enough.

"In elementary school my favorite 'special' subject was art, I loved going and creating something new. Sometimes I got different drawing books to teach me how to draw things like cartoons and animals. To this day I find being creative relaxing. I paint ceramic sculptures that I place throughout my house. I also still love to color when I have the time, it settles me. My mother and I make flower arrangements for my house and I love baking and decorating cupcakes.

"I think students having the chance to be creative is very helpful for them when learning, especially new material. That's why almost every time I do any project with my students I have them use their imagination to illustrate something, or design and then create something. Creating something without words comforts them because the language barrier is not in art. Also when creating worksheets, PowerPoints, or SMART Board lessons for my students, I always include some graphic design or animation to help get their brains stimulated. The thing I really like about the IM of teaching creativity and IBR strategy, well, they're not the same old stuff on the SMART Board because this IBR method has students producing things that are three-dimensional."

8. *O. K. Carhart* is a multitask man from Oregon and someone I've known for over five decades, (an artist, builder, land sculptor, with extensive business backgrounds in photography and newspapers plus). In response to my question about his process of creativity he said, "Here's an example: I was building miniature fir trees for my model railroad that's taken over the family room in the house. It's a fairly simple process using tapered pieces of wood and inserting compressed furnace air filters in different sizes onto the wooden shafts to build a fir tree. After a while it almost becomes automatic, and then I start to think beyond what I'm doing. I'm somewhat tunnel visioning. So in this case, the fir tree construction led me to start thinking about the fact that not all trees are planted in great locations. Some actually take root in unusual places . . . like rock faces. And that kind of thinking led me to creating and building a new kind of model tree that I'd only seen in nature. What I call my 'multilevel mind,' in the meantime started me thinking about the next stage. This is: 'what happens when these trees are logged?' And the answer, of course, is 'they're stumps!'

"Next, I carved some small pieces of wood and plaster and made stumps. This led to my thinking that there has to be a faster and simpler way. This evolved into making molds, to easily make as many as I wanted. Then I stared at the color pallet next to where I was working and thought about something my wife had asked about earlier when she was making greeting cards. . . . So the list goes on, and on, and on . . . with one thought, or idea, linking or triggering another.

"When I think about the process deeply, in some ways I find that we are all like the computers or the handhelds we use daily. Our minds seem to have multiple screens percolating or going continuously. Some screens are in front, while others are behind, but they are always there and moving. Our job is simply to look at, visualize, and try to focus on the possibilities and what we want to accomplish."

9. The Siblings and Cousin: *Marisa, Andy F.,* and *Rayna Schiering*:

Marisa, age sixteen, is a three-year-experienced sculptress. She explains that when she's involved in her creative process she needs quiet around her. No interruptions. (Interestingly, this corresponds with the Dunn and Dunn Learning Style Environmental Strand for field independent learners; see chapter 10). Marisa follows a Linear Creative Process up to the point of changing the final piece she sculpted by adding texture and/or color. Although envisioning in black and white and focusing on how to form the clay before firing it, she adds another aspect of her creativity by making lines, painting in varied color tones, and applying shading that's realistic. Each of her pieces is different and she explains that her final product is a pride-filled creation that she enjoys and finds others do as well.

Andy F., age thirteen, is a computer guru and programmer since age ten. He explained he once made it to the front page of scratch.com for his creation of a program. Becoming interested in computers when he was three years old, he took typing instruction when five or six so he could manipulate the computer keyboard easily. But, overall, he said, "the computer is just fun to play." His dad was an influence and he thinks some beginning ideas came from him, but taking an afterschool technology program, he enhanced his skills with this play and learning tool. The Tech Club was involved in robotics and competition with mind exercises.

"You know what, I wanted to make a game on the computer and I'd use my memory of things I'd seen before and think of styles while going from platform to platform and jumping from place to place of the game I was making. I'd see images and these would connect to other ones." (When I heard Andy say that during his interview I thought of O. K. Carhart's "Personal Creativity Perspectives, #8," likening creativity to a computer screen that has multiple images on it simultaneously, and he just chooses the right one for the project he is doing).

Andy continued with "I think about how I want a character to look and how to integrate that into the style of the game. I envision these invisible sensors around a character and how I want to implement ideas, and that action results in my experimentation and fixing problems that may arise or get involved in 'debugging.' Then I try to design content or levels of a game and I go back and forth with problem-solving and decision-making.

"I'm 'in-the-zone' when I'm being creative as I figure out what I'm doing with tools I have and with my programming language I can do this efficiently. And, just so you know, to stay calm, I have to have classical electronic music playing on my headphones all the time, or I'd go crazy talking to myself. Bottom line, I like my mind, my ability to create, and recreate, trusting I can improve things makes me feel good. I like to produce a finished product and know others can take on this challenge as I did. Sometimes I have a sense of control by using computer creative design."

Rayna Schiering, age thirteen, has been taking art lessons in drawing and painting for three years. She likes drawing eyes and finds that she envisions her drawings or paintings before doing them and focuses on what will come next. Unlike other creative entries in this section, Rayna, will get up and take breaks, moving away from her work to do something else. Then, she'll return after a while to complete the project and will not veer from it until it's done.

Rayna explains that until she's done with her work she's not satisfied, but when she has completed her project she enjoys looking back on her process and the finished piece, which she'll more likely than not keep in a sketchbook rather than hanging it up or giving it away. She will share her art endeavors with other artists and enjoys conversation about their creative process. Candidly, Rayna explains that she compares her own art to others' artistic creations, and finds this sharing to be very inspirational!

10. *Anthony J. Ferrantello,* an architect for several decades writes: "With every design challenge, whether it be a humble vegetable stand for the local farm to be built by the local Boy Scouts or volunteer group, a school, a mess hall in a military base or a historic renovation/preservation project, I set out to obtain some mental satisfaction and desire for joy from the creative process. Yes, ultimately that joy came in the morning after laboring throughout the night as to how this design was going to develop.

"I think obtaining joy has been the desire of every artist throughout the flow of time. For me, joy is obtained because the work produced brings a feeling of beauty and then beauty becomes the value I give to the work. I judge the work as beautiful. As a value, I elevate beauty to other values such as goodness and truth. So to make a full circle, beauty is then connected to morality and love. Creativity, well, to achieve this end, a purposeful attitude of mind that seeks value is essential in any endeavor be it visual or performing arts, music, literature, and the architecture in which I'm involved."

11. *Mary Fleckner*, wife, mother and grandmother, as well as foil-leaded stained glass designer, explains her creativity as follows: "I liked looking at this art type and took several classes in it starting twenty years ago. You learn something different from each art instructor. I thought, 'whoever does this is creative.' I read 'pattern books' about foil-leaded stained glass work, as I modified examples given to my taste, size and color-wise desires. I'd combine ideas by, let's say, having a hummingbird and trees in the background. I begin with an idea of what I want to create and have to find glass that matches the scene or object of what I want. After picking the subject and making a pattern, the hardest part of this art form is picking the glass and *envisioning* how it is going to go together.

"There's exactness to doing glass work. The idea is 'measure twice and cut once.' I need the proper tools and the steps of a) relying on the original picture and drawing, which are influenced by b) *memories* and *discernment*. (Looking at your figures on Linear and Reciprocal Processes of Creativity, it is at this juncture I switch from the former to the latter).

"Next, I'd say I liken glass design to geometry in that the cut line, let's say for a butterfly, is part of the design. I have to think that out in advance. I won't remember where everything goes, so I need to follow the pattern and design closely as I cut and grind the glass. Frequently I change patterns and I go *back and forth in my creative process* while remaining focused on technical aspects of my creation.

"Emotionally, I block out feelings while working and have a flood of satisfaction when the project is completed. There's a joy-of-giving the finished work to others or keeping the work for myself. I also feel euphoria and pride in the accomplishment of my endeavors." And, asked why she continues to do this exacting type of work, Mary replied with, "It's the challenge that keeps me doing this form of glass work." On a side note, people who have seen her work remark that it's extraordinarily beautiful!

CONNECTING PERSONAL CREATIVITY PERSPECTIVES WITH CREATIVITY VIEWPOINTS

The contributors who gave their thoughts on being creative, you'll notice, have the elements of the bulleted areas that appear in the section Creativity Viewpoints in the previous chapter. These include Maritza's thinking she's not thinking when being creative, and that's true for Anthony as well. That experience references the "flow or white time" (Csikszentmihalyi, 2009); and the concept of "suspended animation" (Schiering, 2014).

David, however, focuses on changes of an existing domain, and working with others. He does each of these, as he refers to Hargadon's idea of there being a good deal of context resulting from interacting with others, and adding pieces of context to create something new. David uses his memory to influence his creativity for projects he assigns in his class.

O. K. Carhart, in his first few paragraphs about his creativity, appears to follow the Linear Process mentioned in chapter 2. An example would be when he related his *conversation* with his wife influencing his construction of trees. Hargadon (2003) mentions conversation as a component of creativity. Then again, in the closing comments O. K. made, he referenced how "we're like computers with multiple screens showing." This reference causes one to see that his thinking, creative cognition, is more of the Reciprocal Creative Process. Subsequently, for this particular individual, both creative processes are evident and in-play at the same time.

Mary Fleckner went from the Linear Process, doing things step-by-step in sequential order, and then into the Reciprocal Creative Process. She remained with that reciprocity until the glass work was completed.

Overall, the eleven categorized creativity contributions demonstrate application and awareness of memory influencing their creativity, and an unawareness of using it as well. Each one imagines, invents, designs, and self-actuates. Each one follows his or her own processes or combination thereof, as listed in figures 2.1 and 2.2 in the previous chapter. Creativity, we may recognize, is done differently by individuals and there is no right or wrong way to be creative. Just as one has a particular feeling, creativity just is. We are all innately creative. Some express it to more degrees than others.

Experiment: Read the *Personal Perspectives on Creativity*, if you've not already done that. After reading, take a piece of lined paper and make two columns. At the top of the left one put your name, and write a paragraph or two about your own creativity. This would be something you imagined and then actually made. Next, do the same for a friend you know to be creative. Describe how he or she or you envision his or her creativity. Then, using the section on Creativity Viewpoints, see what matches you can make and write these in the right-hand column for you and your friend.

How many matches have you made? Is anyone's viewpoint repeated? Do you see a pattern? For the creative person you wrote about and for the one you did for yourself, were there similarities? Why or why not, do you suppose, is this the case?

CREATIVITY, CLEVERNESS, AND FUNCTIONS OF CREATIVITY

In chapter 1, synonyms regarding one's being creative were listed. Further conducted research disclosed that an individual being "clever" was a defining attribute and appeared along with functions of creativity. In a blog by Dustin Staiger (*Casual Fridays*, 2012), he relates that the *functions of creativity* included such characteristics as "originates, forms, embodies, evolves, sustains and is purpose centered. Cleverness functions included its being entertaining, distracting, informative, reflective, and attention getting."

Perhaps while one is being creative he or she is being clever, but it's not necessary to have the latter for the former to exist. The mainstay of creativity is the idea that one is producing something, as opposed to gaining notice.

CREATIVITY AS ENTERTAINMENT: EXAMPLE ONE

This following story was told by a comedian on a ship about a waitress and a man having dinner in a restaurant: "A customer has just finished what he states is a terrific meal and offers compliments to the chef. Then he comments that the dessert menu has hot fudge sundaes on it and questions if these are really good. The waitress replies that they are truly delicious, as the patron states that he'd like to get this and asks to get 'extra hot fudge' on his hot fudge sundae. The waitress responds with 'We only serve our hot fudge at one temperature.'"

This "joke" was told to 124 people. Many of these were teacher candidates. When asked what they thought the waitress was going to say, each expressed the idea of the customer wanting more hot fudge on his hot fudge sundae. Regardless, the idea of addressing the temperature of the hot fudge is what made this a joke and expected answer given or not, all thought the creative waitress's response was entertaining.

CREATIVITY AS ENTERTAINMENT: EXAMPLE TWO

The following anecdote is about a mom in her early thirties explaining about how her son answered the house phone for the first time. While the story is true, it is the telling of it that finds one being entertained. Perhaps this is because of the commonality of a social reality or just because of the innocence of the child involved. Nonetheless, the creativity is present in the response from listeners with their laughter.

The mom had decided to train her four-year-old, Josh, about proper phone etiquette. The house phone was mounted on the kitchen wall a bit out of the boy's reach. Subsequently, the mom provided a step stool in front of the phone. When the phone rang, she instructed him on how he was to get on the step stool, wait for the third ring, then pick up the phone, and listen to the person say, "Hello." This was to take place prior to his responding with, "Hello, this is, Josh, may I help you, please?"

Several weeks of multiple daily practicing with a toy phone were about to be tested. This was done with Josh's dad walking up the street to the little store to pick up some groceries, and then calling the house where his son would answer the phone and say:

"Hello, this is, Josh, may I help you please?"

Cued as to the procedure of this endeavor, up the street the dad went. About fifteen minutes later the phone rang in the house. Mom told Josh to go ahead and answer the phone as he'd been instructed, and she watched.

Josh got on the step stool and at the third ring picked up the phone. He nodded as the person at the other end said, "Hello."

His own voice was a little shaky as he responded,

"Hello, this is, Josh, PLEASE HELP ME!"

REVIEW OF EXAMPLES

Both of those examples fall into the category of being entertaining and clever by demonstrating reflection and a style of delivery that was attention getting. Gathered opinions note that while the first story was contrived and got a laugh or smile, the second one was a demonstration of a cute experience . . . happenstance . . . a touch-of-life incident that depicted a common social reality: telephone etiquette. Both of the examples showed ingenuity. This resourcefulness was evidenced with the formation, scope, and sequence, and/or perhaps interest in the anecdote, as much as the way the story was told.

QUESTIONS

What was your reaction to these examples? Why do you suppose you had that reaction? Did you share either of these examples with anyone and what was that person's reaction? Were you in agreement? What do you think makes the examples given indicative of creativity in the format of entertainment or even attention getting?

ASSIGNMENT

The idea of this assignment is to demonstrate how your thinking may involve creativity. Address creative cognition in your own fashion through storytelling or an anecdote, or by producing something to show others. At the completion of your presentation, explain what the term "creative cognition" means to you, and if given the opportunity, how you'd teach it.

JOURNAL AND/OR DISCUSSION QUESTIONS

1. Have you had some creative cognition experiences? If so, what are these? If not, how do you suppose one might develop these; linearly, reciprocally, or a combination of the two?
2. Have you or someone you know designed an object or an idea and then created it? If so, which one of these? Which of these do you suppose is most viable and why? How did you or this other person feel when the creativity was completed? What was the reaction of others to it? What impact did the reaction of others have on you?
3. Is Creative Cognition a learned process? Explain your answer.
4. When you think of creativity, who are the people that come to your mind as having this trait and why is that?
5. Can you think of any times in your own life when you have been in a state of complete hyperconcentration or experienced being "in the zone?" If so, what was it like? If not, what do you suppose it'd be like?

FOUR

An Introduction

Creative Cognition's Interactive Methodology and Book Report

The Child That Dreams

I am still the child
And I shall spend these years
In wondering about and dreaming
Of what I have not
But wish for and could be.
And you shall teach me
So that I may grow with
Truth and knowledge
To become the person within my being
Who will turn one day to teach another
Who is still the child that dreams. (Schiering, © 1965)

CHAPTER OVERVIEW

We are all learners and teachers of something. And, there are multitudes of ways one may be creative. This chapter focuses on the concept of thinking creatively using, as a product, the Interactive Book Report (IBR) which is a result of implementing the Interactive Methodology (IM). Both involve project and performance-based learning and teaching. Combined, these two invite each learner, teacher, or individual to engage in his or her inventiveness and creativity development.

An examination of each of the aforementioned is provided so creative cognition's IBR project may be visualized with respect to its components being utilized in a school setting or when away from it involving academic and social literacy. Next, basic components of the IM and IBR are given attention along with the discipline of reading and Common Core learning standards with the IBR. These are followed by a little history and uniqueness of the IBR. The aforementioned commentary is provided by Anthony Marino, a doctoral graduate in Instructional Leadership from St. John's University. Danielle Rosenberg, a teacher-candidate at Molloy College, shares her Interactive Book Report in a narrative that provides detail about this project. Journaling and/or Discussion Questions complete the chapter.

EXPLAINING THE ACRONYMS AND BASICS OF THE IM AND IBR

You may be looking at these acronyms and wondering what they are and if there's a difference between them. If you are, then the answers are that the *IM* stands for the *Interactive Methodology,* which is a means of learning and teaching that addresses one's doing "hands-on" type of work and also being creatively involved in the cognitive/thinking process. The IBR frequently accompanies or is part of this methodology, and it is a learner self-constructed binder-style book. Its pages are interactive, instructional resources/educational games that address the topic of a unit of study or a book read. Learners make the IBR working alone to design, imagine, create the pages, or work with a partner or in small group format to do this. Each page of the IBR's activities is self-corrective or has an example of the completed page.

When referencing a methodology, as with the IM, there's a lot to consider. Most importantly this is to realize that a method is "how" something is done. In this case, the IM is a creative cognition, interactive means of learning and/or teaching. With a bit of detail, the IM's approach involves a student or one who's learning through inventing for the purposes of being creative, sharing ideas, exchanging visions, and engaging participants in the process of information retention.

POSSIBLE IM COMPONENTS AND IBR ACTIVITIES

What are you envisioning now that you've read these first few paragraphs? Write down or share these first impressions and then see if they match what comes next. The IM may involve role-playing, puppetry, or personally made educational games, including floor and wall games. What's frequently evident is that there's a presentation of work, such as a project made for display or sharing. Dance and art may be part of these IBR page activities, or three-dimensional mazes, dioramas, diagrams, drawings, and technology, which are used as tools to assist with these constructions. However, the main components require tactile/kinesthetic, as well as auditory and visual involvement in learning with use of any or all of the four modalities at the same time.

As stated earlier in this chapter, this method of learning and teaching, as well as the IBR itself, requires, as a key component, creativity. There's the use of one's cognition to produce evidence regarding thinking skills such as, *basic awareness* and *critical analysis*, too. These serve as simultaneous connectors to the *metacognitive* (higher-order thinking) skills of evaluation, advanced decision-making, reflection, and self-actualization, to name just four of these.

All three thinking skills sets are part of the IM and recorded in the IBR as one identifies what thinking skills are being applied when designing the interactive pages and playing them as well. This cognitive and metacognitive skill information is provided in detail in chapters 15 and 16. Chapters 17 and 18 provide a detailed listing of the thinking skills used for the interactive pages provided in these chapters.

A LITTLE MORE IBR INFORMATION

As you already know from the previous paragraphs, the IBR is a binder-style book and most frequently accompanies or is connected to the methodology addressed in this book. A regular three-to-four-inch binder serves as this book, and it then has twenty to forty pages, which are *mostly* the educational games/interactive instructional resources learners have made. These are placed in page protectors or laminated so one may use a dry-erase marker to play-the-pages when instructions explain whether this play is required or not.

The IBR pages are those invented through imaginings, design, and then creativity application of an individual, partnerships, small groups, or entire classes of learners. Pages are done to be self-corrective. When this self-correction is not possible, an example of how the page should look, when completed by the player, is provided.

HISTORY AND UNIQUENESS OF THE IBR

The strategy being presented in this book was first titled "The Interactive Book Report" (Schiering, 1996). Then, in 2003 it was copyrighted and called *The Interactive Book Report: Playing the Pages* (M. S. Schiering). As the name changed, the words "interactive methodology" were introduced by Schiering, because it is a way of learning and teaching. When applied in the academic and social setting, the method brings about interaction and communication among and between those who participate in it. This creative method of instruction promotes the use of creativity through addressing one's mind's eye and decision-making. The IBR with creativity at its core is one strategy or technique that has the power to take over one's attention, remain in someone's thoughts, and capture one's imagination, simultaneously. The focal point is the concept of creatively *learning-through-play*.

Robinson (2006), in his first video of seven on the topic of creativity, questions: "Do we grow out of creativity or are we educated out of it?" I'd tend to favor the latter of these. I also find that this idea of the IM and accompanying IBR is unique because each, when practiced, is for the use of creativity and designed to teach, develop, structure, enhance, and adapt imaginings for the purpose of creativity. The atmosphere of the creative setting has provision for opportunities to be creative, whether in the classroom setting or at home. There's cohesiveness in the learners' thought patterns that allows for experimentation, acting on visualizations, and promoting intuition.

Concretizing memories of presented material for the learning of the learners is evidenced. Subsequently, when the learner is involved in creating, his or her "recalling" things that apply to the creative project are brought to the foreground. With you practicing this and reflecting for a moment, what do you suppose makes you remember some things and let go of others? Probably it was the significance of the situation that caused you to recall and retain it. Was that your answer? Why or why not?

SENSE OF LEARNER GRATIFICATION

The creativity involved in the methodology and the construction of the IBR pages brings about a sense of gratification for the learner, which happens as the individual "takes the lead, and has faith in his/her resources being at his/her command." These resources include the aforementioned intuition, strength of thought, and belief and determination that goals can be reached. And, breaking through the wall of fear and criticism that threatens to stop one is evident, "because the IBR encourages acceptance of one's efforts to invent and create" (Schiering, 2000). "When creativity is affirmed as being a positive, there's courage to pursue the goal, and finally compassion, which enables one to collaborate and work with others while valuing their ideas" (Goleman, Kaufman, & Ray, 1992).

One further unique point of interest about the IM and IBR is that they involve thinking to the point of there being an ongoing awareness of knowing "what" one is thinking when *learning-through-play*. The Interactive Methodology and any accompanying materials for this focus on the reciprocity of cognition at beginning, intermediary, and advanced levels being intertwined.

EXPLAINING THE IM AND IBR: A PERSONAL PERSPECTIVE: ANTHONY MARINO

Anthony Marino (Summer, 2014), before earning his doctorate at St. John's University, was a Molloy College teacher-candidate. He used the Interactive Method by designing and making an IBR in EDU.506A: *Integrated ELA and Reading for the Diverse Learner*. Schiering was his professor, and Anthony writes the following about the IM as it involved interaction, imagination, and creativity. He explains, "The idea of interactive teaching and learning, as represented in the IBR, for those using it or creating it will find this technique to teach and learn most effective. It's a way to learn for friends, family, and others. More importantly, those doing it find it appealing because it's something of one's own making.

"When first introduced to the IM: I asked myself, 'What does a method of teaching involve and what is the focus of this learning method? Does it require you to listen, read a textbook, memorize something, or actively involve you in some project?' Then I questioned what others might think, "Now, what does a book report look like to you and your students? Let me guess . . . colorful title page, perhaps with an illustration? Then there comes the summary of the story. Of course, don't forget to include the main characters, setting, pages and pages of details and quotes directly from the book. Lastly, why don't you tell us why you did or didn't like the book?

"Finally, I thought of how I perceived this method of learning and teaching and how I'd promote it by saying, 'Tired of the same old format, which involves listening at your seat, not moving around? Sick of reading a book report that just regurgitates facts from the original story? Do your eyes tear when you have a stack of papers to read or you're writing a book report and evaluating it? (If you're the teacher, don't forget the act of grading all those reports and trying to write different comments for each one.) If your answer to these previous questions is 'Yes,' then this IM is 'the' method for you!

"Fundamentally, we are addressing a new concept—well not really a new concept, it is actually a concept that was developed in the 1990s and used by fifth grade students. Over the past twenty plus years it has evolved into what is known as the Interactive Method (IM) and IBR book. Both have been taught to hundreds of teacher-candidates in the United States and in Europe and South America. Children on both sides of the Atlantic Ocean have benefited from this method and reporting style, to be quite honest, they've been learning by having fun."

READING: USING THE METHOD: DR. MARINO'S PERSPECTIVE

Marino, in a conversation with others not familiar with the IM and about how the IBR is a reporting strategy that actively involves the students, explained, "I think the first thing that needs to be talked about is how the teacher thinks and feels about reading. While the actual teaching of reading may be an art form, if you do not love to read, you are probably not going to have fun teaching it. So, first you have to know about yourself with respect to your attitudes about reading. If they are positive ones, then your class will know that as much as they'll know if they're negative. Before assigning reading and then the IBR, the teacher needs to be vested in the process.

"Therefore, it's important to know one's literacy history and see if it helps the students in doing the reading and follow-up review of literature assignment. Why, you ask? Enlightenment! Finding out your attitudes about reading can help YOU determine how YOU will teach reading to others and react to the IM with an IBR.

"I'm also thinking it's important to know about your class's literacy history, brief as it may or may not be. I think the IBR creation encourages students to read so they may self-actuate by using their imaginations. If your students do not like to read, the most likely outcome is having a negative reaction to what is read. What do you think we should do? Would you assign a book to read that you know that a student dislikes? Perhaps before we assign an IBR the learners need to know how they think and feel about reading and realize themselves that an IBR can change a poor attitude to a 'plus' one."

NOW WHAT?

"Okay, you reflected on what you like, and now have an idea of what your class likes, I'm asking, and you are probably asking, 'Now what?' Great question! Let's look at the IM. It's INTERACTIVE . . . HANDS-ON . . . TACTILE/KINESTHETIC, AUDITORY/VISUAL! Student engagement is important when teaching reading or any subject! The new Common Core learning standards are not just about making a simple connection or summarizing the contents of a book being read, or a unit being examined. They're about dissecting the topic, making inferences, analyzing what has been read, realizing or speculating about the author's intent, and supporting by providing details as evidence for any statements you make. The IBR does all of that! This method and activity hits on all the Common Core learning standards.

"All of this involves moving from basic understanding and awareness (cognition) to thinking about what one is thinking through recalling and reflecting (metacognition). Activities for the IBR pages are selected not just because they are fun. They are selected to give the designer and creator of the book report's playable pages an opportunity to experience the book or unit being studied, through a variety of modalities.

"The pages of the IBR are self-corrective so that when others 'play-the-pages' they too will experience the book from a different perspective. The IBR fits the bill whether it is a review of the material that was contained in a piece of literature or new material to be studied. This meeting of expectations is evidenced by critical thinking skills being practiced, or allowing others to experience the book as a way of motivating them to read the book.

"Concisely, the IBR is constructed about a piece of literature, but is not exclusive to that! The IBR may address units of study, including social studies, science, English, and foreign language, and yes, even math can benefit from this method. Any topic can be developed and learned through use of the IBR reporting style of learning and teaching.

"It is a product, a REPORT, for lack of a better term. Students become active participants in their learning! You can't hope for a better environment than that!" (Marino, 2014)

> *When students become active participants in their learning, they later recall what has been presented* (Schiering, 1974).

NARRATIVE EXAMPLE OF THE IBR: DANIELLE ROSENBERG

It may be difficult to visualize the IM and IBR. Explaining them without pictures and only a reference to the website (www.creativecognition4U.com) or E-book video to see examples would be like this narrative from Danielle Rosenberg, a teacher-candidate who made an IBR in 2013:

"As you know, The IM is an interactive way to learn and teach. By interactive I mean hands-on instructional strategies being applied as the foremost instructional style. Delivery of information is animated and engaging with acceptance of students' ideas and thoughts on pages to be used in the IBR. This learning technique provides evidence and experiential learning that is intended to facilitate the learners' ability to grasp and retain concepts in varied disciplines. The IBR addresses all modalities in its creation, knowing 'who' one is as a learner, and a self-corrective means of teaching in any discipline, and the joining of learning styles with academic and social cognition components.

"In a manner of speaking, the IBR mimics the activities when we were preschool students and learned through playing at a friend's house or in our own place. Overall, being involved and engaged in something helps us to recall information and obtain a deep comprehension of its components.

"The IBR that I made is based on the book *In the Year of the Boar and Jackie Robinson* by Bette Bao Lord. The IBR is designed for fifth graders. It begins with a short biography about the author, followed by a summary of the story. Next, there's the Reciprocal Thinking Phases (see chapter 10). Each activity involves thinking skills, and these are identified on a chart that names the activity and lists the cognitive and metacognitive skills developed when playing that page (see Task Card figures in chapters 10 and 16). The student learners will then be presented with an invitation to play the pages of the IBR. This can be a rhyme or written as if the main character is talking to the page players, or just a 'hello' and 'come play these pages and have fun doing this.'

"The first of five required creative interdisciplinary interactive activities in my IBR is The Scoop on Bandit Pic-A-Dot. (See chapters 15 and 16 for interactive resource illustrations and explanations.) The Pic-a-Dot has story comprehension questions with three possible answers. Pick the correct answer dot, which is beneath the answer, and the card easily slips out of the Pic-A-Dot Holder. If you're wrong, try again later. The interaction is picking the right dot and holding the card to try and pull it out of the holder (chapter 16).

"The next activity is Vocabulary Flip-Chute with vocabulary from the story going in the top slot and the definition coming out the bottom one. This activity is a 'question-in' and 'answer-out' type of game. I see it perceived as being magical. When the student releases the Flip-Chute card he/she has a moment to think of the answer that will appear. It's that letting-go of the card where the wonderment occurs. The activity is different from a 'flash card,' which requires a turning over of the hand to reveal an answer. For a brief moment, a second at most, the card is not visible and then the answer 'appears like magic!'

"The third activity is Math Word Problem Matching Task Cards. This matching is where students will have the opportunity to answer mathematical word problems based on NYS Common Score standards. The Task Cards are individualized puzzle pieces put together to form a shape-match (Dunn and Dunn, 1992).

The fourth activity in the IBR is in the social studies discipline with the Map Electro-Board. Students use this game to locate a variety of geographical places on a teacher-created map of Brooklyn and China, the setting of the book they read about Jackie Robinson. Using a continuity tester, the student touches one end to the map location and the other to the name of that place. If the light lights up, the correct place has been selected. If not, try again!

"The fifth activity is Over the Moon Wraparound. This is where students read and study the recipe to make moon pies and use the Wraparound on the back of the game to check their memory for the sequence of the ingredients in the recipe. The last two activities are creative ones that I designed and constructed. The first one has student learners making their own Chinese New Year envelopes. Supplies include markers, crayons, glitter, and different sheets of Chinese characters to design these envelopes, which are presented in the book they read. The second creative activity I made up requires use of chopsticks. Each student selects a variety of paper Chinese food items from a plastic plate. As items are selected, they're placed in a Chinese food container by using the chopsticks.

"The IBR closes with a note of congratulations for playing-the-pages of the IBR and learning-through-play." (See chapter 16 for details about how to play these games.)

JOURNAL AND/OR DISCUSSION QUESTIONS

1. How would you explain the IM and IBR?
2. What were key points of Anthony Marino about the topic of this chapter?
3. What were your favored activities mentioned in Danielle's IBR?
4. What do you think are the two most important aspects of using interactive instruction and creating a book report that's interactive?

FIVE

An Overview

IM and IBR

CHAPTER OVERVIEW

This chapter explains the brain-mind connection for creating memories. It goes into detail about the retention of information, which involves one's ability to recall things through attention, orientation, and decision-making. Specifics of the IM are followed by the IBR with regard to reflection. Then, a good number of questions are asked to have readers examine their personal memory on a variety of topics.

Anthony Marino, EdD calls attention to today's hot topic of Learning Standards (Common Core) application to the IM and IBR these: product. Two types of IBRs are given attention along with four specifics of the IM. The chapter then addresses an explanation of comprehension and the three types of literal, applied, and implied are defined with examples. Lastly, there are Journal and/or Discussion Questions.

RETENTION OF INFORMATION

Frequently, students or whoever is involved in using the interactive, creative, and multimodality IM will retain information because he or she has experienced the designing and creating of an IBR. Still, those exposed to it for the first time will likely recall and retain information because they are actively playing-the-pages and this "doing" fosters memory. To better comprehend that concept, this next section addresses the components of memory by way of defining and then examining them with respect to the brain-mind connection.

BRAIN-MIND CONNECTION

"The brain is the core of thought and the organ that perceives sensory impulses and regulates motor impulses," so stated Schwartz and Begley in 2003. "Simplistically, the brain is a physiological function which is made up of matter. The mind is housed in the brain and comprises awareness and consciousness that physically influences and interacts with the brain's function." Million in 2010 explained in one *Brain World* magazine article that, "Hence we have cognition that stimulates creative thinking as one looks back on things and recalls them." As Doidge (2007) relates in *The Brain That Changes Itself: Stories of Personal Triumph from the Frontiers of Brain Science*, "The brain and mind, unless something happens to them, continue to operate until they don't. During the years of our lives there is constant change in brain/mind function. This is how it works."

For the connection of the brain-mind to the IM, one might relate that through memory of past experiences we are provided with new thoughts, ideas, and opinions in order to create, to imagine, to explore, to invent, and to be involved in designing and making the pages of the project-based IBR. (See chapters 16 and 17 for further information.)

THE BRAIN-MIND AND MEMORIES

Much like modeling a piece of clay, the brain changes and the resultant behaviors are altered, but the previous ones experienced may be returned to, although not in exactly the same manner. This ongoing and continual reconfiguring of the brain and mind results in what will be our memories.

The overall concept of the brain working with the mind is that there's continual growth and refining so new challenges can be met. You might equate it to growing up. How? Well, you're constantly getting taller or wider. If the latter and you want to be trimmer, then you modify your intake of food, or you may exercise, and later your appearance is changed. The brain does this in conjunction with the mind by being transformative. "The brain continually refines its processing capacities to meet the challenges with which it is presented. This increases the communicative power of neurons and circuits that respond to oft-received inputs or that are trapped for habitual outputs.

"It is the brain's astonishing power to adapt and change, to carry with it the inscriptions of our experiences, that allows us to throw off the shackles of biological materialism for it is the life we lead that creates the brain we have (Schwartz and Begley, 2003), and all of this involves the brain and mind's memory of experiences."

IBR: MEMORY: THINKING CONNECTIONS

Memory involves a thinking connection to what is being examined and creating the IBR on a topic stimulates that use of memory. Subsequently, one is led to ask, "What is memory?" Memory is the ability to recall information or experiences from the past. For example, when going ice skating with three of my grandchildren, I watch them intently as they skate in front of me. The six-year-old falls and as I rush forward to help her up, my mind regresses to a similar incident so many years ago when I was learning to skate. I remember crying and the skating teacher coming to help me up to resume the process of one foot in front of the other and gliding around the rink.

Memories are recalled all the time based on recognition of connected and similar events—this happens in daily life and with the students in our classrooms—framing what they will learn and how they will learn. It happens when we have similar experiences to some media format exposure of a like event, or see people we recall and make associations based on those times spent together. Then again there's memory triggered by reading and conversation holding. Although we may not think of it, even young children have memories.

Not so long ago, using the Internet's Skype, I asked the little sister (age three) of a former teacher-candidate now teaching in upstate New York, "What is your happiest memory?" She responded quickly with "Having an ice cream at Abbott's Custard by the lake." I must say that from that question's answer I realized that having memories wasn't age specific. What was needed was for one to ask the question to trigger the memory.

How often do we, as individuals, parents, relatives, or friends ask a very young child, between two to five years of age, a six- to nine-year-old, preteen, teenager, or adult about his or her early memories? And if we do not do this, which would give us so much information about a person when answered, do we skip over it? For that matter, do we do this for ourselves—ask ourselves questions about what's remembered? Are you a person who recalls through practicing "reflection"? That exchange of information, sharing, builds community and a sense of well-being between those sharing. It's a teaching tool the IM uses to establish or enhance camaraderie.

Cognitively, memory involves recognition, recalling, and reflection. Did you know that memory may be initialized prior to birth? It is! Numerous studies evidence a recalling of smells and sounds initially introduced during a mother's pregnancy, and later evidenced as recognized in newborns when they are "experimentally" presented with these sounds and smells.

Developmentally, a baby coos and the parent interprets what is meant by this sound. As the baby matures to become a toddler, the cooing is replaced with language that expresses what is wanted, or needed, thus leaving the comprehension to be less interpretive and more established over time and experience. Memory serves as the baseline for what is liked or not liked.

Each of us holds different memories. The context of how subject matter, or classroom material and/or environment may trigger different memories in different students is obvious. Different reflections may positively or negatively impact learning. The IM is such that it triggers memories of positivity, success, enjoyment, creativity, and inventing. You already know that, right?

Generally memories, both plus and minus ones, can influence how we act and how we approach a given set of content or situations. We love to teach what we like best, we love to experiment and explore with the means of instruction that most influenced optimism. I'd like to ask you to take a moment and look back, as you're invited to recall/reflect on your earliest memories. I realize this task may be difficult because memories are most frequently triggered by a present experience, but let's give it a try. Make a list of those memories and share them with someone. Is your list the same as another person's? How? If not, how are they different? Looking at that list, what's the most significant memory you had and why do you suppose that's true? What was the first thing that came to your mind when asked to make this list?

IBR AND REFLECTION:

This word "reflection" is very important for this book you're now reading as, in order to make the IBR, one needs to reflect on the piece of literature being addressed or the topic of a unit of study. So, I'm thinking it may be helpful to clarify that this is not the image one sees in the mirror. The type of reflection referenced is "one's ability to stand back from what one has created and look at it 'assess it'" (Hegarty, 2014) and see if it represents effectively the information studied. Assess its worth. As the IM is employed through the use of making an IBR, one's reflection is "vital" by recalling what one knows about the material being addressed.

Reflection is a looking-back-in-time and a looking-forward and realizing some life experiences have made us *who* we are in the present, and influence personality characteristics for actions to be taken in the future. In that context, "We are our experiential past and people can only address, perceive particulars, configure generalities, respond through emotions and interpret what they find to be important in their life experience through the viewing—reflection on previous experiences. One's points of reference are based upon his/her reflection" (Schiering, 2000, p. 5).

APPLYING MEMORY AND REFLECTION: QUESTIONS

These next set of questions can certainly be fun to address, either in partnership, or small-group format, or if you're alone, then try it with yourself. Make a list and recall as best you can the answers to the following questions: Where did you live when you were growing up? What was the neighborhood like, and did it change over time? Why do you suppose it did or didn't do that? Who were significant people in your life? Who are significant people now and who do you think is important to children you know? Why?

When did you learn to read and write? What were your experiences with these? Did that change over time and if so how? (How do you suppose learning to read impacts children now? Why do you think that? What's your reaction to the Common Core (CC) learning standards? Do you think these help children learn? Why or why not? Interestingly, the CC learning basic and intrinsic standards are addressed when creating and playing the pages of an Interactive Book Report, but more on that later.

Some more questions for you to answer include: Did you like school and if so when were the best years? As you matured did you learn to ride a bicycle, or were you walking here and there? What was funny to you then and what's funny now? Did you think about driving a car . . . what kind and what was your first experience as a driver? What about relationships? How do you form them? What are things that bring others to your attention in a negative and/or pleasant way? What do you think about the future based on your past?

When it comes to teaching you might think about these questions involving memory: What style and manner of interaction with a teacher gave you a positive self-image and motivated you to learn? What made a person a good teacher; a master teacher—how do you emulate this? Based on your own personal experiences of learning, what are your three top "to do's" and three "don't do's"? Finally, did you ever wonder how your memory is formed? If so, what are your thoughts about that?

MEMORY, SUCCINCTLY STATED

"Succinctly, the act of remembering occurs in three ways:

1. Attention: the ability to focus on a specific stimulus without being distracted.
2. Orientation: the ability to be aware of self and certain realities and facts that manipulate the information. These are commensurate with the ability of a person to respond to stimuli and interface with everyday life-experiences.

3. Decision-making and Problem-solving: the ability to understand a problem, generate a solution or two, and evaluate these" (Schiering, 2003b).

SOME SPECIFICS OF THE IM

1. The IM involves reacting to information given whether it is through the use of an educational game or computer program, or video, app, using a SMART Board, and/or interacting with others in a communicative manner with a giving and taking conversational exchange. The "key" word is "interactive," as opposed to persons being sedentary or passive recipients of information.
2. The purpose for the previously stated interaction is to create memories. As a result of nearly fifty-years of teaching and learning, it's been noted that when an individual, small group, and sometimes even large ones are "emotionally" involved in the learning process, memory acquisition occurs readily. More importantly, this type of learning, the "being involved" type, as opposed to memorization for a test or drill work, lasts indefinitely instead of being short term.
3. Subsequently, retention of material presented is a vital component of the IM. Student learners from any grade/age level find that they're able to recall and reflect on what is learned. This is by originally being involved in the learning process. *The memories we have of past experiences shape our personalities. We bring our memories with us wherever we go and they are part of whatever we think and feel, say, and do.*
4. Realizing numbers one through three of the IBR in relation to the IM is a *memory creator*. It becomes part of a person when making it and afterwards as well.

TYPES OF IBRS

a. An IBR on literature: the learner reads a book and then reviews the main elements of the story.
b. An IBR on a curriculum area: a study of the systems of the human body, for example, is introduced through pages in the IBR that inform the learner of the components of that system.
c. An IBR in a particular discipline: this would be an IBR in, perhaps, math, with pages that revolve around different mathematical functions such as pages addressing word problems, addition and/or subtraction, geometrical shapes, fractions. Or maybe an IBR in English language arts, on parts of speech and types of sentences, would be another discipline worth addressing. Then there's social

studies with study of foreign countries, the USA, pioneers, or science IBRs with emphasis on planets, storms, ecology . . . there are so many topics that it's impossible to list them here.

THE IM AND LEARNING STANDARDS: DR. MARINO'S PERSPECTIVE

"Although times have changed, new and old educational methods have been introduced/reintroduced, and new buzz words have been used. The goal of education has always remained the same, at least for me. I remember the very first conversation with my building principal: Keep your eyes on the prize.

"At first I thought I knew what the prize was . . . how wrong I was. Over the past decade the 'name' of the prize has changed but the purpose has not. Terms such as: student-centered, real-world/project-based/inquiry-based, data-driven, college- and career-ready, and Common Core–aligned are all the buzz, and have been used to describe the prize. I will ask the question again: What is the prize?

"Currently, most USA states are adopting and implementing new standards to 'raise-the-bar' on the education of our youth. These are a set of standards that, in the opinion of their creators, will assist students in getting ready for the real world. In examining the remediation rates of freshmen in universities across the country, it is easy to see why these standards are being modified and implemented in our elementary and secondary schools. The thought behind the standards is a noble cause; however, there have been a variety of reactions (both good and bad) to how states are implementing these new standards. Some states have jumped in quickly, while more and more are beginning to slow down their implementation because of political blow-back from constituents. While we presently have a good deal of testing to decide the ability of student learners, there has been a lack of information on how to meet the learning standards. What is the prize? I think 'It's [a] teaching style that produces good learners.'"

FROM NYS COMMON CORE WEBSITE

http://www.p12.nysed.gov/ciai/common_core_standards/pdfdocs/p12_common_core_learning_standards_ela.pdf, page 7.

New York State, one of the first states to implement the new "Core" has defined some characteristics that students who are college- and career-ready in reading, writing, speaking, listening, and language possess. "Students will: demonstrate independence, build strong content knowledge, respond to the varying demands of audience, task, purpose, and discipline, comprehend as well as critique, value evidence, use technology and digital media strategically and capably and come to understand other perspectives and cultures." What methodology does all of that should be evident from what you've read so far in this book.

The Common Core states that the aforementioned characteristics "will be evidenced after students have successfully met the standards in the disciplines of ELA, mathematics, science and social studies. Students will be asked to work toward mastery of these standards, developing an ability to cope with the rigor associated with them" (NYSED website).

I respond with, "Yet there are very few methods that address the needs of students that are aligned with this new notion of 'the Core.' So here are some ideas as to what to do. Use the Interactive Methodology and IBR strategy. After examining each stage of their evolution, the method and technique have always addressed the philosophy of getting students ready for the real world. How? Well, these criteria or standards were accomplished through teaching critical thinking skills, giving students ownership of their education, building content knowledge in a variety of disciplines, teaching tolerance of others' methods of learning by collaborating and sharing, as well as conversing with one another, creating and evaluating evidence, comprehending and critiquing, using primary and secondary sources, using technology appropriately, creating resources through design and engineering, and most importantly—having fun!

"For example: In the NYS Writing Standards K-5, 'Students will write narratives to develop real or imagined experiences or events using effective techniques, descriptive details and clear event sequences'" (Common Core, p. 28).

"Using the IM, there are a variety of IBR pages that can be created and included that address this standard. Students can create a Story Map graphic organizer, or a Sequence Map, or Character Analysis Web. They could also create a Team-Learning activity or complete a Cloze read activity that addresses this standard.

"Grade six students in reading are expected to 'compare and contrast texts in different forms or genres in terms of their approaches to similar themes and topics' (p. 49). Cause and Effect and Venn diagrams can be created and included (see chapter 10). My major question is about your reaction to the Common Core Learning Standards? Do you think these help children learn? Why or why not? Do you think the IM is designed to meet these standards? Why or why not? From my perspective, interestingly, the Common Core learning basic and intrinsic standards are addressed when creating and playing-the-pages of an Interactive Book Report, but more on that later" (Marino, 2014).

COMPREHENSION AND THE IM

The Interactive Methodology relies on comprehension for a creation of the pages to be played. (Schiering, 2000–present)

Comprehension involves memory, cognition and metacognition. Remember, you've read about memory, and its being the storing and then recalling and retrieving of thoughts and feelings too. Thinking . . . having thoughts, ideas, opinions, and judgments are cognition represented by such skills as realizing, comparing and contrasting, prioritizing, and classifying. And then, there's metacognition, which is thinking at a higher level and includes advanced decision-making, evaluation, and self-actualization.

Comprehension is recalling stored information and application through reflection of these aforementioned reciprocal thinking processes. This is done with the ability to understand or have knowledge about something. Comprehension is the main goal of education and the overall basis of the formation of personalities through understanding concepts, ideas, thoughts, opinions, and emotional responses to stimuli.

We, as individuals, want this comprehension for ourselves and schools demand it for students. As such, school is not the simple acquisition of facts, but rather a place where students come to understanding something in connection with how it works, can be used, or the connection to other things. "Thinking/cognition is recognized through 'comprehension' to produce understanding" (Allport, 1937). Comprehension may or may not be verbalized, but regardless of this, it's demonstrated through things said, and/or actions and behaviors in three applications, which include:

1. Literal Comprehension: Fact-based evidence of comprehension.
   Example: The Yankees are a baseball team.
2. Applied Comprehension: Comparison and contrast comprehension, resulting from making connections to one's own experience, read material, conversations, and/or mixed media presentations.
   Example: Reading about the first forty USA presidents, I think Abraham Lincoln was better than many leaders when it came to presenting ideas on liberty for all citizens.
3. Implied Comprehension: This is inferential comprehension, based on context or illustrative material being presented in oral, visual, tactile, or kinesthetic formats.
   Example: When I saw bird footprints on the beach's sand, I thought that earlier in the day there were birds walking on the sand.

These three applications then form the definition of comprehension, which Olsen (1995) and Li (1993) relate as being "the activity of thinking with decision making and problem solving as receptive and meaning-making orientations."

Think for a moment and list four things you comprehend about your learning and teaching as an educator, or as one who learns and teaches through life experiences. What did your thinking produce?

JOURNAL AND/OR DISCUSSION QUESTIONS

1. How would you define retention of information, memory, reflection, and comprehension?
2. What are three types of comprehension and examples of each one?
3. What are the three types of IBRs?
4. How do the Common Core learning standards apply to the IM and IBR?

SIX

Advantage Points of the IBR and Leadership Building

CHAPTER OVERVIEW

This chapter addresses the definition of something being an "advantage." Five of these pluses are recognized in the creation of an IBR. Then in a more general listing, there are over twenty additional gains in using the IM and IBR. These are referred to as upsides. One special consideration and an ultimate upside is then presented. Technology, considered to be interactive, is given attention as a tool for learning and as being part of the IM and IBR. Advantages of this form of learning as well as disadvantages are addressed. Then, how this IBR project and performance-based activity involves developing leadership qualities is discussed.

EXPLAINING "ADVANTAGE"

What does it mean to have an advantage? Some might say it's simply a benefit or having a lead over something else, and they'd be correct. Realizing that the IBR involves learning and teaching that is interactive serves as the center point of the advantages or "pluses" regarding this endeavor. The following five areas are addressed as being gains of this project for learners and teachers alike at any grade or age level. Following this listing there are over twenty continuing upsides of the IM and IBR listed.

IBR Advantage Point 1: Preferred Groupings:

If you're one who prefers working alone or with another, or in small groups, or like being on a team, your preferences are met with the IBR.

Any grouping is possible for the making of this instructional resource. Things to remember about this IBR include that educational game pages are self-corrective. Then, with ideas put in place, the images are brought forth to creation for playing-the-pages, as one would play a game. This is done, topic wise, to review a piece of literature, as much as serving as an introduction to those who've not read the book.

Or, the IBR may address a thematic unit of study. Whichever, it is interdisciplinary in that there needs to be at least one interactive page involving reading, English language arts, math, science, and social studies. Those pages may be made in any group or singularly. The pages are bordered and titled with attractive lettering and design. Titles should mention the discipline being addressed, as Danielle did in her example of IBR activities in chapter 4. Then, the pages may be different colors or the same, but there needs to be something eye-catching in the overall makeup of the page. Chapters 16 and 17 provide ideas for pages, and the steps to be taken to create an IBR.

IBR Advantage Point 2: Convenience and Engagement:

The IM may be used every day in the classroom or wherever one is trying to learn new or formerly presented material. It may also be used once a week or a few times a month, or once in a while, for most of a semester or throughout the year. Primarily, this decision depends on the one using the methodology and the appropriateness of the IBR for learning new material or reviewing something already presented.

The idea is to use the IM and IBR whenever it's handy or expedient, as it's quite open-ended . . . you use the method and the book when it's appropriate, in your opinion, to use them. The big thing is . . . you decide if it works for you and if, as a teacher, it works for your class, by realization of how this method is practiced and the IBR is made for teaching one's self for learning and retention of what's been learned!

One other thing is that this book addresses the idea that creative cognition is developed, as well as enhanced by making an IBR. It is! But, one should also know that the IM involves "engagement" in learning and the pages of the IBR individually adhere to learning and teaching interactively whether or not in a book format. The pages may be separate projects connected to new or formerly presented parts of a curriculum at any age or grade level.

Additionally, these interactive pages of an IBR involve learning and teaching being intertwined with the roles of the teacher being connected to those of the learners. As Delialioglu (2012) stated, "Students are more engaged when the instruction increases the contact between student and teacher, provides opportunities for students to work in cooperation, encourages students to use active learning strategies, provides timely feedback on students' academic progression, requires students to spend quality time on academic tasks, establishes high standards for acceptable academic work and addresses different learner needs in the teaching process."

With the pages of the IBR being self-corrective, as explained in an earlier chapter of this book, the instant feedback on one's academic acuity is clearly provided. Additionally, the active engagement of one's mind is predominant as the inventiveness and creative thinking, and imagination incorporation abound.

IBR Advantage Point 3: Belonging/Classroom Community:

The IBR gives an opportunity to have class-room togetherness. This "sense" or feeling of "joining" is primarily due to the individuals in the class working on the IBR project. There is a common goal of creating the IBR. Even if one is working to design a page without the help of others, the final product is entered in the book with all the other pages.

This "sense of belonging" occurs with each learner's different abilities and areas of interest being appreciated for the common good of the practiced IM. There's an emotional component of enjoying what one's creating, collectively. The making of an IBR meets and then, when completed, fulfills this emotional component of togetherness.

IBR Advantage Point 4: Reflective Practitioners and Socialization:

As the page or pages of an IBR are being made, there is ongoing reference back to personal experiences regarding the topic that is addressed. There's recalling whether it's from a specific happenstance or situation, or one read, or shared as an experience that someone else had. This reflection and practice of it is done through use of memory, and, if working on a page with another or others, there's shared reflection. These recollections help to form ideas for creation of pages and, of course, the socializing that occurs when there is sharing of thoughts and ideas, perhaps opinions, judgments, and feelings as well. The final result is collaboration.

A portion of learning in a classroom or really in or at any place is that it's a social experience, which involves "thinking about one's own thinking" (Olsen, 1995, p. 134). Subsequently, the creators of the IBR are socializing reflective practitioners. This reflective partitioning means looking back to influence what one is presently doing. And, with learners cooperating with one another to create pages for this book, there's ongoing communication. As we already know, learning is not just an academic experience, as there's interaction between individuals with discussion on the contents of the IBR; conversations.

When working with others, the idea of using one's imagination to create leads to discourse, both verbally and nonverbally. Conversations tend to expand from the topic of the IBR to daily thoughts, ideas, opinions, and sometimes judgments and feelings. Meaning and perspectives are shared. Information is exchanged and problems are solved in a cooperative manner (Glatthorn, 1995). This process takes place in the classroom and wherever learning occurs, which is pretty much everywhere!

Perspectives about self emerge as the IBR is being created. Since learning is frequently a reflective practitioner process, as stated previously, sharing is colored by individual perspectives, including perspectives about self and others. These come to be recognized as the composition surrounding the "social" part of learning.

Socialization Questions: Think of those who are your friends. How did each person become part of the socializing partnership or group? Where and why did the caring begin and what was the setting? What solidified the socialization? Were there any projects you worked on with friends or what is a project you'd like to work on with a friend?

IBR Advantage Point 5: Cooperation:

The IBR instructional style and the strategy call for learners' cooperating and doing this through discussing, conversing, sharing, prioritizing, examining, evaluating, deciding, informing, synthesizing, conjuring, realizing, risk-taking, comparing and contrasting, classifying, recalling, inventing, imagining, designing, and creating activities to facilitate learning. The IBR reporting style calls for cooperation's being an intrinsic part of the methodology and creation of pages for learning-through-play. "With the use of the interaction and acceptance through cooperation, as well as creative thinking ideas regarding one's self and others, the IBR learning community is one that is most favorable for those involved. It's not just cooperation, but a comfort zone" (Schiering, 1996).

CONTINUATION AND CULMINATION OF ADVANTAGE POINTS

The Upsides, Special Consideration, and Ultimate Upside of the IM and IBR:

Upsides 1–10

1) Learners, teachers, all those involved in the IM or making of an IBR have the opportunity to talk WITH one another, as opposed to talking at someone or to others. The key expression is talking "with" because there's collaboration, and sharing.

2) Individuals, partnerships, or small groups are contributing participants in their own learning-through-play.

3) Learners are creating educational games of their own design.

4) Proud ownership of work is evidenced.

5) One's imagination is constantly in-play.

6) Learner-empowerment as well as self-efficacy are evidenced with retention of material being long-lasting because students are making their own learning devices.

7) By being active participants in their learning, a new form of assessment is realized.

8) Transformation of self may be evidenced as thoughts, ideas, opinions are explored and impact one's personality through creative design.

9) The nuts and bolts of the IBR revolve around the use of auditory, visual, tactile, and kinesthetic instructional resources being designed and constructed, thus thoroughly involving a sensory-motor approach to learning. The neuroplasticity of the brain is therefore evidenced; and 10) Retention is enhanced when "doing."

Upsides 11–18

11) IBRs may be done individually or provide opportunities for conversation and collaboration, subsequently, enhancing "social cognition."

12) A positive classroom atmosphere is created through sharing. A sense of togetherness ensues;

13) Free-range of creativity is employed.

14) Self-valuing, is clearly evident.

15) Being a reflective practitioner is emphasized.

16) Work is project- and performance-based with evidence of the completed work being provided in a touchable format. This equates with experiential learning.

17) A variety of disciplines are experienced by the designer/creator and player-of-pages.

18) Evaluation of comprehension may be attributed to the designer and creator of the interactive pages addressing the topic and/or being in alignment with material from other sources.

Upsides 19–26

19) Beginning awareness, critical and creative thinking, as well as metacognitive processes are addressed with the IM.

20) No judgments are passed on the quality of work.

21) This method allows for the expression of one's self.

22) The opportunity to focus, in a finite manner, on what's to be examined brings forth comprehension of a topic.

23) There's a digesting of one's thought processes and those of others as different IBR pages are "played."

24) State and National Common Core learning standards of project- and performance-based learning is provided through evidence of the IBR.

25) Sharing the ideas brings forth trust.

26) Students are teaching and learning from other student-learner endeavors/IBRs and the teacher acts as a facilitator.

Special Consideration

The use of the method by creating an IBR relating to a piece of literature or a thematic unit of study is time consuming. It's a project for inside and outside of school. If done at home and used to assist you in a specific subject, the making of interactive instructional resources requires concentration. While I personally do not see this as a downside, the fast-paced everything-must-be-done-now society in which we live might define this IBR learning and teaching strategy differently.

Ultimate Upside

****Important to remember: *Again,* it's important to remember: "If you're the user of this Interactive Method and ultimately the *designer* and *creator* of an IBR, then you are the owner. Once you are in possession of something, it's yours, you created it, and your invention becomes valuable because it is of your own making" (Marino, 2000).

THE IM AND IBR CONCERNING INTERACTIVE TECHNOLOGY

In our present interactive technological age, we first need to realize that "technology is a tool and not a strategy" (Bowen, 2014). We have use of cell phones or smartphones, tablets, and iPads in most classrooms, along with SMART Boards and multimedia-style presentation systems. These learning tools are available through the Internet with social media being at the ready. These may be good things, as the advancement of technology has had a profound effect on our society. And, interactive technology is part of the IM and may be a page or pages in the IBR! On the other hand, there are a few drawbacks.

Frequently, it seems that technology is practiced as a method in and by itself, as opposed to being an instrument to enhance or display a methodology or the IM. And, in upper grade level classes, teachers proclaim that students are so into social media that it and texting have become their predominate means of communication. They use abbreviations with abandonment. A dictionary of acronyms used to keep messages brief has been memorized. These abbreviations appear in essays, in creative writing, and even in notes from one person to another. Decision-making and problem-solving seem to be at a minimum, partially due to minimized communication between individuals or whole groups, even societies. When does all this inability to converse effectively stop?

It's difficult, but perhaps there isn't an answer to that question because means of expression have become so minute that the art of lengthy or meaningful *in-depth* communication is seemingly lost. This is true for upper grades, college undergraduate and post graduate students, and middle to lower elementary learners as phone games occupy time, and the SMART Board and other advances in technology reach the classroom and are touted to be "in the zone." This is considered a plus/advantage, although students may be "zoned-out" when using the technology.

While an individual, partnerships, or small groups learn to be brief in expressing thoughts, ideas, opinions, judgments, or feelings, they are still expressing and having some form of communication. Nonetheless, this brevity may not serve them well in the overall scheme of things, or it may hinder their development in other ways.

Most profoundly, the IM and IBR are for having opportunities focused on holding conversations or problem-solving, evaluating, synthesizing, and active listening. Not that the methodology and/or book report are a *cure all,* but they are a method and a strategy that go together and go a long way in providing opportunities for collaboration, hearing others' ideas, and discussing as well as weighing their viability while talking about everyday things.

While technology may serve as a vehicle for designing pages of an Interactive Book Report and thereby may be "popular," it may also not be needed to create pages. Or, there *can be a joining of technology and hands-on activities*. Regardless, the advantage of an interactive method of learning and teaching is that it's one which involves the learner in a multitude of thinking skills and touchable and manipulative means for that learning to occur. It stimulates conversation for the purpose of communication skills being developed! The IBR does not abbreviate, but rather encourages discourse to solve problems, make decisions, use one's imagination, be creative, or just share ideas.

THE CREATIVE COGNITION'S IBR: LEADERSHIP BUILDING

Let's take a look at leadership and the IBR with creative cognition. In an article for *LinkedIn,* an Internet publication, Matt Schiering (2015), writes about the traits one might possess for this guidance role. Using his numbered "Leadership Qualities" ideas, the author connects them to the IBR in the following listing with explanations.

1. *Singularity of purpose*: The IBR is designed to develop creative cognition through imagining and inventing the pages to be played. The goal is to design and create interactive pages.
2. *Encouragement and Reassurance*: When working on the IBR in a classroom setting or elsewhere at any age/grade level there is the overall concept of one's being successful built into the project. The IBR, once begun, has a support system that is supplied by the

learners and teacher. Giving confidence through knowing what is to be done and doing it is built into the one's achieving.

3. *Collaboration:* Presenting ideas and images in a linear or reciprocal format for the IM and IBR to others allows for their input. Assistance may be given and cooperation builds strength in purpose. Learners talking "with" one another builds confidence as ideas and thoughts, as well as opinions, are shared. Alliances are made and relationships form a classroom community.
4. *Optimism:* The IM and IBR promotes and supports positive thinking with the idea that this making of pages/learning-through-play can be accomplished. Learners develop confidence in their own endeavors.
5. *Good Planning:* The IM and IBR pages are designed to address varied disciplines. Therefore, the connection between the topics of the IBR pages to be reviewed, learned, or taught must be subject to comprehension of them. Organization of the IBR is presented in a rubric with what pages come first, second, etc. The IBR requires preparation and sequencing for a comprehensive scope of the project.
6. *Persistence:* When using the IM for making an IBR by one's self or working with a partner or even in a small group, there is an end product that needs to be present. This requires goal setting and working to complete the project, which encourages continually moving forward with purpose to produce or reach a goal. One's determination builds with each page created.

JOURNAL AND/OR DISCUSSION QUESTIONS

1. What was your favorite "Advantage Point" of the IM or IBR and why?
2. How do the IM and/or IBR promote socialization?
3. How do the IM and IBR support technology?
4. What are four leadership qualities that the IBR helps develop?

SEVEN

A Guide to Learning and Teaching Creative Cognition

CHAPTER OVERVIEW

If you are not particularly creative, then how do you teach creativity? Perhaps it's best to recognize here that being creative and using one's imagination is part of who we are. Guidelines for having a creative classroom are presented. See how many of these guidelines are practiced that you've personally experienced. Two suggestions are made before several sections on teaching creativity/creative cognition. An "evolution" of concepts on how to do this is provided. Examples of in-practice IM that are decades apart is primarily accomplished with several teacher reflections. Test preparedness with using the IM and IBR are given attention.

Then, this chapter addresses the creative classroom environment, student engagement in learning, and classroom "interrupters" of creativity. These aspects are given attention and explained. They are followed by a section on characteristics of creatively cognitive people, vital components for a creative cognition IM classroom for the teacher and learner. Settings where creativity abounds, and viewpoints on this with yours included is presented. End notes and a Reflection Exercise are followed by Journal and/or Discussion Questions.

Suggestion 1:

Regarding the use of the IM and IBR for learning and teaching creative cognition, I believe that "Using the IM may be practiced each day, everywhere. Making and using the IBR strategy should be done when it seems appropriate for the development of creative cognition."

Suggestion 2:

Keep in mind Sir Ken Robinson's statement in his 2006 video, "We educate the whole being. Creativity is as important as literacy."

TEACHING CREATIVITY

I am not a teacher of how to be creative, but I am one who may lead you to discover your own creativity. I do this discovering by giving ideas, presenting techniques, sharing talents, expressing opinions, inspiring, motivating, and collaborating. Here are some additional thoughts on being one who stimulates creativity in others . . . one who inspires another to be all he or she can be without fear of repercussions. This stimulation is accomplished by using the IM. At this juncture, you, the reader, in all likelihood comprehend that this interactive and creative method requires opportunities to be inventive and have hands-on instructional resources at the ready.

REVIEW OF IM AND IBR

The IM calls for creative cognition in its overall concept. It's a way of instructing that involves the learner in his or her learning process through active involvement. And, the IBR usually is part of the methodology with learners creating a report-style book addressing a review of a piece of literature or an introduction to it. The IBR may also be about a selected topic, such as a thematic unit of study. You could even address several topics or pieces of literature if you choose to do that. And, if you don't actually make the IBR, you may use and have learners construct their own interactive instructional resources/educational games. This would be done separately such as in a *learning center* to facilitate engagement in learning with development of learners' creative cognition. Dr. Patricia Mason used the idea of using interactive instructional resources separate from the IBR and her work is explained in chapter 8.

Remember, the IBR itself is a book one creates to review or teach something new, but simultaneously is made to learn material for one's self or others. In each of the chapter sections, the IBR and the IM are inherent in what's related. This IM is one focus of this book. It's a method that may well change the educational world through the idea that when learners are involved in their own learning, their retention of material lasts a lifetime.

This retention happens because what has been made is the learner's idea and the ownership of that makes it part of who he or she is as a learner, and maybe as a teacher as well. Then, the individual or whole groups using this method may build upon this comprehension for advanced understanding of a variety of topics. They may also share their creations with others and thereby result in learners teaching learners.

EVOLUTION OF THOUGHTS ON TEACHING CREATIVITY

Over thirty years ago, while teaching in the sixth grade at a middle school on the east coast, this author was asked by a supervisor, "Can you teach creativity to your students?" I had been told from my earliest childhood that I was a very creative person. This was a huge plus for me, so considering my impression of being something others were not and having this exclusive 'gift,' my response was an emphatic "No."

My supervisor then told me my answer was incorrect and that I should think about how to enhance and/or develop the student learner's more imaginative side of the brain. He suggested I "Teach them to be creative thinkers!"

"Give me a break," I thought, and I continued this thinking and yet wondered, "Aren't I presenting the curriculum in a way never or rarely presented before by others I've observed? How can I make someone else have this 'gift' I have? Besides doesn't *my* creative cognition and being creative make me unique and rather special? And, if I do discover how to make students be creative, do I really want someone else to have this ability?" (Reflectively, this seems to be a rather selfish viewpoint, and looking back on the "me-of-then," it was.)

Sustained thinking on whether it was possible to teach creativity and develop students' cognitive skills, simultaneously, plagued me. Was my "No" response to my supervisor correct? Then, in a moment of either clarity or enlightenment, I realized my original answer should have been "Yes." In fact, I realized that I'd been doing this creative cognition instructional method—teaching children to be creative and use their imaginations—for all of, or nearly all of, my entire career as an educator; I just hadn't labeled it as such.

TEACHING CREATIVITY/CREATIVE COGNITION: THE CLASSROOM ENVIRONMENT FOR THE IBR

One of the components of teaching creativity and/or creative cognition depends on the assignment one gives to stimulate a person's thinking. Teaching creativity also relies on the classroom atmosphere being one where there's personal engagement in the learning process, flexibility, and positive attitudes about learners sharing their ideas involving the process of learning that best works for each of them. This, I wholeheartedly believe, is best done through having project- and performance-based instruction.

Overall, a congenial classroom atmosphere and these types of assignments stimulate students to be imaginative, inventive, and interactively involved in the learning process. This is done most frequently through educational gaming, which today's educational terminology refers to as using "interactive instructional resources" or "hands-on" techniques.

The IM is fully engaged in this process with evidence-based learning the result. The creators of the IBR or even makers of instructional resources related to a topic of study, without being in a book format, show their work and use it to assist in knowing about the subject area being addressed. Then, sharing the hands-on resource with others so they will gain knowledge about it brings the IM and IBR to the point of learners teaching learners, whole classes teaching other classes . . . it's a sharing experience. (See chapter 20 for a study conducted on using the IBR to learn about ecosystems and sustainability.)

EXAMPLES OF IN-PRACTICE IM: DECADES APART

When do particular learning and/or teaching styles take hold? How do you best learn and if/when you teach, what is your most favorable way of doing that? These questions were asked at the start of this book and perhaps now, if not then, you've a more expansive idea for an answer. For this author, in a 1972 first grade class, the idea of making educational games for learning just surfaced naturally. Well, maybe not so naturally, but as an alternative to a programmed learning sequence we were required to use for teaching students to read. While I'd used this educational games form of instruction in years previous to this, the formalization of learning-through-play took place.

First there was keeping "games" in a labeled cardboard six-drawer box. Students would simply select the game they wanted to play at a desk or on the comfy corner carpeted floor. Most often for these six-year-olds the games involved tactile and kinesthetic flip cards, a variation of Tic-Tac-Toe, and puzzles for learning-to-read activities that addressed recognizing reading, science, social studies vocabulary, consonant blends, sentence structure, parts of speech, story character identification with picture and name cards, character analysis through actions matching, decision-making, and sequencing, or number identification and how to add and subtract symbols.

The years that followed, 1976–1998 in sixth grade and then fifth, found me practicing the IM fastidiously. Students made interactive instructional resources on different topics; these included board, wall, and floor games, and/or role-plays with scenery, as well as the IBR in the 1990s. We'd play these games together, as one might play a game at home, or they'd be played with a partner or by one's self. The type of grouping or lack thereof really depended on the material and instructions for how to play the particular interactive instructional resource. Or, it relied on how to use the technique appropriately for instruction. Each game had a set of instructions. Each game involved creative cognition in its design and makeup for effective learning.

The eight interactive instructional resources presented in chapter 16 of this book give another twist on this previously mentioned early 1970s–present time classroom practice of using games to learn. Once having IM knowledge and information on types of educational games, each student in the fifth grade class (1991–1999) made a Flip-Chute (F.C.).

The F.C. was Velcroed to their desk. Then, F.C. cards were made by each learner and addressed such things as science terms, parts of speech, word opposites, vocabulary from a selected piece of literature or social studies unit, math word problems, or equations in picture or numerical formats. They also made Electro-Boards and Velcroed these to the wall, or Wraparounds, Pic-A-Dots, and Task Cards kept in a bookcase in appropriate holders. Then, each day, at a class-voted-upon-time, we'd have "Creative Cognition Time." This was FUN!

This meant that we'd either exchange with one another our envelopes containing the Flip-Chute Cards we'd made, or took from the bulletin board an Electro-Board, or Wrap Around that one wanted to try. The other games were simply the most desired ones a person wanted to use for that hour and were taken from their room's shelf for playing somewhere in the classroom.

During that period, what students experienced was teaching other students using the IM with interactive instructional resources as the focal point. And while playing, there was socialization, conversations about school, home, things that mattered in one another's lives. This brought a sense of everyone belonging and community to our space. This community feeling was enhanced by a poem I wrote in 1976 and is titled, "One Classroom Rule" (Schiering, 1976; 2009). I wrote the poem and incorporated its message into our daily experiences. The message was to say things that are positive with this phrase at the forefront being: "No Put Downs . . . ONLY Lift Ups!" This meant to be complimentary as opposed to finding fault with oneself or others.

Practicality encourages each and every one of us to practice that rule wherever we might be. Acting kindly incorporates not making negative statements, but positive ones when talking about others or one's self. "It serves no purpose to put yourself down," I'd say repeatedly.

Character development is part and parcel of the IM and IBR construction. This following of being positive through caring, fairness, being trustworthy, responsible, respectful and kind towards one another and ourselves makes one's learning environment safe and a place where learners want to be. Our classroom, because of the overall attitudes about learning, as well as the IM and learning/teaching games, that developed creative cognition, was like being at home base. And, let me explain here that the classrooms were diverse in that some were in inner-city locations while others were in the suburbs and rural centers from Ohio to North Carolina and then New York, which was followed by adult learning locations in South America and several European countries.

For those making errors when playing the pages of an IBR, it simply meant going back and trying again with the same learning resource or one in a different educational game format. Since there were a variety of topics available, the students had free choice about learning new material or reviewing topics presented earlier. Textbooks and conversations, first-person interviews, and teacher-talks were a few of the sources for information gathering regarding what would be in the games. Later, the Internet became a viable source for obtaining information.

In 1998, "hot" topics were ecosystems and sustainability. They still are today. But back in 1990s, as Earth Day was approaching, the students separated into partnerships or small groups of three to four and each made a poster on foam-core board that was 3 1/2 feet by 5 feet. Each of the eleven panels had an educational game addressing how to keep our planet safe for future generations. The project was called *Our Interactive Earth Day Book,* and panels were taped together to have the book stand up like an accordion-style book. You could sit on the floor and play a panel, or put the accordion-style book on a few long tables and stand in front of the panels/pages to play them. The project was entered into the *NYS I'm a Green Nation Earth Day Competition* and took first place.

The games or interactive instructional resources call for involvement that is Independent, Self-directed, Self-sufficient, Self-regulating, and Self-ruling. What better way to learn than through teaching decision-making skills along with self-reliance and governance?

In college classes, as these learning tools were constructed in IBR format, the class had the opportunity to play-the-pages of one another's IBRs, following their oral presentations of their work. Here we were, at college, learning about a topic or piece of literature, maybe vocabulary (Spanish/English) by sharing and collaborating and teaching each other, simultaneously, and enjoying doing so. The best way to learn, I believe wholeheartedly, is through setting an example and is called teacher modeling.

LEARNING STANDARDS AND THE IBR

National learning standards, while stating what skills are to be developed, do not necessarily offer suggestions for how to impart knowledge or have students develop these skills or comprehension strategies. However, the delivery style or use of interactive instructional techniques begs to be used for "project- and performance-based learning," as originally stated in the Common Core standards. These projects and performances provide evidence of learning and they are there to assist in the development of one's thinking skills. Such cognitive skill application leads, in a natural manner, to enhancing one's creative abilities and aptitude/talent while being engaged in the process of learning. This activity-based method is in opposition to teaching-to-the-test or learning a set of procedures with emphasis on rote memorization.

TEST PREPAREDNESS THROUGH THE IM AND IBR

Do you want to have students prepared for a test and do well on a test? Then, the best learning is done by having them *involved in the learning process*! My learning and teaching experiences have presented that concept to be true. And, national statistics from as far back as eight years offer evidence that high-achieving students in other countries attribute the level of excellence to involvement and, additionally, parental interest and involvement in their children's education. "Interaction with homework guidance, ongoing communication with teachers, and even visits with the schools proved to be most beneficial, as the student-learners saw their parents' interest in their personal children's academic and even socialization endeavors in the school setting" (O'Connor-Petruso, Schiering, Hayes, & Serrano, Cyprus research and presentation 2004).

Yet another component for good classroom instruction for creative cognition students, and for that matter all students, is promotion of self-awareness and high self-esteem. This is done by providing information that will create amicable relationships between students and students to teacher(s) and vice versa. As stated in *Teaching and Learning: A Model for Academic and Social Cognition,* (Schiering et al., 2011), "Teaching is not just having what's in a textbook being learned. Teaching also involves the communal interactions of a classroom influencing and being conducive to an environment that promotes, through discussion, definition and modeling, the ability to have interaction with others."

"For six and more hours—five days a week from kindergarten through grade 12, and sometimes before and after that—parents put their most precious gifts, their children, into the teacher's hands. What happens in that classroom shapes those in that space. This develops a desire to gain knowledge and the formation of attitudes, belief and value systems and dispositions and demeanors" (Schiering, 2000).

What happens in that classroom serves as the catalyst regarding a desire to learn. The combination of an individual's and the whole group's thinking and feelings forms the interrelationship of teaching and learning. And, combined, these form creative cognition. The IBR, in one neat little package, promotes and provides this interrelationship by bringing learners together to share ideas, modify them, have a goal, design and create learning tools . . . pages to play and have fun, simultaneously.

That "having fun" part, as mentioned in the last sentence is truly important. The reason it's important is that the IBR creates a classroom community that has support of one student for another through working collaboratively. The atmosphere in the room is positive and a sense of security prevails.

*****The IM of teaching revolves around being persons of good character; respectful to others and self, responsible, trustworthy, caring, and kind. When a student or any individual is in such a setting, then the comfort of such is relaxing, enjoyable, and often pleasuring. Eradicating testing fear and elevating self-worth through a nurturing classroom environment are two by-products of using the IM that promote creative cognition* (Schiering, 2000–present),

TEACHING CREATIVITY: STUDENT ENGAGEMENT IN LEARNING

This engaged-in-learning concept is supported by many teachers I've encountered or learned about through research endeavors. One of the latter is Linda Naiman. She relates that creativity skills can be learned. We may also learn to be solely noncreative. This learning is done with high structure and instruction that does not allow for leeway. True learning is not developed from sitting in a lecture, but by applying creative thinking processes. Common Core refers to this as "Project- and Performance-Based work." In later chapters of this book, as in previous chapters, these ideas of creativity and Common Core are addressed through the IM and IBRs.

These ideas include storytelling and educational gaming with focus on development of cognitive skills and the heuristics involved in skill application, as well as using realistic exercises appropriate to the domain at hand (Scott, Leritz, & Mumford, 2004, pp. 31–38). I would refer to these domains with an acceptance-of-effort by the students with their implementation of an assignment. Most importantly there needs to be flexibility in the classroom; teacher open-mindedness when using the IM and having student learners making IBRs. Goleman, Kaufman, & Ray, in *The Creative Spirit* (1992) relate that "there needs to be a "nurturing" experience in the classroom." This nurturing encourages creativity.

NOT TEACHING CREATIVITY: STUDENT NON-ENGAGEMENT IN LEARNING

So, what happens when this nurturing, acceptance, and encouragement of using interactive instructional resources does not occur? What happens, I've witnessed, is all too often in today's classroom learners are instructed in accordance with the following (Schiering, 2000):

1. "When things are to be done,

2. What these things are, and
3. How each one is to be done, as well as
4. Who is going to do what, but not why something is being done"

One can simply say farewell to creativity with such a structure, as what naturally follows is negative judgments or stringent evaluation. The following section addresses inhibitors of creative teaching of creativity in the classroom, as the numbered items directly above are practiced.

TEACHING CREATIVITY INTERRUPTERS: THE REVERSE OF THE IM

Over-Watching

Constantly watching children's work and commenting on the lack of ability they're conveying is one of the first ways to eliminate creativity. These approaches may be followed by pitting one child against another for individual competition with a resultant winner and loser. With enough losses, the creativity is smothered. Then, there's "over-control," as noted in the book *Creative Spirit* (Goleman, Kaufman, & Ray, 1992), and this may include stifling curiosity and pressure to complete work in a "timely" fashion, which eliminates children's sense of "having enough time" to do work.

"Frankly, the concept of being 'enough' is entwined in this allotment of time, as the child comes to realize that he/she is a failure, because meeting of goals is not possible. Frequently, the individual gives up trying with an attitude, justifiably grounded in the idea of, 'If I can't meet goals, then I might as well give up trying. I'm not enough'" (Schiering, 2009). Teaching and learning interactively are the reverse of the approaches mentioned in this paragraph, as there's not a stringent time constraint.

Transition Time

From personal classroom observation, teachers were evaluated, and still may be, on "transition time." This meant how much time was given between the switch from one subject area to another, "If too long, by Principal standards, the chastisement was evidenced in the teacher's evaluation. And yet, looking at this from this time period just think of what happens when a student is embroiled in a project and told to 'stop'" (Schiering, 2000–present). It is my opinion that when everything to be done during a class day is scheduled from the minute it begins to the minute it ends, the creative and often teachable moment doesn't exist.

If this transition time is so strict then after a while the learner's attitude changes from getting engrossed in the work to "why start?" Acceptance is a key element in developing creativity, and so is being supportive of students' work. Positivity is exceptionally helpful. The IM promotes and allows for nonjudgmental evaluations, but rather approval and appreciation for creativity in the design and implementation of the work. And if it takes a moment or so longer to complete the work, then let that happen.

Negative Evaluations and/or Judgments

All too often, there are judgments that occur in the classroom . . . a good or bad reaction or statement from the teacher can influence a student in his or her academic or social structure, feeling comfortable or not comfortable. The negative comment will undoubtedly thwart the creative person's attempt at being creative, or approaching a topic from a different perspective. But, let's look at what Anthony Romano, who contributed earlier in this chapter, has to relate. (As his former professor, I asked Anthony for his comments, as every teacher-candidate in our class saw him as a creative person, whether it be through his storytelling or the projects he imagined, designed, and created.)

It was during the fall of 2013, but the commentary below is Anthony's viewpoint as a result of reflecting on his childhood and adolescent memories in school and some from college years as well. I asked Anthony, "What has it been like to be a creative person in a classroom?" He answered:

> Creativity is an interesting topic, and I personally think that the term goes hand in hand with the idea of being different from my classmates. I think up until recently I associated myself more with being different than creative. When you think creatively, you are looking at a specific task in a new and unique way, you are thinking about it in a way that perhaps no one else is thinking about it, so it is different. It is human nature to *judge* something that is different from the norm. It is at this point where being creative may not work so well in the school setting.
>
> Growing up and still to this day I have been very cautious about presenting creative ideas to anyone, because of the inevitability of facing a negative judgment for it. I think with any creative project that time has been invested in there is doubt and fear of evaluation and negative comments.
>
> Creative individuals move and shake to the beat of a different drum and sometimes it is hard not to wonder what everyone else thinks of their dance. Maybe one of the greatest creativity inhibitors is discrimination in the form of a judgment that's not uplifting.

Testing

Ah, testing! There's a huge topic to address, as testing students in American schools, with the advent of state and national Common Core

Learning Standards, has become the mainstay for educators' consideration. In a January 2014 issue of *Reader's Digest,* Gray (37), relates that one of the reasons for children disliking schools and parents' following suit was the amount of end-of-year testing that occurred. The comparison of students in the school district at the same grade level also seemed to be distressing, as all students were given the same test, regardless of ability level or learning abilities or disabilities. Teacher's evaluations are based on 40 percent of these test results. Subsequently, the pressure to do well is considered a detractor from the Linear and Reciprocal Creative Cognition Processes.

TEACHING CREATIVITY: CHARACTERISTICS OF CREATIVE COGNITIVE PEOPLE

You may recognize each classroom as being unique because of those occupying that space having different abilities and personalities. Schools become places of diversified personalities joined in one space. Since one of the teacher's responsibilities is to balance these differences in a way that promotes learning being enjoyable and a process that's worth one's involvement, it's helpful to know, for this book, the characteristics most commonly attached to one's being creative.

Mihaly Csikszentmihalyi (1996b) writes in *Creativity: The Work and Lives of 91 Eminent People* that he has "devoted 30 years of research to how creative people live and work, to make more understandable the mysterious process by which they come up with new ideas and new things. If I had to express in one word what makes their personalities different from others, it's 'complexity.' They show tendencies of thought and action that in most people are segregated. They contain contradictory extremes; instead of being an individual, each of them is a multitude."

The following are from a survey taken using Csikszentmihalyi's list of contradictory creative cognitive characteristics. The participants in the survey noted these sixteen statements as those that are indicative of being a creative person. Those asked were familiar with the IM and IBR as a method and strategy dealing with creative thinking for developing imaginations, or the application of the one or the other, or both in a home, work, or school setting.

Creative People _____________:

1. have a great deal of physical energy.
2. have the ability to focus for many hours on one thing or work on many projects at the same time.
3. tend to be smart and appear naïve, simultaneously.
4. generate a great quantity of ideas.
5. show flexibility.

6. are able to switch from one perspective to another.
7. demonstrate originality in picking unusual associations of ideas.
8. demonstrate a combination of both playfulness and productivity, which can sometimes mean both responsibility and irresponsibility.
9. work late into the night and persist when less driven individuals would not. (Usually this perseverance occurs at the expense of other responsibilities or other people.)
10. combine fluency, imagination, and fantasy that are rooted in hyperawareness of reality.
11. pay personal attention to real details, allowing a creative person to imagine ways to improve them.
12. individually tend to be both introverted and extroverted.
13. are genuinely humble and display a strong sense of pride at the same time.
14. are both rebellious and conservative.
15. appear very passionate about their work, but remain extremely objective about it as well. They are able to admit when something they have made is not very good.
16. have the ability to enjoy the process of creation for its own sake.

(Take a moment and see if you identify with any, some, none, or all of these statements. Then show them to others, who might include students and friends. If you've the inclination and time, conduct and record responses of those who respond. Compare them to others who've done the same thing or to this list on this page. What were the results? Was there full agreement or not with the idea of creative people having these characteristics? Were any other comments made and if so what were these? Use your responses as a reference point when learning and teaching.)

VITAL COMPONENTS FOR AN IM CREATIVE COGNITION CLASSROOM

As a result of teaching creatively for many decades, I have found that there are seven very important components for the practical application of cognitive creativity. In teaching, or any learning situation that results in creativity, there must be the following:

1. Few, if any, restraints that extend to an embracing of open-endedness of assignments and flexibility.
2. Project- and performance-based assignments stimulating thinking and interactivity.
3. "We learn to be creative by experimenting, exploring, questioning assumptions, using imagination, and synthesizing information" (Land, 1968).

4. Teaching students to be creative may act as an inspiration for oneself to try other ideas and be inspiring to others as well.
5. Eliminate fear of repercussions for work done: verbal or nonverbal.
6. Foster all class members making positive statements to one another by adhering to the idea of "Only lift-up" type statements being acceptable. There's a way to make evaluative comments without being negative or taking away from one's positive self-image. Think of how to word your comments in an uplifting way and set this example resulting in teaching your students to do the same in their conversations or communications.
7. Be a change agent in your teaching by incorporating through modeling number six (6) above.

TEACHING CREATIVITY: SUBJECTIVE OR OBJECTIVE EVALUATION

Do you remember Anthony Romano's comments on creativity from chapter 3? He continues here with his thoughts on creativity, subjectivity, or objectivity evaluation. In 2013 he said: "In my opinion, what should be more focused upon within society, especially in school classrooms, is how one's creativity is neither good nor bad, it just is.

"Creativity is not something that can be graded objectively or even subjectively. For example, I enjoy writing. Yet, in the past, I have been extremely cautious as to who reads my work. Maybe they won't like my word choice? Maybe they won't like my style? If enough people don't like it maybe it indicates that writing is not my forte? In reality, none of that matters. It is, for the most part, their opinion based on their experiences when if there's any evaluation it should be by addressing only whether I met the criteria of the assignment. That is what should be important."

CREATIVITY IN THE CLASSROOM: FOR THE STUDENT LEARNER

Dominick Toscano (2014a) writes on creativity for the student-learner when thinking about the IBR method. "To do work that is creative and true to oneself and to continue to be able to do that work without fear of judgment is empowering and long lasting. However, I think it is difficult to reach that point. I struggle with this even today. To have that ability to say that you create a piece of art for yourself and no one else, that is perhaps the most difficult stage to reach, yet in my opinion, the most true and honest. Freedom to do that, be one's self in a classroom, is what I think needs to happen in schools.

"Overall, my concern is that children are afraid to express their creative abilities in the classroom, not only due to the judgment of their teachers, but also from their peers, leaving them to develop their skills independently. I add to that the comments on challenges I face with one of these being in my classroom. My students are embarrassed to have others see their work because all too often students will make fun of each other. In fact, it should be the opposite; the classroom is exactly the place for creativity to flourish and grow, I believe.

"The classroom is the place for children to see that when they write, paint, draw, sculpt, or whatever they prefer to do, they cannot be graded. It is the place to let them own their work from within and create their own unique style. It is the place where we can develop children's confidence so that they may become 'creatively free' and move forward so that they keep creative practices in their lives. This is essential as I think that, the more creativity is fostered, the longer it will last."

CREATIVITY IN THE CLASSROOM: FOR THE TEACHER

In the paragraphs before this one, teacher and teacher-candidate Anthony Romano wrote about his heart-felt opinions of the latitude needed for creativity in a classroom setting. That may, as well, apply to teachers, but is often met with administrative restraints, from financial decisions because of newly purchased curriculum materials as well as standardized state testing (Toscano, 2014b) and, unfortunately, other teachers' jealousy.

How to address this has been a concern of mine, writes this author. This concern is from experience while being a public school teacher who taught creativity through applying open-ended assignments. These open-ended assignments followed instruction on use of strategies such as research, gaining information, and direct and indirect instruction (teacher-focused distribution of material and student-focused application of using that instruction), but also resulted in the student learners enjoying the process of inventing and investigating to create. That freedom to do so, once expressed outside the classroom causes other students to question what is being done in their class. If the restraints are stringent, talk about which class is more fun comes to be discussed. The comparing and contrasting are brought home, and then the issue of creativity or lack of it becomes a home and school situation.

All too often the teachers in schools today, both private and public, have a requirement to teach the same thing in the same way in their classrooms. This is with the idea that the ending test scores on state-wide instruments will be high. When there are not rules that result in several same grade-level classrooms being on the same page, having the same lesson presented, then creativity may exist.

END NOTES ABOUT CREATIVITY

- With the trend in education being accountability, to teach effectively one needs to be able to connect creativity to cognitive function. However, with an emphasis on test scores and performance on standardized instruments to measure one's achievement, ability, or intelligence, the opposite is observable. Low test scores equate with inability.
- Because high test scores equate with one's being smart, creativity is often not appreciated and/or recognized. But, using creative instructional techniques will provide a most viable means for achievement on the aforementioned tests. Why? It's because interactive learning, experience-based learning, with the IM and IBR, causes retention of presented material.
- It will be those persons with creativity who will change the course of history with inventions and new ideas to further humankind. "If we are to reverse this trend of negativity with respect to one's being creative, then, when talking to people or giving an assignment three simple guidelines for fostering creative cognition are provided here:

1. *"Avoid rigidity and do not allow only highly structured and sequential processes to dominate.*
2. *Allow for, encourage, honor, and respect, elasticity and variables through engagement of one's imagination.*
3. *Know what one is thinking and feeling and the factors that influence creative cognition by addressing the inner components of* A Model for Academic and Social Cognition, *as well as* The Reciprocal Thinking Phases" *(Schiering, 2011; 1999).*

REFLECTION EXERCISE

And, what about "you" with respect to creativity? What creative ideas have you evidenced in you and/or others? Make a list of these, and share them. Reflecting, try to find the original idea. Then, examine how it developed to be what it is now. See how one idea leads to another? Or, did you go back and forth in your creativity? When you construct this list of steps taken to come up with a new idea, you are experiencing creative cognition in a structured format.

JOURNAL AND/OR DISCUSSION QUESTIONS

1. What's your opinion on whether a teacher can teach creativity? Explain your reasoning. You may cite examples from this chapter.

2. What are examples of a creative classroom environment?
3. As an educator and learner, are you willing to meet Common Core content in creative ways? Why or why not?
4. What is meant by student engagement in learning?
5. What are three inhibitors to teaching creativity in the classroom?
6. What are at least five characteristics associated with one's being creative?
7. What are at least two vital components of a creative classroom?
8. What are four differences between being clever and being creative?
9. How might creativity and cleverness be combined? Include the focal point of creativity?
10. How do you suppose an educator would demonstrate, in the classroom, honoring of individual's creativity?

EIGHT

Creative Cognition with Special Needs Children

Linking Learning Styles, the IM, and the IBR

CHAPTER OVERVIEW

What is meant by special needs students extending to an example of the author's history concerning a student's experience with this label is explored. This chapter then moves on to categorize characteristics of these types of learners. This is followed by how the IM and IBR in general address each of these components. Next is a clarification of the Dunn and Dunn Learning Style Model and how the IBR relates to and/or is linked to each of its strands or elements for assisting learners learning-through-playing. This is done in conjunction with special needs learners, regardless of age or grade level. The chapter culminates with Processing Style Identification and the IM with processing style scenario. Questions about this scenario follow with the chapter closing Journal and/or Discussion Question section.

QUESTIONS FOR YOU CONCERNING SPECIAL NEEDS

What do you think of when reading or hearing the term "special needs" student, regardless of age or grade level? Aside from a physical impairment in an academic setting, do you automatically envision "special needs" as someone who is learning disabled in a particular area, or doing poorly in school in general, or who doesn't seem too quick to catch on to things, or has socialization problems? Or do you think of someone who is very bright, gifted and/or talented, creative, and an out-of-the-box thinker? Perhaps you think of someone who just doesn't fit the mold of what you expect. Maybe that "special needs" person is both learning disabled and gifted, as opposed to being one or the other. The truth around here is that if someone needs special attention it's probably due to his or her not doing well on tests or being slower than other students in the academic and perhaps even social behavior arenas.

A "SPECIAL NEEDS" EXPERIENCE: REFLECTIVE NARRATIVE

1. During elementary years of education a close friend of mine was termed as being a *special needs student.* Although that hardly seems possible now, at the time, others (teachers and classmates) had judged her that way. Why? I think it was because she was highly creative and this was not something honored. Additionally, she was unable to read until she was eight years old. A year or so after that, she "couldn't read exceptionally well," at least not as well as her classmates and maybe not reaching this status until she was in the eighth grade.
2. The truth of the matter was that her creativity abounded, but by then the pattern had been set as to what was considered to represent someone who was smart and someone who wasn't. So she saw herself as "less than" instead of "equal" to her classmates, kids on the block, others her age in general. Whatever she was, it wasn't enough.
3. For many creative persons, such terms as "dumb, stupid, a waste of time, too different, and/or lacking intellectually (adult categorization) prevail when referencing overall academic skills. Sometimes the comment may be that the person thinks too far out-of-the-box. For this individual, she relates that "These monikers were difficult to handle and that would be putting it very mildly."
4. Her parents' reaction to this lack of academic acuity initially was embarrassment, as they believed her performance reflected on their own intelligence and/or ability to parent effectively. To their credit she was supplied with private tutors and that helped a bit, as being highly creative was acknowledged, but was not considered a particularly impressive factor. Nonetheless, she explained, "The social stigma of being one who needs more attention than classmates, in some subject matter areas, was devastating."

   This author explains that such social stigmatization is still prevalent or at least part of today's educational systems. These special needs learners are grouped together as underachievers, overachievers, learning-disabled, mentally challenged, but definitely "different." That difference, whatever it may be, sets them apart in a place called "alone." While some hunger for or appreciate it, others do not.

5. When in the school setting, overall, this special needs individual was a good listener, naïve, and when permitted to converse, "rocked." In fact she recalls being able to purposefully make people laugh, children and adults alike. Once questioned as to how she could do that, she said, "I don't know, I just can. Ideas and words, they come to me quickly as to what to say. I was also a good storyteller."
6. Nonetheless, even with those abilities, this student was retained in second grade, and required to have tutors and classroom accommodations made for her in order to pass to the next grade. For the longest time she honestly thought she was stupid, certainly a *failure.* As did others, she devalued her creative and imaginative qualities.
7. She learned that the negative name calling (dumb, retarded, . . .) doesn't necessarily go away even when it stops. It may remain with a person, forever. Subsequently and generally, it's my opinion that stored somewhere in the psyche, one's impression of him- or herself may be dramatically influenced by those early beginnings . . . positive and negative alike. Over time this might work for or against a person in the academic and social arenas encountered.

   In grade ten after doing abysmally poorly on a social studies test, she recalls her teacher talked with her awhile about this grade of three points she'd given her. This was for having the courage to put her name on the test paper. "Harrumph," she thought. But the teacher went on with telling her she knew she was smart by the demonstration of reasoning she continually exhibited in class discussions. Her next words encouraged this teenager to study more and if she had questions, to come and ask her. She closed with the four words that changed this student's life. She said, "I believe in you."

   Somewhere within those next few moments or shortly thereafter the student explained what she thought of the teacher's comment, "If this teacher can believe in me maybe I can believe in me." On the next test in that class she earned a 100 percent. From that result she knew having that first success was vital, because one success brings another; there is no ending point for success. Another thing learned is that she was not "stupid," but perhaps a "late bloomer. Not everyone advances at the same rate," she said (see Gladwell in *Reader's Digest* on this topic, September, 2014 issue).
8. The truth of the matter for this student was that in later years she came to realize some of the effects the original academic misdiagnosis and name calling had on her. I think that maybe the metho-

dology being used to teach her was not appropriate for her way of learning. "If children don't learn the way we teach, we must teach them the way they learn" (R. Dunn, 1978; 1996). The IM would have worked, I believe, and the IBR too would have been a project for her achievement. I wonder if perhaps the reason for the national and state learning standards being based on *project and performance instruction and the teaching of thinking* is because that's what we need in education systems: personally active and involved learners.

9. This "special needs" student went to college and became a teacher. She explained that this was doable because along her educational path she had some teachers who emphasized her areas of academic strength. They also were accepting and created an environment around her that was comfortable for learning.
10. I have often wondered, after hearing this student's story, of the learners in our classrooms or people we know who have talents not recognized. How many are misunderstood, or challenged? How many think it's best to conform to a system that doesn't necessarily encourage thinking that's out-of-the-box? How many try to discourage or stop their thinking that's creative, or a bit different from the established "norm?" What are your answers to those questions? Are they unanswerable? If so, why?

A FEW AFTERTHOUGHTS

Being labeled "special needs" is a term attributable to many different persons for different reasons. Some may be challenged in academic areas or others in physical or behavioral ones. Perhaps labeling that's done of individuals is something that's "not necessary" in the overall scheme of things. Since it's nearly impossible to speculate on what would have happened had the aforementioned student not been called dumb and retarded, one is left to question if she would have striven so hard to prove to others that she wasn't these "names"? Do you suppose this student would have tried to be a better academic and socially cognitive person if that were the case? Why or why not?

SERIOUS CONTEMPLATIVE AFTERTHOUGHT

Do you suppose the same experiences, feelings, and thoughts expressed in the "special needs" scenario would apply today in educational settings? Why or why not? What are the programs and conditions in schools that enable such a described-in-detail experience to occur or not occur? What limits as learners and teachers do we set upon ourselves with thinking one can't achieve? One thought is everyone is special in his or her own way. It's one's attitude that often shapes the space. So, in thinking it's best to select a positive attitude . . . one that says I or you shall achieve and then set about to do just that.

Under the circumstances provided for you, could this person have invented, in later years, something like the methodology described in this book? A five-person consensus opinion is that while this individual rose to the occasion of proving the "titles" given her as incorrect, other similarly labeled persons will not. How many learners do we lose in the abyss of negative classifications? What are your thoughts on this topic of "special needs?"

****In chapter 7 some characteristics of creative people were given attention. Being smart while demonstrating naïveté is one of those referenced characteristics. Going back to that point in this book, try observing how many of the sixteen listed creative contradictions you identify with, or someone you know does. Here's a thought: Individuality needs to be honored, as opposed to ignored or given short shrift.

A SPECIAL NEEDS SCHOOL EXPERIENCE: AN AFTERTHOUGHT

Before leaving this topic of "special needs" I recall visiting, on several occasions, many years ago, a special needs school. The limited population was wheelchair bound. Some of the children only had the use of a finger pad to move their chair. But, move them they did in a huge rubber-mat floor gym. The cognitive ability was present and the creative cognition abounded as the room was arranged for "cardinal directions" to be viewed and followed. Moving the wheelchair forward was to go "north," etc. The atmosphere was fun and the accommodations for learning quite appropriate, as students felt successful. Again I call to mind the idea of teaching to one's strengths . . . honor individuality!

IDENTIFYING CHARACTERISTICS OF SPECIAL NEEDS LEARNERS

Do you know characteristics of special needs children? In a class given by professor Rita Dunn in 1995 the following were listed as characteristics most often observed, and this includes gifted students: 1) Can't remember what they hear, 2) Can't read well, 3) Move while they are sitting, 4) Can't follow directions, 5) Can't work well with others, 6) Require, but don't follow, structure, 7) Nibble while they concentrate, 8) Talk or sing to themselves and to others, 9) Appear to be, or are, hyperactive, 10) Don't do what they are told to do, 11) "See" different ways of doing things, 12) Take frequent breaks, 13) Stop, start, stop, and start activities, 14) Require a lot of attention, 15) *Want* to, but don't work well with others, 16) Are either "into" everything or withdraw, and 17) They are not attracted to academic learning.

IM AND/OR IBR FOR SPECIAL NEEDS LEARNERS

For those who have difficulty learning by listening there are other modalities to be put in play, such as visual, tactile, or kinesthetic ones. For those who have difficulty with reading, there may be use of an audio tape where the individual listens to the story or book to be read. When you're making an IBR book and using the IM you are moving around while sitting, and for those who require, but don't necessarily follow structure, the chart on *Reciprocal Creative Process* may be applied (figure 2.2). For those who require frequent breaks, are hyperactive, require attention and nibble while they concentrate, the IM is perfect, due to its propensity for flexibility, acknowledging one's creative process with use of imagination, and consideration of these so-labeled students "seeing different ways to do things."

You may be stopping and starting work and can't follow directions or not work well with others, but you want to do that, because one is fully engaged in use of his or her imagination. A person may work best alone, or show preferences for moving from one topic to another as a matter of conditions of processing styles, which are respected and/or honored. As for talking and/or singing to one's self, this accompanies seeing different ways of doing things.

The two remaining parts of the list are "Special Needs students are either into everything or withdraw and are not attracted to academic learning." Both of these are easily addressed with the IM and IBR itself. How? For the first of these, when one is designing and creating through use of his or her imagination, they are being reflective practitioners, which stimulates being multi-involved. For the second of these, the interaction of making the pages of the book constitutes involvement in academic learning in an imaginative way so participation is appealing.

Also, the problem of not being attracted to academic learning is addressed through the submersion of social cognition, which is a major component of the interactive method and interactive book. This involvement has to do with having the opportunity, without restraint or judgment, to collaborate with others, to discuss and be discerning, respecting opinions and trusting in the creative process to realize one's being "enough."

All in all the IM and IBR work as a method and strategy for special needs students, at any age and grade level regarding those having the previously listed seventeen *Identifying Characteristics*. In fact, differentiation of instruction pretty much addresses these special needs students. For more information on that see part 2, chapter 17, especially "Kinds of Instruction."

OVERALL VIEW: IM ASSISTS SPECIAL NEEDS STUDENTS

How the IM addresses these situations is through its use of creative cognition and the act of providing lessons promoting one's being creative, acknowledgment of the way students learn and/or process information, and flexibility in instructional styles to meet the learning needs of the persons participating in the instruction. Perceptual preferences are addressed along with room design being formal (desk and chairs) and having an informal section (comfy corner with cushions, possibly carpeting, and an area with soft illumination as well. Additionally, the necessity to complete something immediately or in a specified order is not emphasized so open-ended direction is operational. This informal or formal component of the environment may take place in school, home, or job location when self- or group-learning is happening.

GENERAL LEARNING STYLE OVERVIEW

Over time many educators have noted that different individuals within their classroom perform better at some tasks than others and that an individual who performs well in one discipline may perform badly in another and vice versa. Drawing from these observations, educators and theorists have concluded that individuals possess varying learning styles that correspond to the individual's differences in perceptive ability, cognitive processing, information management, and sensory variability. Keefe (1979) noted the learning style movement emerged from the reform movements of the 1960s and 1970s as a key element toward increasing instructional responsiveness to individual students' needs.

"Keefe and Languis (1983) describe learning style as the consistent patterns of behavior and performance by which an individual approaches educational experiences. Learning Styles, therefore, is the composite of characteristic cognitive, affective, and physiological behaviors that serve as relatively stable indicators of how a learner perceives, interacts with, and responds to the learning environment. It is formed in the deep structure of neural organization and personality that molds and is molded by human development and the cultural experiences of home, school, and society" (Schiering, 1999).

A MISCONCEPTION ABOUT LEARNING STYLES

Before moving forward to discuss a particular learning style model, a clarification is necessary. In my actual teaching in public school and college professor years, I noted that most people thought that "learning styles" referred to whether someone had a preference for a specific modality. This would mean while some liked to listen (auditory), others may like to learn by reading (visual) or touching things (tactile), or have whole-body (kinesthetic) involvement. However, this is a misconception, as learning styles, such as in the next section of this book, are much more than that.

DUNN AND DUNN LEARNING STYLE MODEL

A popular learning style *Model* in the United States since 1976 is that of Dunn and Dunn. It rests on research conducted during the past three decades. The theoretical cornerstone of the Dunn and Dunn *Model* is based on the brain lateralization theory, which notes that within an individual a particular hemisphere of the brain may be more dominant than the other, or in another case a dual brain dominance where both sides of the brain function equally. Additionally, this *Model* relates that: most individuals can learn; different instructional environments, resources, and approaches respond to different learning styles strengths.

In adherence with the lateralization theory and the first strand of the *Model*, Environmental, there are those who are considered left-brain dominant and these are Analytic or Field Independent (FI) Learners. They prefer no sound when learning new material, with a formal room design, and bright illumination. Their counterparts, the right-brain dominant, Global Learners or Field Dependent (FD), would have the opposite preferences. The Emotional strand addresses the elements of motivation, responsibility, persistence, and structure, which over the decades have all been attributed to indicators of bilateral or left-brain dominant learners.

The Sociological strand includes what type of work collaboration one prefers, or for which there is a low tolerance. For example there's working by one's self, in pairs, with peers, on a team, with an adult authority, or in varied groupings. The first of these is given attention by FI learners and the remaining ones by FD processors.

The defining Psychological strand elements are: perceptual preferences (auditory, visual, tactile, or kinesthetic modalities), which are non-indicators of either FI, or bilateral brain dominance (FI and FD). Intake of food or water is connoted with the FD learners as they work on many projects at the same time and exhibit a holistic view of projects or assignments. The FI learners like to work on one project at a time, sequentially, before beginning any other work. A preference for no interruptions whether for food or water, or going to watch television would be happening.

The two Physiological elements in the *Model* are: Analytical (FI)/Global processors (FD), which equates with left- and right-brain dominance, and whether one exhibits behaviors that are usually impulsive or reflective. The strands and elements represent factors that in different combinations can influence the learner in the process of learning. The *Model* is not an alternative to established theory of learning but seen by Dunn and Dunn as a complementary *Model* based on neuropsychological and cognitive theories.

Overall, when a student is learning new and difficult material by reacting to certain elements within the strands, brain dominance is evidenced through learning preferences. Analytics and then Global processors demonstrate respectively: a) no sound being present or some sound—even the whirring of a fan being necessary, b) high intensity lighting, or soft illumination—such as a table lamp, c) formal room design with a desk and chair, or informal room design where one studies while sitting in a chair or lying on the carpeted floor, d) no snacking or food intake as opposed to taking frequent breaks for food, and e) being structured, completing one project at a time to completion, sequencing material, or working on many projects at the same time, not necessarily to completion and needing to seeing the whole picture.

EXAMPLE OF LEARNING STYLES: COMPARISON OF FD AND FI STUDENTS

The teacher has assigned the students to create an educational game to help assist them in learning about the life cycle of a butterfly. The field dependent students would work with a partner or in a small group where there was a portion of the room for an informal design, such as a comfy corner. These students would prefer to have soft illumination and sound present when working on the game. Additionally, they'd need to see the entire picture, as opposed to the structured sequential order of constructing this game. They may take frequent breaks and want a snack time while working, in order for their attention and persistence to be formidable.

Conversely, the FI learners would show a preference for working alone in a high intensity lit area with no sound interfering with their concentration. They would want to work on this project to completion before beginning any other assignment, and they would want a formal room design. No snacking or taking frequent breaks would be acceptable, as they demonstrate a high level of responsibility for completion of the task at hand.

IM AND IBR CONCERNING LEARNING STYLE STRANDS/ ELEMENTS

Examining the Dunn *Model* the following may be observed as meeting the processing and learning styles of learners of any age.

1. The Environmental strand is "covered" by the IM in that when working on an assignment, there may be bright lighting or soft illumination in the classroom or at home. The need for a formal or informal room design may be accommodated with desks and chairs for the former and a comfort corner for the latter. Sound is a bit difficult to control in a classroom, but individual CD players could be used for those preferring sound and sound-blocker headphones for those needing quiet while working on the IBR or for any project. Room temperature is controllable at home, but less so in the classroom.
2. The Emotional strand is perhaps one of the easiest for the IM or IBR to cover. First the project- and performance-based IBR serves as a motivation through its calling on students to use their imagination and creativity, sharing ideas and collaborating. Responsibility is evident as are persistence and structure when realizing the guidelines for what's in an IBR and the steps taken to produce it.
3. Sociological strand asks the question if one prefers to work alone, or in a partnership, with a team or having an authority figure present. The flexibility of the design of the methodology allows for any of these factors to be given attention. And, conveniently, the IBR may be done by an individual or not.
4. The Psychological strand: The pages of the IBR, which are in different disciplines on the same topic may require varied modalities or perceptual preference to be utilized. Intake at home or a preferred time of day, and mobility may be accommodated using this interactive and hands-on method with reaching a compromise through discussion as to how this can be accomplished.
5. Physiological strands involving Analytical, Global or Dual Hemisphericity processors come down to those who prefer working alone, having bright illumination, no intake, working on one project to completion, having structure, and being reflective or not, for any of these preferences. Certainly, from the previous chapter it can be discerned that each of these desires or needs may be met through the engaging method or creation of the IBR which allows for tremendous laterality in its composition.

(The IBR emphasizes the elements of the fourth strand with attention to perceptual preferences. In this instance this interactive method of learning, and yes, teaching, has the designer and maker of the IBR using all perceptual preferences: auditory, visual, tactual, and kinesthetic. This is so each one playing the pages will find comfort in the experience).

OTHER IBR FACTORS THAT ADDRESS LEARNING STYLE PREFERENCES

1. Success is provided by pages being self-corrective and the page-player only needing to repeat until digested any area of difficulty.
2. And, each page is in a different discipline so social studies, reading, ELA, math, and science, as well as art and possibly music and physical education are all experienced when creating the pages and/or playing-the-pages.
3. Teachers who adhere to a learning-style philosophy create a classroom design that has areas for comfort and those that are more formal. These respectively address preferences of global processors who like soft illumination and an informal room design with sound present, and analytic processors who like to have high-intensity lighting and a desk with a chair for learning tasks. This informal area may be referred to as a Comfy Corner and has carpeting, throw pillows or the like, and accommodations such as individual headsets for listening to music softly played while concentrating on material.
4. Other classroom accommodations would include the opportunity for healthy snacking with the rule of "if you abuse this privilege—you lose it" being applied. Of course, the losing it would only be for a short period of time, as opposed to a full day or week. The child that is hungry is most definitely not able to concentrate on learning. Analytic learners would not respond to this particular "intake" provision, as they are not in need of snacking.
5. Learning-style teachers provide opportunities for working in partnerships, as global processors do not like to work alone, as do analytics. Since perceptual preferences are neither indicative of right- or left-brain dominance, teachers would be sure to have all modalities implemented for application of varied instructional techniques. This means that some projects or assignments would require tactile/kinesthetic involvement, as well as auditory and visual ones.
6. Realizing that the analytic processors are usually highly structured, motivated, responsible, and persistent, the teacher would want to create assignments where different processors may work together in small groups or on a team, and allow for some "alone" time for analytics. The basic premise within the classroom and at home regarding learning styles is that the elements represent preferences that should be acknowledged. A learning style inventory may provide preference information, as well as teacher observation. Children who are physically comfortable in their learning environment are more likely to learn and approach it in a positive

fashion than those who are continually working without recognition of these preferences.

A FEW QUESTIONS

A few questions for your active mind at this juncture may include: What are your strongest perceptual preferences? How do you know this? Are you equally strong in several modalities and if so, which ones? What are things you've noticed about your friends, students, coworkers, and family members' perceptual preferences? Are these the same or different from your own? How do you suppose this influences your learning?

PROCESSING STYLE IDENTIFICATION AND IM

Scenario Directions

1. The following is an example of a fictitious student in a sixth grade classroom. Can you tell from the narrative what type of processor she is, what her learning preferences are, and if she's an FI or FD learner?
2. Discuss your answer with a friend or write down your response, and be sure to state why you have the opinion you do.
3. Compare with others and see how many agree or disagree with your thoughts and ideas.

SCENARIO

Karen, reentered the classroom, and walked reluctantly to her desk. The task that awaited her return from the drinking fountain seemed impossible. She'd entered the first category on her map-system chart very neatly. And, she'd copied this from the SMART Board. The remainder of her paper, although divided into sections or columns, was blank.

Tom, was seated to her left, and Sue, seated to her right, were swiftly and systematically entering data to the various sections of their charts. In front of Karen was her text, which contained the needed information between pages sixteen and twenty-four. However, Karen had difficulty synthesizing the information. She lacked structural skills and while making the chart was a "breeze," the reading and dividing of material into proper categories was a "drudge." She could do it, but it would take forever, or so she believed.

The room had intense lighting and her chair was extremely uncomfortable without any cushioning, just hard wood. This type of setting made Karen uneasy and seemed to enhance her inability, or at least desire, to do school work. "If only I could stretch out in a corner or work with a friend out in the hall," she thought.

CHALLENGING ASSIGNMENT

- From your perspective as a learner, teacher, educator . . . whomever, what accommodations would you make for Karen and why would the IM work for her (list at least five factors)? Then, once again being a *reflective practitioner,* take a moment and explain how the IBR would work for each processing style and the learning style preferences of FI or FD students.
- Now, take a moment and separate a piece of notebook paper into two columns, or work on your laptop. Label one column FI and the other FD. Write the learning style preference and then reasons, one under the other, why you think the IBR works for that type of learner.

JOURNAL AND/OR DISCUSSION QUESTIONS

1. What did you learn from the section about the author's history concerning special needs students?
2. What are four or eight characteristics of being a learner with special needs?
3. What are the five strands of the Dunn and Dunn Learning Style Model?
4. How do the IM and IBR address perceptual preferences, and the other factors related to learning styles?
5. What do you consider key points in this chapter? Why do you think that?

NINE

Learning and Teaching Creative Cognition

The IBR's Cognitive Collective: Thinking and Feeling

Joining Thinking and Feeling

I think . . . therefore I am.
I feel . . . therefore I am.
Where did I learn that?
Perhaps it's not as important as realizing
What we think and feel.
By knowing that . . .
You come to realize who I am
And
I come to realize who you are.
All said and done
We are a combination of what we think and feel. (Schiering 2010)

CHAPTER OVERVIEW

Definitions of the Cognitive Collective and thoughts, ideas, opinions, judgments, and feelings are given with the latter five having examples of each one. Thinking and feeling are part of the IM in that each is relevant in creating activities for an IBR. A paradigm within *A Model for Academic and Social Cognition* is given attention in a narrative. Figure 9.1 provides an illustrative perspective. These are for comprehension of the importance of thinking and feeling being impacted by Common Social and Societal Realities and one's Belief and Value Systems. The Cognitive Collective and effective pedagogy as well as key points of thinking and feelings are emphasized. A scenario concerning a practical example of the Cognitive Collective is given, as the chapter closes with Journal and/or Discussion Questions.

THE COGNITIVE COLLECTIVE: DEFINITION

Each of us is a combination of what we think and feel, and there's an accepted, effortless, and innate movement between and within these. There's not much refuting of that concept. The Cognitive Collective is exactly that, the combination and interplay between and within what one thinks and feels. "Often, what we think and feel becomes what we say and do" (Schiering, 1976). With that in mind the Cognitive Collective term was first developed by this author and copyrighted in 2003 as a paradigm, in the same year, within her then graphic organizer on teaching and learning, *A Model for Academic and Social Cognition.* Years later, working with Bogner (2007), president of Molloy College, the two devised definitions for the thinking and feeling skills. These include thoughts, ideas, opinions, judgments, and feelings and follow with examples of each definition.

DEFINITION OF THOUGHTS, IDEAS, OPINIONS, JUDGMENTS, AND FEELINGS: REVIEWED AND EXPANDED WITH EXAMPLES

1. **Thoughts:** Immediate conscious responses to reflection, which involve memory. Reflection is further defined by Schon (1997) as having two forms, which are reflection "in" action or thoughts occurring now in the present, and reflection "on" action as referencing something that happened in the past.

Example: From my experience, I have thoughts that pizza is one of my favorite foods.

2. **Ideas:** A prediction of future responses or speculation based on one's perspective as a result of reflection "in" or "on" actions.

Example: She got the idea about going shopping when her daughter asked for a new dress.

3. **Opinions:** A combination of thoughts and ideas in that a formulated concept results from one's or a group's thinking that helps shape opinions.

Example: The teacher's opinion about using interactive instructional resources resulted from experiences using these in the classroom.

4. **Judgments:** Concretized or solidified thoughts, ideas, and opinions which are a result of reflections brought forward. Often, they are based on one's level of attachment to a situation. Judgments are not easily changed, but they may well change. If easily modified,

then you've expressed a thought, idea, or opinion, as opposed to a judgment.

Example: My judgment is that learners like learning through play. (Until evidence of this is demonstrated on a continual basis not to be true for you, the judgment will remain a judgment—solidified thought.)

5. **Feelings:** A sensory and/or emotional response to stimuli that may be descriptive or classificatory.

Example: Sensory Response: The water felt soft as it slid through my open fingers.

Feelings are also defined as being the quality that something has in that one responds in a manner that connotes feeling of an emotional or intuitive nature and/or reflects on something to establish a formed response that is rooted in thought, ideas, opinions, and judgments.

Example: The roller coaster ride made her feel uneasy like there was a knot in her stomach.

Subsequently, feelings and emotions are similar with feelings connecting to a physical reaction of one's body and emotions being a sense of something being experienced. They may be observed or defined as being joined or being different from one another. These then are transrational responses to stimuli in that a sensory response to situations occurs at the same juncture as deeply held thoughts, ideas, opinions, and judgments (Schiering & Bogner, 2007). Bogner (2007, p. 21) refers to feelings and emotions as "root responses" to stimuli.

And one other thing: Knowing these definitions of thinking and feeling types addresses the Common Core learning standards in a detailed manner. How? You may question. This is accomplished as learners are able to make the transference through mental imaging to the project and performance of the IBR through using the IM. Subsequently, all three are linked together.

The paradigm within the aforementioned model deals with anyone's thinking and feelings being impacted by common social and societal realities and belief and value systems, as seen in figure 9.1. The overall idea was that it is our thinking and feelings that influence our behaviors, as "What we think and feel becomes what we say and do" (Schiering, 1976). Therefore, the use of the IM and the designing and creating of the IBR pages for playing, when completed, are examples of one's thoughts and feelings. The paradigm below is a graphic representation within the model previously mentioned.

THE IBR'S COGNITIVE COLLECTIVE'S INTERPLAY OF THINKING AND FEELING

What do you think of this idea? "Thinking and feelings are the most natural of human processes" (Bogner, 2011). Also, you are asked to address this, "When did thinking and feelings begin?" After some thought you might note that it's apparent that even in the infancy stage, individuals are naturally and almost immediately conscious and responsive by making cognitive connections and feeling responses relating to, for example, differentiation of voices.

Those having been heard, mutedly, in the womb, now have become classifications between the mother and father, and later, between males and females. This categorizing becomes apparent as a result of beginning awareness and rests with identification in an infant's reactive mannerisms.

The same can be said for classifications based on the sense of smell and touch, which is a "feeling" or sensory response to stimuli. Additionally, the reaction to favored persons is evidenced as prioritizing (thinking skill), resulting in the baby's being more eager to be held by one individual than another. Although language is not yet exhibited by the infant, certainly reciprocity of cognition and metacognition, as well as imagina-

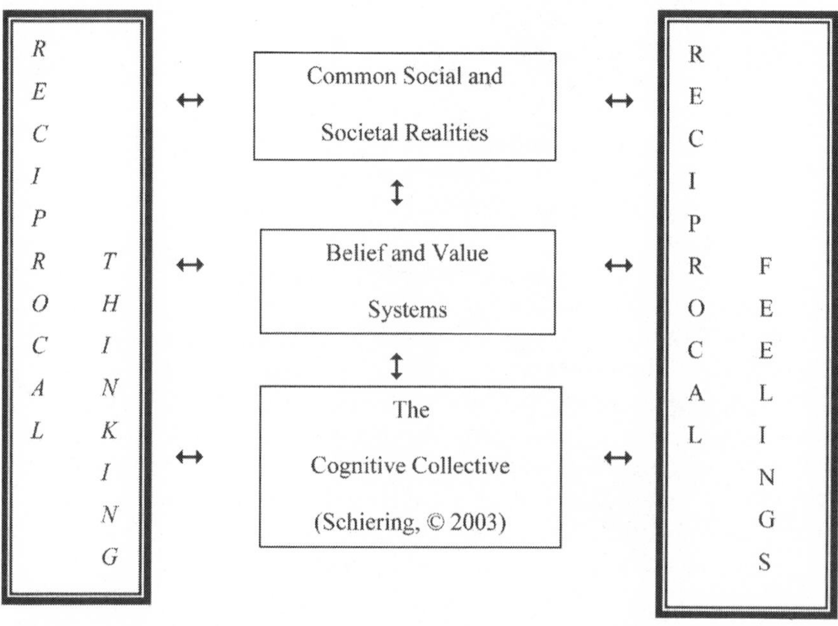

Figure 9.1. The Cognitive Collective Paradigm

tive thinking are "in-play," resulting from one's observable responses to any given experience.

In later years, in the academic setting, when one is using the IM and the IBR, the interaction and relationship between a learner and learning-teacher is continual; if you would, there's an ongoing exchange of what one is thinking and feeling. What brings about optimistic thoughts and emotions is in direct proportion to an individual's positive self-esteem, which an individual develops through the interactive learning and IBR. The concepts referenced by using the methodology are those involving motivation, a sense of security, self-respect, success, and acceptance through use of one's imagination and the processes of creativity.

THE RELEVANCE OF THE COGNITIVE COLLECTIVE TO EFFECTIVE PEDAGOGY

How Feelings Impact Thinking and Vice Versa

Examples of the relevance of the Cognitive Collective are apparent every day and in every environment. Within the classroom, teachers are confronted with students who are dealing with feelings as well as cognitive processes. These interactions shape the dynamics of the classroom and the likelihood that students will achieve the desired learning outcome. Casual observation may attempt to delimit the episodes of strong feeling to early grades where students are more immature, or to middle grades or high school where students are struggling with definition of self. Nonetheless, one truth is that what one is thinking and/or feeling is present in all settings, and truly evidenced in educational ones with students of all ages.

THE COGNITIVE COLLECTIVE'S KEY POINTS

- The Cognitive Collective is the "interplay" of thinking and feeling. It occurs during pre-language and progresses to language acquisition.
- It involves the Reciprocal Thinking Phases and Reciprocal Feelings.
- Reciprocal Thinking and Feelings are the thoughts, ideas, opinions, judgments, and emotions you and everyone have, which result in a continual structuring and restructuring of his/her reality—beliefs and values upon which we take action.
- The reason for using the term reciprocal is that there's movement between and among what one is thinking and feeling. Each impacts the other, and individuals move simultaneously through and around these.
- What one is thinking and or feeling is so closely woven together it's often difficult to discern one from the other.

- Thinking impacts one's feelings and vice versa.
- These interactions of feelings and thoughts shape the dynamics of the classroom and learning in general.
- What one thinks and feels results, oftentimes, in what one says and does.
- The presence of thoughts and feelings is a representation of the reality that human beings feel as well as think, and this reality happens everywhere . . . (Schiering et al, 2011).

All and all, sharing thinking and feelings makes us not just human doings, but human beings . . . humans in the act of being.

A PRACTICAL EXAMPLE OF THE COGNITIVE COLLECTIVE: SCENARIO

Sue, a young adult, was walking with her friends in a local shopping mall. She realized the area was one she'd visited regularly (thought). She'd been to other malls, but she'd evaluated (thought) this one was most attractive (opinion). Once there, the group decided (thought) to explore the entire area, as some hadn't been to this particular set of stores (idea). Since Sue had been here previously and knew of one store that was most extraordinary, she urged everyone to go to this spot first (judgment). It was here that she figured everyone would have the same reaction as she did, because there was a sense of comfort there for her (feeling). Explaining this to her friends she asked them to vote on whether or not to go to that area. Majority ruled, as everyone decided to go to this spot (thoughts, ideas, opinions, and feelings).

The interplay of thinking and feeling, in Sue's case using past experiences, and in the case of her friends relying on her ideas, opinions and judgments is clearly evident. The collection of these, with reciprocity between and among them formed new experiences upon which memories would be established (attention, orientation, decision-making: chapter1). This would add another dimension to what was recognized, when thinking about the mall visit, through their Cognitive Collective. In this instance, with a pleasant experience had by the group, they'd be motivated to revisit the area, together or individually, based on their memories.

JOURNAL AND/OR DISCUSSION QUESTIONS

1. What is the Cognitive Collective?
2. What are brief definitions of thoughts, ideas, opinions, judgments, and feelings?

3. When do you believe thinking and feeling begin? Explain your answer.
4. What are three key points of the Cognitive Collective?
5. What was your opinion of the scenario with Sue?

TEN

Learning and Teaching Creative Cognition

The IBR's Reciprocal Thinking Phases

Two Questions

Born from a thought
On a day of reflections
In solitude amidst a crowd
There emerged, within myself,
Two pervading questions.
These tickled the cortex of my brain and then . . .
spread slowly to block out
Any surrounding or extraneous thoughts or interferences.
These questions imposed an insistence and intensity,
which could not be ignored.
The questions were:
How do I think?
And
What am I thinking? (M. Schiering, 2014)

CHAPTER OVERVIEW

Review of the Cognitive Collective is followed by a definition of Reciprocal Thinking. Then, the remainder of the chapter addresses the *Reciprocal Thinking Phases: Cognition and Metacognition* with definitions of the *Phases* and skills within these. Three figures are provided that address a graphic organizer of the *Phases*, Task Cards, which is an IBR-suggested activity, and the *Reciprocal Thinking Identification Chart.* When the *Phases* graphic organizer is utilized, one comes to an understanding of what creative cognition skills are used to make the IBR activity. These may or may not be recorded.

When the Identification Chart is used, the creator of the game/interactive page is reflecting on and using cognitive skills on the *Phases* graphic organizer to discern what cognitive skills are being used by the player of the page. Some of this discernment and deciding may be up to one's conjecture, but after recognition of the definition of each skill, a comprehension of each skill readily comes to mind. The definitions of cognitive skills that appear on the *Reciprocal Thinking Phases Chart* are presented in this chapter.

An explanation of how we, as adults, move seamlessly between the three *Phases* is discussed by asking, "What are you thinking?" Then, creative cognition linked to the IBR comes prior to the chapter's "Questions" section.

REVIEWING THE COGNITIVE COLLECTIVE

> *Reciprocal Thinking and Feelings are the thoughts, ideas, opinions, judgments, and emotions you and everyone have, which result in a continual structuring and restructuring of their reality—beliefs and values upon which we take action. This is accomplished through personal and shared reflection. In some instances, it's important to note that thinking and feelings are so interwoven it's difficult to separate one from the other" (Schiering, 2003b).*

Human beings think as well as feel. The result is that this unity of thinking and feeling happens within the classroom, as well as outside it. Throughout a person's day, individuals move between varying cognitive processes and emotions. As teachers, we must address this natural progression and interplay by recognizing, first, that they occur, and, second, that in order to be effective teachers or human beings, we must know how this process happens and attend to it. The Cognitive Collective is the interplay between and within an individual's or a whole group's thinking and feelings.

RECIPROCAL THINKING: DEFINITION

The reciprocity of thinking refers to the ongoing exchange of comprehension that forms memory. This exchange occurs within and between the *Phases* of *Beginning Awareness, Critical and Creative Thinking*, and the *Metacognitive Processes*.

What you are thinking may not be what I am thinking, but awareness of what is transpiring, cognitively, empowers learners and teachers alike. This empowerment happens while providing self-efficacy. Knowing what one is thinking helps to clarify learning with the individual's acknowledging the finite identification of the cognitive and metacognitive processes being experienced at any time.

The use of the word "reciprocal" in the title "Reciprocal Thinking Phases" demonstrates that the processes of cognition and metacognition are occurring simultaneously, as opposed to being developmental with one evolving from the other. The use of the word "reciprocal" emphasizes that thinking is ongoing and conducted within and between the phases. The movement between and within phases is occurring naturally, as one does not purposefully go from one thinking skill to another; it just happens. In the IBR, the beauty of these named and defined skills is in the identification of what one is thinking.
I think, therefore, I am.

THINKING AND THE IBR

With respect to the IBR, the acknowledgement of one's thinking, the realizing of this thinking, makes it possible to create interactive pages that are designed to facilitate one's imagination and make or even invent interactive instructional resources/educational games. But, most importantly, the designer is aware of what is being thought when a page is played, and this is done through comprehension of the definitions and practical applications of the skills. Creative cognition is evidenced when the pages are designed and created and later learning-through-play occurs to solidify the IM and practical use of the IBR.

Comprehension, as explained previously in this book, is occurring continuously and providing comprehension through analysis, evaluation, comparing and contrasting, prioritizing, and self-actuating to name a few cognitive functions. Overall, comprehension is done by realizing the differences between types of thinking and feelings.

THINKING COMPLEXITY

"Thinking occurs in varying phases of complexity that are reciprocal in nature with the individual moving seamlessly between and among them. Each individual's thinking can be characterized by a number of specific cognitive skills that can be identified by individuals. This being the case, one can hone and develop these skills, identifying when he or she is using each and becoming more proficient in its usage.

"Tasks for the learner and the teacher, therefore, would seem to be attending directly to helping one 'know what he/she are thinking,' helping each learner to identify when he or she is using a particular skill and assisting him in developing mastery over it" (Bogner, 2008).

PHASE ONE: BASIC AWARENESS AND ACKNOWLEDGING

This first phase involves skill development in recognizing, realizing, classifying, comparing, and contrasting, as well as information gathering and acquisition. It emphasizes a beginning knowledge of learners' and teachers' competencies by implementing a targeted number of thinking skills. These skills relate to fact finding and ordering techniques that include initial classifying and cause the learner to start making connections to personal experiences and those presented orally or in written formats. Learners are able to respond to various stimuli in conversations, as well as configure answers to literal comprehension questions with accuracy. This phase takes into consideration an individual's earliest forms of awareness through differentiation of voices and sound (comparing and contrasting), the feel of animate and inanimate objects, and later, verbalizations that address aforementioned skill areas.

PHASE TWO: CRITICAL AND CREATIVE THINKING

This phase involves the transcendence and inclusion through movement from and within their beginning awareness. Learners process skills through visualizing and verbalizing the connections they have made from prior experiences and awareness with prioritizing, communicating, inferring, predicting, generalizing, sequencing, initial deciding, and initial problem-solving. It can be determined that the combination of critical and creative thinking relies on past awareness to construct new meaning. The learner may hypothesize, imagine, or visualize making connections from his or her own experiences or reading material for applied comprehension. Subsequently, determining outcomes from actions taken provides a comprehensive set of thoughts for problem-solving, a matter which is addressed as a metacognitive process.

PHASE THREE: METACOGNITIVE PROCESSES

This phase occurs when the thinking goes beyond the cognitive and the learner actually knows what he or she wants to realize—exhibiting a control over his or her intake of material. There is critiquing accompanied by self-actuation through evaluation and synoptic exercises (general and summative overviews) occurring. There is a realization of action or actions that need to be taken to facilitate the acquisition of knowledge. Metacognition is domain dependent as it is instantiated (firmly grounded) in a context or learning task (Tobias & Everson, 1995).

This being grounded refers to learning that addresses a specific subject area and refers to students working in a format that is structured and sequential. Abedi and O'Neil (1996) defined metacognition as consisting of strategies for planning, monitoring or self-checking cognitive/affective strategies, and self-awareness. The metacognitive process in phase three requires self-assessment and self-adjustment through evaluating, organizing, critiquing, collaborating, tolerating, deciding, risk-taking, inventing, analyzing, synthesizing, advanced problem-solving, recalling, reflecting, and self-actualizing.

PHASE THREE AND IMPLIED COMPREHENSION

The result of learners and teachers' identifying and implementing the higher-order thinking skills in this phase is evident in their ability to address implied comprehension questions. This is where the answer is made obvious through conjecture or clues that lead one to think that a specific answer is viable. An example would be a sentence about seeing a bird's footprints on the sand. It's implied that previously a bird had walked on the sand, because of these footprints. Implied comprehension is based on context or illustrative material being presented in auditory, visual, tactile, or kinesthetic formats.

BASIC AWARENESS AND ACKNOWLEDGING SKILLS: DEFINITIONS

Recognizing helps a person to be aware of or identify things from previous experience and also to acknowledge something as being new to the one doing the recognizing. Realizing focuses on the skills that help a person make something real and to comprehend the importance of something that one did not know previously. Classifying refers to arranging things into groups according to established criteria, for example, to arrange by age, height, color, type of clothing, or some category. Comparing includes examining or judging between two or more things in order to show how they are similar. Contrasting focuses on the difference between two or more things. When you combine comparing and contrasting there is discernment, a distinguishing between one thing and another or perhaps one idea from another so as to differentiate and perceive.

CRITICAL AND CREATIVE THINKING SKILLS: DEFINITIONS

Prioritizing deals with or lists something in order of its importance. Communicating refers to the exchange of information or conversation with other people by using words, signs, or writing and expressing your thoughts or feelings clearly so other people understand them. Inferring is the formation of opinion based on the information one has previously

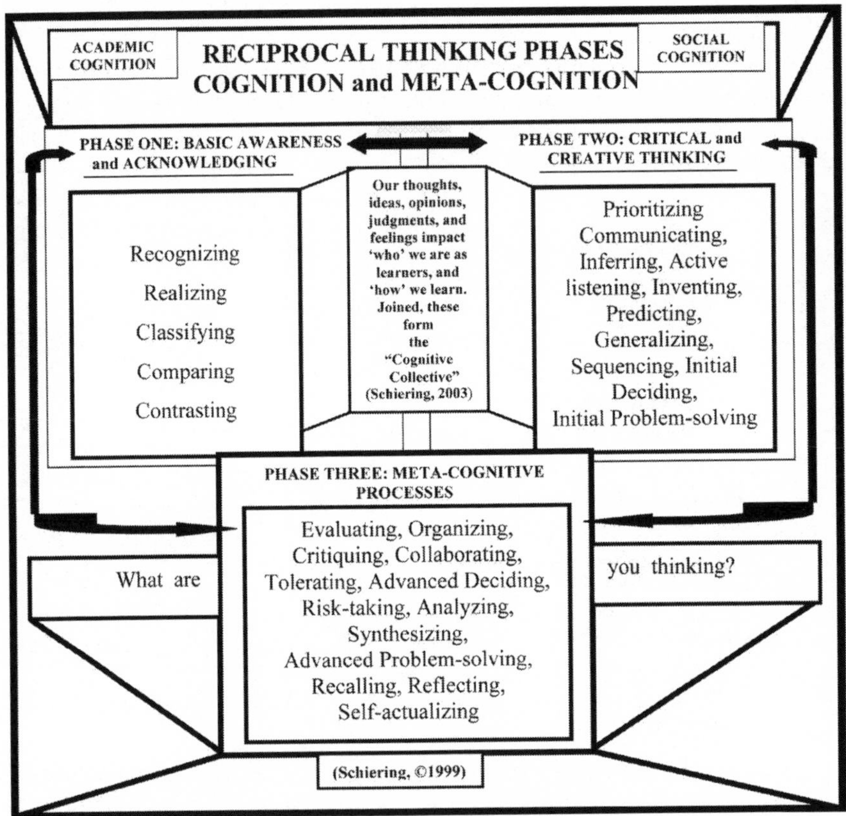

Figure 10.1. Reciprocal Thinking Phases: Cognition and Metacognition

experienced, or indirect evidence being present. Inventing equates with originating or devising.

Predicting relates to the formation of an opinion that something will happen before it actually is a reality or has occurred. Generalizing refers to forming an opinion after considering a few examples of it. Sequencing is a series of related events, actions, or the like that happens or is done in a particular order. Initial deciding is beginning choice. Initial problem-solving is beginning thought, dealing with, and/or providing explanation about a difficult situation or person. It is finding the correct answer to a question, or the explanation for something that is difficult to comprehend.

METACOGNITIVE PROCESSES SKILLS: DEFINITIONS

Evaluating has to do with judging or determining the quality of something, as to assess or appraise its worth. Organizing is to make into a whole with unified and coherent relationships or to arrange thoughts in an orderly fashion and is sometimes referred to as a person's being logical or sequential. Critiquing refers to the formation of a thought or judgment as to whether something is good, bad, or somewhere in-between those two places. Critiquing may also be an opinion that's given and connotes whether something is favorable, unfavorable, or possesses both of these components. Collaborating is to work together with another person or group in order to achieve or produce something. Tolerating concerns the pattern of recognizing and respecting behavior that is not pleasant, is not to be interfered with, or that is to be allowed or permitted without bringing comment.

Advanced deciding and problem-solving involve the processes of reaching a high degree or level of difficulty by providing choice, judgment, explanation, and/or resolution to a situation, specifically reaching a high degree or level of difficulty concerning one's thinking. This is accomplished by providing explanation about a tough or challenging situation. Or, it could be with respect to a person and finding the correct answer to a question, or the explanation for something that is difficult to comprehend. Risk-taking is the action requiring grabbing a chance without knowing the outcome of that action or verbalization.

Inventing is to discover, think up, devise, or fabricate in the mind, think out, produce something new, or originate through experiment. Analyzing concerns the careful examination of something in order to comprehend it. It concerns also the examination of thought and feeling components to ascertain their general composition for comprehension of them. Synthesizing is to form by bringing together separate parts of a situation in a concise manner.

Advanced problem-solving includes recalling to bring back to one's mind something from the past, as in reference to a memory, whether from a moment earlier or some longer expanse of time. Reflecting is to realize something after thought or contemplation. Self-actuating has to do with one's self going forward and taking action, doing something as opposed to remaining stationary. What Are You Thinking?

CONNECTING LEARNING AND TEACHING CREATIVE COGNITION TO *CONSTRUCTING THE IBR PAGES*

When making pages for the IBR, one wants to recognize, using the *Phases* graphic organizer, what creative cognition skills were involved in making the page. Looking at each section of the graphic organizer, examining each skill, the person making the page practices attention, orientation, and decision-making with use of his or her memory. These are utilized with discernment to determine which skills are being applied to the making of the IBR page. These may be listed or mentally noted. By listing or noting, the designer and maker of the page is teaching and learning himself or herself about which creative cognition abilities are present and being utilized. This happens for each of the *Phases* skills as the activities are imagined, designed, and constructed.

CONNECTING LEARNING AND TEACHING CREATIVE COGNITION TO *PLAYING THE IBR PAGES*

One of the major principles of the interactive methodology presented in this book is to realize what one is thinking through cognitive awareness, to recognize and give attention to what's happening when a particular page of the IBR is being played after it has been made. Subsequently, perhaps the best way to explain that is to give an example.

Let's say that there is a science page for the thematic unit addressing ecosystems. Activity: A set of "Task Cards," or puzzle pieces are made on 5x8 index cards that are the same color. These are made with one side having a word related to the topic of ecosystems, and the other side having the definition of that word. Some of the words might include ecosystem, ecologist, sustainability, recycle, reuse, reduce, community, environment, biodegradable, succession, and nonbiodegradable.

Then the cards are cut in half, but each one has a different shape (figures 10.2 and 16.4). Two examples of Task Card *definitions* would be placed, respectively, on the *right side* of the first and then second cut cards: "This is everything that surrounds and affects a living thing," and next, "A scientist who observes and then studies the impact of living and nonliving things." The definitions, placed, respectively, on the left side of the first and second card would be: ecosystem and ecologist.

It is the student's responsibility in this activity to read the word and try to find the definition. If the cards fit together, then the match has been made, and the word and its definition are realized. Learners would make twenty to forty Task Cards, each having a different shape match, but done on the same color card and using the same font and font size, as well as color for printing. If doing Task Cards for math equations or word problems, identifying quotes from a book, word opposites, or English and foreign language meanings, each have the same requirements applied.

It's important to reiterate that the cognitive and metacognitive skills used are occurring mentally, simultaneously. The reciprocity of thinking is just that, a give-and-take from *Phase* to *Phase* for within and between applications of thinking skills. The cognitive skills utilized in this shape-match activity page involve the following for the making of the activity as well as later playing the IBR page that has it:

1. Recognizing the word and the shape-match definition.
2. Prioritizing by matching the ones that are most familiar to the activity player.
3. Comparing and contrasting each card's definition.
4. Inferring that the definition will match the word before making the match.
5. Predicting which definition will match the ecosystem-theme word.
6. Initial and advanced deciding when reading the word, defining it, usually through recalling, and then making the match.
7. Problem-solving by analyzing the words and definition.
8. Generalizing that these words are all part of ecosystems, as opposed to some other topic such as storms.
9. Evaluating one's selection of matches.
10. Risk-taking when trying the match.
11. Reflecting on the words and their definitions.
12. Self-actuating by spreading the cards out on a section of a table or the floor and putting the pieces together with words and corresponding definitions.

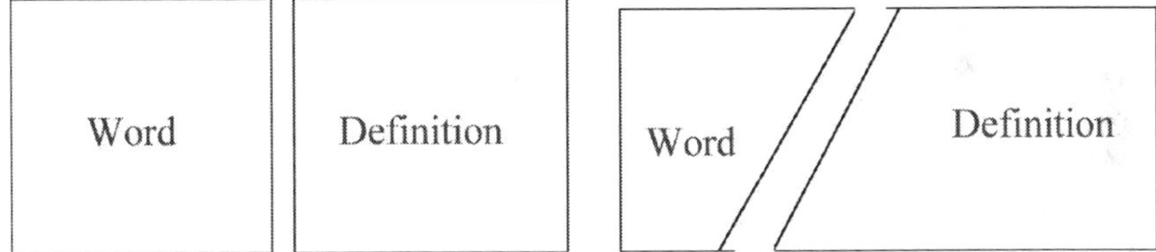

Figure 10.2. Task Cards

IDENTIFICATION OF RECIPROCAL THINKING SKILLS CHART

The Reciprocal Thinking Identification Chart (Schiering, 2000) addresses what cognitive skills are being used and/or developed when the page is played. In this way the person involved with learning-through-play addresses his or her thinking skills by making the page, and then playing it. Doing this identification, the individual is involved in the teaching and learning of creative cognition through inventing, at the very least. The chart serves as a recording device for this teaching of thinking.

This chart fill-in may be initially challenging, due to one's lack of familiarity with knowing what one is thinking. However, practice makes perfect and having the previous sections of this chapter with the skills definitions makes the "doing" of completing this identification chart easier than one might anticipate. Of course, the idea is to complete the chart with the activities listed that demonstrate the corresponding reciprocal thinking that's done for this particular activity.

In the preceding section with ten cognitive and metacognitive skills listed, this becomes quite doable, as the chart is filled-in with the activity placed next to each skill that is applied when playing the page. In this case, it'd be the Task Cards, but there may be other activities and skills used to play-a-page, and here is the opportunity to decide which ones are being utilized (figure 10.4).

This Identification of Thinking Skills Chart section of the IBR is best done when all the interactive pages/activities, usually a minimum of ten, have been made. The student or students making the IBR would collaborate with others to problem-solve as the skills used to play the page are discussed and decided upon. In figure 10.3 on the following page, 26 cognitive and metacognitive skills are listed. The chart is shown with the "Task Cards" activity placed next to each applicable skill area. There may be other activities listed that are used to play the page. It's up to the creator of the IBR pages to decide what cognitive and metacognitive skills are being experienced.

Please note that in chapters 15 and 16, more than twenty-five activities are listed with corresponding Reciprocal Thinking Skills. The "Identification Chart" appears in two different formats and can be distinguished by the #1 or #2 at the end of the title.

ANALYZING THE IDENTIFICATION CHART #1: TASK CARDS (T.C.)

In the first *Phase,* each section has the T.C.s mentioned because each of the cognitive skills was recognized, realized, compared, and contrasted by category for classification. In the second *Phase,* when putting the cards together, there were inferences made when one was looking to match the shapes. Then, predicting what half of one card went with the other was made clear when a "match" was made. The T.C.s were sequenced when they were put in order for initial deciding and problem-solving as to which card went where.

The activity involved the learner with the movement of the cards and then the reflecting on the definition of the word for correctness once they were all together. Let's see if you and a partner can explain why the other metacognitive skills were selected for Task Cards. You're invited to collaborate and discuss your reactions by knowing what you're thinking, just as a learner playing this page would do at home alone or with others inside or outside of the classroom. Remember, all the activities in an IBR address the Interactive Method and one is learning-through-playing these educational games.

IDENTIFICATION OF RECIPROCAL THINKING SKILLS CHART (Source: Schiering, 2000)	
Phase One: Basic Awareness & Acknowledging	**Identification of Cognitive Skill: What's the Thinking?**
Recognizing	Task Card
Realizing	Task Card
Classifying	Task Card
Comparing	Task Card.
Contrasting	Task Card
Phase Two: Critical and Creative Thinking	**Identification of Cognitive Skill: What's the Thinking?**
Prioritizing	
Communicating	
Inferring	Task Card
Predicting	Task Card
Generalizing	.
Sequencing	Task Card
Initial-deciding	Task Card
Initial Problem-solving	Task Card
Phase Three: The Meta-cognitive Processes	**Identification of Cognitive Skill: What's the Thinking?**
Evaluating	Task Card
Critiquing	.
Collaborating	
Tolerating	
Advanced Deciding & Problem-solving	Task Card
Organizing	Task Card
Synthesizing	Task Card
Risk-taking	Task Card
Inventing	.
Analyzing	
Recalling	Task Card
Reflecting	Task Card
Self-actuating	Task Card

Figure 10.3. Reciprocal Thinking Identification Chart (*Source*: Schiering, 2000.)

IDENTIFICATION OF RECIPROCAL THINKING SKILLS CHART #2 (SCHIERING, 2000)

CHART OVERVIEW FOR THINKING

Each of the three *Reciprocal Thinking Phases* contains definable cognitive skills that can be identified and honed over time by answering the exemplified question about what you are thinking—this thinking is observ-

ACTIVITIES	PHASE ONE	PHASE TWO	PHASE THREE
Story Map	Acknowledging, Realizing, Recognizing, Classifying, Comparing - Contrasting	Prioritizing, Communicating, Predicting, Generalizing, Initial problem-solving	Advanced-deciding, Analyzing, Synthesizing, Problem-solving, Reflecting, and Self-actuating
Electro-board: Who Said That	Realizing, comparing and contrasting	Prioritizing, Initial Deciding and Problem-solving, Generalizing	Evaluating, Organizing, Advanced deciding and problem solving, Recalling, Reflecting, Self-actualizing
The Fantastic Flip-Chute Vocabulary	Realizing, Recognizing, comparing and Contrasting, Classifying	Communicating, Predicting, Generalizing, Initial Deciding and Problem-solving	Evaluating, Organizing, Advanced deciding and Problem-solving, Risk-taking, Recalling, Reflecting, Self-actualizing
What You'd Do: A Role Play	Acknowledging, Recognizing, Comparing and Contrasting	Prioritizing, Communicating, Inventing, Inferring, Generalizing, Initial-deciding and Problem-solving, Synthesizing	Tolerating, Recalling. Advanced Problem-solving and Advanced-deciding, Collaborating, Organizing, Critiquing, and Self-actualizing
Sequence of Events Floor at Table Game	Acknowledging, Recognizing, Realizing, Comparing and Contrasting, Classifying	Prioritizing, Commutating, Inferring, Generalizing, Initial-deciding and Problem-solving	Organizing, Advanced-deciding and Problem-solving, Recalling, Synthesizing, Collaborating, Sequencing, Reflecting and Self-actualizing
Pic-A-Dot: Story Comprehension Questions	Recognizing, comparing and Contrasting	Prioritizing, Communicating, Generalizing, Initial-deciding and Problem-solving, Synthesizing	Risk-taking, organizing, Advanced-deciding, Collaborating, Sequencing, Self-actualizing
Make a Story Character Puppet	Realizing, Comparing and Contrasting	Initial-deciding and Problem-solving, Communicating, Inventing, Inferring, Self-actuating	Organizing, Evaluating, Synthesizing, Collaborating, Self-actuating

Figure 10.4. Eight-Item Reciprocal Thinking Identification Chart

able. Asking this simple question illustrates the importance of being aware of one's cognitive function for later enhancement. This awareness is accomplished through knowing which cognitive skill the person is using at any given moment when playing an IBR page.

Developing greater facility in each of these cognitive skills allows the individual to be thinking in a most effective manner. The final cognitive skills result in reflection through self-accounting and self-actuating. These skills provide empowerment and self-learning with attention given to gleaning information from the presented material's content, as well as implementation and application of skills for decision-making and problem-solving.

"Two essential observations flow from this idea. First, the learner will learn better if he can identify the cognitive skills being used while practicing and honing this skill. Second, the teacher can structure and teach lessons that do these things by using the chart or having peer-to-peer, or student-to-teacher discussions that address these skills" (Bogner, 2011).

SOME FINAL THOUGHTS ON THE RECIPROCAL THINKING PHASES

The reciprocity of thinking occurs within and between *Phases* at all levels of cognitive and emotional development. However, this reciprocity is not age specific. It is not developmentally imposed. Some may exhibit the Critical and Creative Thinking skills at a very young age. This also applies to metacognition being evidenced. Conversely, a person of forty years, or younger or older, may not evidence reciprocity of thinking in these *Phases*. Reasons for this are unknown.

However, teaching students and ourselves about these *Phases* and the cognitive skills within each one, as well as practicing them, develops all types of thinking skills. When involved in the IM, a person is continually experiencing reciprocity of thinking. The IBR enhances the skills necessary for thinking through playing-the-pages, designing them, and/or creating the pages. Whichever is being done, the reciprocity of thinking is happening, along with one's creativity being recognized. Perhaps the most important thing is to call one's attention to this process of thinking awareness.

THE IBR AND *THINKING PHASES* POSITIVES

The skills within the *Reciprocal Thinking Phases* are a major portion of the IBR's cognition and creative cognition applications for learning and teaching. This is because of the identification of the skills within the *Reciprocal Thinking Phases: Cognition and Metacognition* figure 10.3. Applying these skills to practical learning experiences and being able to identify what cognitive and metacognitive skills are being used when making an IBR, "one sees that a sense of security emerges and takes hold in the psyche" (Bogner, 2008). You may question why this would happen, and the answer would be that there is empowerment, self-efficacy, and one's ownership in realizing what one is thinking, as well as knowing what interactive pages develop which thinking skills.

As the IBR method is applied through the construction of an Interactive Book Report, the designer(s)/creator(s) come to feel a sense of authority as their creativity is examined and explored. As an overall sense of security ensues, learners feel successful as a result of active engagement in the process of the IBR, accomplishing tasks set forth that address and ensure their being successful.

One thing about being creative with an IBR is, when applying that creativity to a project, there is no right or wrong way of doing things. The way things are being done is in alignment with what one is thinking. Subsequently, feeling secure with the techniques employed and/or having a sense of well-being about the learning environment become the mainstay and allow one to have and exhibit self-respect and self-acceptance, as well as having those feelings for others involved in the IM and IBR construction.

CHAPTER DISCUSSION AND/OR JOURNAL QUESTIONS

1. What does it mean to have reciprocity of thinking?
2. What are the three headings on the Reciprocal Thinking Phases graphic organizer?
3. What are some of the components of the history of reciprocal thinking?
4. How would you explain each of the three *Phases* of reciprocal thinking?
5. How does the Identification of Reciprocal Thinking Skills Chart assist in recognizing and building cognitive and metacognitive skills?
6. How do you suppose knowing what you're thinking brings about self-efficacy and self-empowerment?

ELEVEN

Learning and Teaching Creative Cognition

The IBR's Reciprocal Feelings Phases

CHAPTER OVERVIEW

Examining feelings and the difference between thoughts and feelings, which are acknowledged as emotions and sensory responses to stimuli, are defined in the second portion of the Cognitive Collective. Then, explanation of how the IBR is impacted by feelings is given attention. This is accomplished by sharing teacher-candidate and elementary students' responses to the IBR. An experiment or two are provided for knowing the difference between whether you've expressed a thought, idea, or opinion as opposed to a feeling. Feelings connected to the IM serving as motivation come before the chapter's closing discussion questions.

THE COGNITIVE COLLECTIVE'S RECIPROCAL FEELINGS

Feelings exist. They are not right or wrong—they just are. They happen sometimes with foreknowledge and other times without it. A multitude of feelings may be realized and/or exhibited during any situation. We know this from personal experience. One's reactions to one's own or another's feelings are what create additional emotions. Feelings are reciprocal and may be cyclical. The important thing is to be aware of what one is feeling and express this awareness through communication involving verbal discourse or even nonverbalization. Learning and teaching rely on this interchange of expressing what one is feeling, as much as conveying what one is thinking.

We are thinking and feeling human beings; in a sense, we're humans in the act of being. The operative words are "in the act of" because feelings relate to our rationality or lack of it when experiencing varied situations about which we're thinking. Theorists have described how feelings about self can and do impact learning. How one perceives a given situation is influenced by emotions and feelings from past experiences and those in the present. Effective learners and teachers are cognizant of individuals' varied perceptions and address them either overtly or subliminally during instructional situations.

SOME THOUGHTS AND FEELINGS ABOUT THE IBR

Perhaps the best way to address this section is to relate what student learners and teacher-candidates and teachers who've used the IM and made IBRs have related over the years.

1. I feel good about what I've created.
2. This was hard work, but I feel I accomplished a lot. I did something and learned that I can be creative.
3. I thought I'd feel terrible about myself because I wouldn't be able to create or contribute to an IBR, but what happened was just the opposite.
4. I learned about body systems from the IBR I made and about other body systems from IBRs of my classmates. We were teaching each other by what we produced. I felt accomplished.
5. I like the IBR Method and wish we did this for a lot of books and units.
6. I learned that I felt so good about making these pages to play that I do these at home on my own for different subject areas.
7. I went back to college after more than forty years and had to take a foreign language. I used some of the IBR techniques, games to help me learn my vocabulary and passed the course with flying colors.
8. It was easy to put facts into the activities.
9. I can use this way to learn in any subject, not just science or the book about *James and the Giant Peach.*
10. I loved this 'cause I learned how to do research and to use it so I'd remember by playing. And, I didn't feel like I was memorizing anything, but my brain was taking in information and I remember it.

These supportive statements have been related because the IM and IBR creations afford all learners the opportunity to explore abilities to be creative, to learn while enjoying what's being experienced, and to be involved and engaged academically and emotionally at the same time.

EFFECTIVE LEARNERS AND TEACHERS

To be effective learners and teachers, individuals may well consider being able to identify how feelings impact learning. The teachers need to address the structure of their learning environments so that feelings and emotions positively assist learning. Bogner related in 2011, about addressing the structure of learning environments when he said that to address the learning structure is at the highest level of complexity. Several things are taken into consideration such as:

- the style of delivery of curriculum,
- the overall classroom environment,
- learner's and teacher's demeanor and dispositions, as well as
- levels of interaction, discourse, and opportunities for a sense of well-being for all those in the immediate environment.

FEELING CATEGORIES

You know about feelings. They are divided into two categories, which are physical and emotional. The physical ones are sensory responses to some stimuli. Examples might be you feeling hot or cold, having a ringing in your ears, tasting something that's spicy and your tongue burns, seeing a balloon fly, or smelling the fire in a fireplace. These physical or sensory responses involve one's senses.

Emotional feelings are usually in a category exclusive to a nonsensory response to stimuli. Something causes you to feel happy or sad, elated, nervous, or excited. The response may be due to external or internal factors. With the latter, it may be a memory that triggers an emotional reaction. And, this memory perhaps will cause a sensory feeling.

To some situations you react in a vibrant manner in direct proportion to the value you attach to the situation. This reaction means that your reaction to, let's say, a roller coaster ride will be different from another person's, or it could be similar. Again, feelings exist. They are neither right nor wrong—they just are.

RECIPROCAL FEELINGS: PERCEPTUAL EXPERIENCES

At the core of the concept of feelings and emotions is the idea that they are perceptual experiences that are presented and displayed through an individual's subjective analysis of a situation. This analysis encompasses one's relating a particular event by conveying it in a sensory or emotional manner—an affecting reaction to life experiences. These may be the same or different from those within our nuclear family, surrounding community, or cultural and general groupings, whether geographic or society-based.

People feel a lot of different things at the same time and may have similar multiple emotions about something. Feelings happen simultaneously within and between what one may be thinking.

IDENTIFYING FEELINGS

Where individuals have language, there's an understanding that feelings and emotions are related through actions and/or explanatory accounts that itemize the experience one is having or has had. In addition to verbal communication techniques for those who have language, there is nonverbal conveyance of feelings and emotions.

For example, there are facial expressions, body stance, or gesturing conveying feelings or emotions. Nonverbal feeling emanations may depict "excitement" with a wide opening of the eyes and mouth, hands in the air, and/or jumping up and down. "Sadness" might be demonstrated with a slumped-over body stance, lowered head, and eyes focused downward with the mouth in the same position. Questioning may be evidenced by raised eyebrows and squinting eyes.

PHASES OF FEELINGS

To link the *Phases of Feeling* to those of Thinking is nearly an impossible task. This is because so many different feelings may be evidenced at any given time for any kind of cognitive skill. However, in a fashion, the following *Phases* are presented to show a progression and interconnection of feelings with thinking with respect to one's being in the act of feeling.

PHASE ONE

An individual's earliest forms of awareness are evidenced through differentiation of voices and sound, and the feel of animate and inanimate objects. Recognizing, realizing, classifying, and categorizing these sensory responses are demonstrated by feeling as if one is discovering something. This would involve one's being orderly, contemplative, supposing, questioning, comparative, efficient, effective, self-examining, and creative. Identifying and implementing the feeling terms/cognitive feeling skills in this phase results in learners and teachers' experiencing a selective range of emotions. These are focused on explicit comprehension with an understanding of what they're experiencing as having certain sentiments.

PHASE TWO

The progression and reciprocity of feelings occurs in this phase as learners come to verbalize connections they have made resulting from prior experiences and acknowledging. These would include being: discriminating, determined, communicative, hesitant, mystified, flexible, sequential, unrestrained, intrigued, resourceful, decisive, critical, creative, positive, predictive, inspired, uncertain, contemplative, and exhilarated.

While some of these feeling terms appear to be opposite from one another, they're presented to demonstrate how a feeling might be construed that way by different individuals in response to their corresponding cognitive terms. The result of learners and teachers' identifying and implementing the feeling terms or cognitive-feeling skills in this phase is their ability to be productive and innovative. Also, there is the ability to address and make connections to one's own experience, or to read material for answering applied comprehension-type questions. There is significant comprehension when connections are made to past experiences for application to constructing judicious decisions.

PHASE THREE

The transference and transformation from beginning awareness and initial deciding occur when learners process the skills that allow them to visualize and verbalize connections resulting from prior experiences. There is awareness of oneself and surrounding persons, as well as greater world environments. Self-adjustment and checking are apparent with one's being evaluative, empathetic, conciliatory, understanding, collaborative, tolerant, sympathetic, adventuresome, inventive, analytical, holistic, critiquing, constructive, disquieted, participatory, discerning, reflective, and self-actuating.

The result of learners and teachers' identifying and implementing the feeling terms or cognitive-feeling skills in this phase is their ability to make inferences, which are based on context or illustrative material being presented in oral, visual, tactile, or kinesthetic formats. Identifying and implementing the feeling/cognitive-feeling skills and/or terms in this phase results in learners and teachers' experiencing philosophizing and hypothesizing. Multiple meanings are constructed resulting from reflection.

MORE FEELINGS RELATED TO THE IM

A wide range of emotions is evidenced as innovative ideas are considered with respect to addressing problem-solving and/or decision-making, which involves acceptance of self and others. Each of the *Phases of*

Feelings is interconnected and exchangeable within and between phases. Also, there is a wide variety of feelings that can be attributed to any phase—such an expanse of emotions that it is difficult to impose an exactness to any reaction for each individual.

Feelings are so closely linked to what one may be thinking that it's often difficult to differentiate one from the other. Give this a try and right now ask yourself, "Am I thinking this or feeling this?"

Things to consider regarding effective pedagogy with feelings include:

1. Teachers need to address the structure of their learning environments so that feelings and emotions positively assist learning.
2. Identifying the feelings that individuals may experience when learning and teaching, which is important for overall success in academic and social settings.
3. Most importantly, it's vital to be aware of your feelings and equally important to be aware of the feelings of others.
4. The feelings one has in the classroom or anywhere serve as the strongest motivator, whether this motivation results in one's taking action or remaining idle.
5. Feelings and thinking are so closely related and intertwined that it's often difficult to know which one is which, as one affects and touches the other.

EXPERIMENT: THE INTERCONNECTION OF FEELINGS AND THINKING

Experiment: a) fold your hands together and mentally label the right hand "Feelings" and the left hand "Thinking;" b) raise and lower the second finger on your right hand, and then do this for the left hand; c) raise and lower the third finger as you did the second a moment ago; d) looking at the Experiment Results below, decide whether you concur with these or not.

Experiment Results:

1. It was relatively easy to move the first and second fingers up and down on both the "Thinking" and "Feelings" hands. This interconnection was evident, as the fingers moved independently from one another and were easily moved, although the "Thinking/Feelings" hands were interlocked.
2. The other fingers on your hand did not move when doing the raising and lowering of the first and second fingers.
3. The circumstances of teaching are related to learning through what one thinks and feels.

4. It was not as easy to raise the third fingers representing "Thinking" and "Feelings," as it was with the first and second fingers.
5. Some Thinking and Feelings are not as easy to distinguish from one another, as they're so closely connected. This closeness was evident and exemplified with the portion of the experiment with the third fingers being raised and lowered.

I feel, therefore, I am.

Feeling Reflection Questions:

What was your feeling and/or emotional reaction to reading this section of the book and doing the experiment? What was your reason for reading about feelings? Was it due to its being assigned, something you were interested in for learning about your own feelings or that of your student learners, to gain insight on best-practice by knowing who one is as a learner and teacher, or for some other reason? As you were reading, what were your physical surroundings like? Were these ones of comfort and ease? Why or why not? Each of your reactions to these questions provides an awareness of your physical sensations, as well as emotional ones, which puts you "in touch" with yourself.

"If one has feelings of attachment to what methodology is being practiced for learning, or what is being said, seen, or generally experienced, then h/she will be involved and engaged" (*Reciprocal Thinking Phases*, M. S. Schiering, 1999).

FEELINGS CONNECTED TO THE IM SERVE AS MOTIVATION

Probably, the feelings one has in the classroom or anywhere serve as the strongest motivation to act or not take action. One would suppose it goes without saying that this sentence is one which will shape and reshape your classroom when it's given attention. Feelings are around us everywhere! They take place in school, at home, when visiting someone or shopping, when seeing a movie which evokes even more physical and emotional reactions. Feelings occur when one is alone or alongside a friend. Feelings are part of us as much as thinking, and they serve to create desire to demonstrate being somewhat interested, or not. If one has feelings of attachment to what's being said, seen, taught, or generally experienced, then one will be interested enough to be involved and engaged.

Feelings and emotions come from any place you go and address a wide expanse of situations. And again, these feelings and emotions serve as the strongest motivation any teacher could imagine!

Children, adolescents, and adults need to feel comfortable with learning. This comfort requires a sense of security, safety, and overall emotional well-being in the classroom. Trust in those who occupy the classroom needs to exist alongside the learning environment being one where each individual feels, in a sensory manner, as well as emotional one, that there is trust, caring, concern, and fairness existing at all times.

FEELINGS THAT IMPACT LEARNING

1. Students need a sense of security regarding their feelings as being safe to share.
2. What others say and do and the dynamics of one's environmental situation may get in the way or help what the teacher intends for the student to learn.
3. Liking one's surroundings/environment, the teacher, and the lessons that are presented often results in a student's attention and attitude regarding wanting to learn.
4. If students don't like the teacher they may not try to learn.
5. If students don't feel a teacher caring about them, and/or the teacher is not excited about the material to be presented, then the learner's performance may not be satisfactory. Student attitude or feelings may result in the idea of, "These are just a bunch of hoops to jump through, and I'm not jumping."
6. There needs to be a personal connection to the learning situation, and the IM provides that through the learner's involvement.

EXPERIMENT: DISTINGUISHING FEELINGS FROM THINKING

Here's what you do to distinguish feelings from your thinking: Substitute the words "I feel" for "I am" in a sentence. If the sentence makes sense in both formats, then you've expressed a feeling. Follow the directions below, and then look at the samples to ascertain whether you recognize expressing a feeling.

The first samples are the ones where thoughts are expressed, while the latter clearly demonstrate the use of this substitution of "I feel" for "I am" for relating an identifiable feeling.

Examples of Incorrect Feeling Statements:

1. I feel that there's a problem here. I am that there's a problem here.
2. I feel it is important to check the work. I am it is important to check the work.
3. I feel that you don't like me. I am that you don't like me.
4. I feel that the teacher is silly. I am that the teacher is silly.

Each of these above examples is either a thought, idea, opinion, or judgment, and not a feeling or emotion, because you can't substitute "I feel" for "I am" and have the sentence make sense.

Examples of Correct Feeling Statements:

1. I feel secure. I am secure.
2. I feel happy. I am happy.
3. I feel upset. I am upset.

Each of these above examples is a feeling, because you can substitute "I feel" for "I am" and see that the sentence makes sense.

There are a multitude of feelings we experience each day whether in a classroom or not, and they occur on a regular basis. You, as the learner or the teacher, or the person who's about to embark on this career path, want and need to be aware of yourself and others, cognizant of how feelings influence the aspects of your life, and for this book, the practicing of the IM and making of the IBR book. You want to do that because feelings influence one's sense of security and well-being, attitude and interest. How learners feel in a classroom in a sensory manner and emotional one too is very important, as Maya Angelou said in 2007: "People may forget what you said, and may forget what you did, but will not forget how you made them feel."

JOURNAL AND/OR DISCUSSION QUESTIONS: RECIPROCAL FEELINGS

1. What are feelings?
2. What are emotions and how do these differ from feelings?
3. What is one major component of each feeling phase?
4. What are four ways a student's feelings may impact a classroom learning situation? (Provide a scenario or situation.)
5. How might one determine feeling of a pre-language child?
6. How does one differentiate feelings from thinking? (Write three examples in sentence format.)

TWELVE

Using the IM and IBR

A Psychologist's Perspective

Audra Cerruto, PhD

CHAPTER OVERVIEW

This section, after presenting about learning-through-play, connects the psychology of using the Interactive Method and Interactive Book Report with learning and teaching. Reference is made to child development being the result of interactions between the children and their social environment. These interactions include those with parents and teachers, playmates and classmates, brothers and sisters.

This chapter section also presents the psychology of imagination for creation of the IBR pages. Researchers such as Lev Vygotsky and John Dewey are referenced with respect to the necessity of learning and teaching through use of activities that require one's involvement and engagement. Mention of video games in relation to being the "in" thing for classroom application, and their effect on our present society is addressed. This is added to with the use of the IM and IBR as a necessity for learners in development of creative cognition resulting in retention of curriculum. *"In actuality, as a practicing psychologist for many years I've found in my practice and research that gaming, in particular the construction of games, might enhance student motivation and promote a deeper understanding of a topic more so than traditional pencil and paper tasks or lecture style lessons"* (Cerruto, 2014).

LEARNING-THROUGH-PLAY

As mentioned first in chapter 3 and then continually throughout this book, people play games. People play imaginative games, card games, board games, playground games, sports games, video games, and the list goes on to infinity. People play games to entertain, stimulate, and challenge. As a result, games captivate, educate and sometimes provide an escape from routines.

Prior to playing games with systematic structure, very young children play. They engage in pretend play as they develop from infancy to preschool. The play slowly shifts from interfacing with toys and objects to utilizing symbolic props and imaginative play schemes. Play is the vehicle through which young children learn. They develop cognitive, social, and linguistic skills through the process of playing alone and with others. As children grow older, the shift in play becomes more structured, goal oriented, challenging, and the emergence of playing games occurs.

The Russian psychologist Lev Vygotsky (1980) purported that play was essential to the learning process. "A child's greatest achievements are possible in play, achievements that tomorrow will become the basic level of real action" (Bodrova & Leong, 2003). Through the process of play children actively construct knowledge, skills, language, and attitudes within culturally specific parameters. Vygotsky's theory of the Zone of Proximal Development (ZPD) and More Knowledgeable Other (MKO) suggest that when learners are presented with tasks that are just beyond their current level of ability and have the assistance of a more experienced learner (MKO), they can complete challenging tasks. Play and gaming, perceived through Vygotsky's lens, have the ability to challenge and stimulate learning with amazing outcomes.

People worldwide are biologically the same and there is a familiarity within all cultures, such as shared customs or traditions, routines, and social structures that unifies people. Dewey in 1937 referred to these commonalities as being "birth, death, success, failure, tradition and love." Schiering in 2003 examined the interconnection of Dewey's areas and added the "equanimity of a world sociology relating to religion, economics, academics and politics" in "Cognitive Collective Paradigm" in *Bridging Theory and Practice.* (Schiering, 2003b). All of these areas that people share, regardless of ethnicity, race, religion, educational experiences, socioeconomic status, etc., interface with learning-through-play.

Yet, cross-cultural differences do exist in psychological phenomena. According to the sociocultural theory, the environment in which one lives shapes the development of behaviors, beliefs, and attitudes. Life experiences within a cultural context *are* the defining factors. The sociocultural theory presented by Vygotsky and supported by developmental psychologists, neuropsychologists, and educators around the world highlights the integration of science of the mind, brain, and behavior within the context of cultural and biological and social development.

At the core of the sociocultural theory is the idea that child development is the result of interactions between the children and their social environment. These interactions include those with parents and teachers, playmates and classmates, and brothers and sisters. They involve relationships with significant objects such as books and toys, and culturally specific practices that children engage in, in the classroom, at home, and on the playground. Children are active partners in these interactions, constructing knowledge, skills, and attitudes.

Through play, early in a child's life, and games as a child matures, development occurs. Play is a universal act that addresses cognition, social skills, and linguistics skills within a cultural context. *The overarching fulfillment of the need to achieve mastery or success makes play universal.* Success within the framework of Dewey and through the ideas presented in this book regarding the IM and IBR, as well as the aforementioned *Model for Academic and Social Cognition* allows for the use of play to promote creativity and imagination. Play is an imaginative forum to use cognition and language to address desires that cannot yet be fulfilled in the empirical environment.

Through the creative process of play, children practice their skills. This is a fun, enjoyable, and exciting way to master skills and succeed at a developmentally appropriate level. It facilitates the advancement of skills and propels children to the next phase. This brings us to the use of games in children's growth and development.

GAMING . . . JUST CHILD'S PLAY?

Play is fun, creative, and flexible. Educational gaming or use of interactive instructional resources that are designed to impart information, due to the structured nature, have rules. These are implicit and explicit. Participants usually follow a predetermined sequence of actions that lead to them achieving success. Games must be viewed as providing an opportunity for stimulation and challenge in the areas of cognition and creative cognition. Furthermore, since they're interactive the IM is fully in swing.

As you may recall from chapter 3, there were different kinds of preschool games mentioned as children through adults shared their recollections. An additional survey of my colleagues found we remember learning-through-play with these structured ones: Classics, such as Monopoly (addresses money management, decision-making skills), Candy Land (matching colors), and Scrabble (letter and word building) allow for practicing important cognitive and social skills. Other favorites, such as Perfection (matching shapes under time constraints), Dominoes (counting and matching), UNO (matching numbers and colors), Clue (problem-solving), and Jenga (visual-spatial planning) may disguise the benefits of gaming but are nonetheless utilized.

"Video games, played on handheld devices, iPads, or game consoles, enhance learning as well. Favorites, such as *FIFA 15*, *Call of Duty*, *Candy Crush Saga*, *Angry Birds*, and *Temple Run* address visual-spatial awareness, degree of response time, planning and attending to multiple sources of information, and decision-making skills.

"Just as educational games [that] involve interactive instructional methodologies have been shown to enhance learning, video games have been found to promote enhanced brain functioning. A wealth of recent research has highlighted the potential use of digital games for teaching and learning. Video game developers have looked at the power of games on motivation, engagement, involvement, active learning, problem-solving, and decision-making. Recent statistics of video gaming are staggering. . . . children in the US played an average of one hour and thirteen minutes of video games every day in 2009" (Bavelier & Davidson, 2013).

Neuroscientists have begun to explore how to transform the high interest in video games to train and improve specific brain functioning. Educators and game developers have teamed up to create "educational electronic games" to facilitate learning. Clearly, video gaming is here to stay. Can it be used as an effective vehicle for teaching and learning?

The question is whether educators need to sugarcoat learning with "educational *video* games?" The field of education is experiencing a tremendous amount of pressure to modify or even recreate curriculums to meet the Common Core standards. Despite the critics who describe the Common Core as "a mile wide and an inch deep," teachers face an uphill battle to address the standards in a timely manner. As a result, teachers often think they do not have the time to implement learning-through-play or promote creativity within the learning process, but they do!

PSYCHOLOGICAL ASPECTS OF THE INTERACTIVE METHOD (IM)

The IM, discussed in this book's beginning chapters, utilizes the concept of learning-through-play. This system, as you've read, is an interactive and creative approach to learning and teaching that incorporates playable instructional resources and educational games that address a topic of a unit of study and/or review of a book. The students create an IBR working alone, in pairs, or small groups to develop an activity to "teach" the topic. In order to "teach," the student should have learned or mastered the topic him- or herself. The process of creating a page in the IBR is in actuality the development of a deeper understanding of the topic (metacognition) and the evolution of the student as a teacher or as Vygotsky called it a MKO, More Knowledgeable Other.

Another feature of the IM is that each page of the product referred to as the IBR has the activity in a self-corrective format. This means that once the student has engaged in the activity, he or she can check the accuracy of his or her work with the answers provided. The game-like structure of the activities taps into the child's inclination to play. The self-corrective feature, providing immediate feedback, offers an opportunity to achieve a sense of success and mastery essential to growth and development. Learning can occur in a low stress, fun, and productive environment!

The system of interactive learning requires the application of cognitive skills to create and engage in "games." It fosters a sense of success and mastery when engaging in and receiving immediate feedback. It promotes social and linguistic skills when interacting with other participants or the MKO. It provides a deeper understanding of the task at hand.

The dynamics between a MKO and a participant on a page of the IBR can promote a higher level of learning. The MKO, the creator of the activity, needs to thoroughly understand the topic in order to create a meaningful activity. Combining the knowledge with an engaging activity, the MKO applies learning and creativity to the task at hand. The learner, on the other hand, through the immediate feedback provided by the MKO, can move to the next level of learning through gaming. *As in the psychology of gaming, the psychology of the IM and resultant IBR facilitates success and mastery propelling cognitive development to the next level.*

ASSESSMENT, THE COMMON CORE, AND THE IM

Standardized testing has taken over schools. Test development is a booming business and enterprise. Many teachers find themselves teaching to these tests, due to the pressures and demands from school administrators, state education departments, and national standards. Test scores are used to facilitate big decisions such as teacher and student promotion. Do these standardized tests provide a meaningful profile to a student learner?

Assessment through nontraditional methods may in fact show the student learner's dynamic and complex process of learning and acquisition of knowledge. Through engagement in the IM and creative cognition applied to the IBR, evaluators are able to analyze the process of learning, the application of immediate feedback, and the active application of new information to form a better understanding of the topic. The system offers an opportunity to view teaching and learning dynamically. Although no substitute for standardize testing, the system provides a rich diagnostic tool to determine the cognitive modifiability of the teacher and learner. The IBR is a diagnostic and prescriptive means of evaluation. When the learner plays the page, if errors are made, it can be observed where problems exist and material presented through differentiated instructional means may ensue (see chapters 16 and 17 for Differentiated Instruction).

CONCLUSION

Children love to play. They engage in pretend play and progress to playing games. Learning-through-play fosters an active and dynamic acquisition of knowledge in a familiar format—games. *This natural method of learning is appealing and engaging to children because the modality is the avenue of interaction that relates "children are masters at playing!"*

JOURNAL AND/OR DISCUSSION QUESTIONS

1. What is your viewpoint of the psychology of using the IM and IBR for instruction?
2. How does this chapter support that viewpoint?
3. What are the viewpoints of Vygotsky and Dewey concerning experiential learning?
4. How may the IBR be used as a "diagnostic and prescriptive means of evaluation"?

II

Part Two

THIRTEEN

Creative Cognition, Neuroplasticity, and IBR

A Scientist's Perspective | Mindfulness and Creativity

Harvey Sasken, MD | Michael Russo, PhD

CHAPTER OVERVIEW

The chapter section begins with addressing plasticity of the brain and creative thinking. Then, a little history is provided. The reader is exposed to how the brain is always changing as "technical" information is given. Teaching and learning activities are addressed along with the IBR and recent neuroscience. Creative cognition regarding innovation and active engagement in learning and teaching comes before the IBR and recent neuroscience. Other realities and principles of neuroplasticity are given attention as a section by professor Michael Russo addresses mindfulness and creativity. Schiering addresses mindfulness with "Thinking Inside My Head" just before closing the chapter with Journal and/or Discussion Questions.

BEGINNING QUOTATION

Dr. Sasken, MD, the author of the first portion of this chapter, states: "*It is now recognized that brain pathway connections can be developed and strengthened through life. The brain changes daily.* One of the strongest ways to cement a pathway of the brain is to learn and teach the subject to others through the use of an interactive methodology."

CREATIVE COGNITION AND NEUROPLASTICITY

What about our brain and creative cognition? How do you suppose these two mix together? Perhaps first it's good to take a look at what this "neuroplasticity" idea is and how it has come to the forefront of recent research topics. As Dr. Harvey Sasken, chief of pathology at Lincoln Hospital in New York writes:

A Little History:

"One cannot learn without thinking. Success must be rewarded by the establishment of pathways with positive feedback. This is contrary to compulsory learning and memorization. The hickory stick is out of tune in our world of today. Thinking and creative cognition serve as the baseline for the ideas of neuroplasticity. But, first let's examine the development of thought on this topic.

"The concept of neuroplasticity was first suggested over one hundred years ago and has developed over the last fifty years with modern methods of neuroscience. The older outdated classic model of neural function was that the brain was fixed and hardwired. It was believed that intellectual capacities were fixed and immutable. This means that when it comes to brain functions, everything stays the same, is stagnant in a manner of speaking. Functional brain cells, the neurons, could not regenerate and once they or their connections were lost, they could not be retrieved or regenerated.

"The concept of neuroplasticity includes the notion that the brain is 'not fixed' and immutably hardwired as traditionally believed, but rather that neural functions are quite 'plastic.' *It is now recognized that connections can be developed and strengthened through life. The brain changes daily. New pathways are made regularly.*"

TECHNICAL INFORMATION

Dr. Sasken continues, "The human brain contains somewhere around eighty-five to one hundred billion neurons or functional brain cells. Nineteen to twenty-three billion of them are in the cortex. The cortex includes the sites of higher intellectual functions, referred to earlier in this book as metacognitive processes. Chimpanzees, dolphins, and gorillas have between five and ten billion such neurons. For the cortex to function it requires complex connections to the older areas of the brain. In addition to the neurons there are even more numerous supporting or structural cells in the brain. Each neuron contains a number of processes, the axons and dendrites which form connections to other neurons. These connections are referred to as synapses.

"There may be one hundred trillion such connections in the brain. There are several dozen recognized neural transmitters which facilitate the transmission of signals across the synapses. These transmitters include substances such as dopamine, epinephrine, various amino acids, peptides such as somatostatin and amphetamine, acetylcholine and nitric oxide. Dopamine transmission is associated with a positive or pleasurable response." Do you remember the chapter on *Reciprocal Feelings*? Well, here is where those "plus" emotions originate. Lower levels of dopamine are associated with a negative or unpleasant response. But clearly, the feelings and emotions one has are triggered by the brain-mind connection, as mentioned in chapter 5. It is this linkage and the ability of these two to establish new pathways and be transformative that defines neuroplasticity and the creation of learning and teaching activities.

TEACHING AND LEARNING ACTIVITIES

According to Dr. Sasken, "Recognizable teaching activities have probably been present in our cultures for hundreds of thousands of years. Classically it was considered that for a species to survive it had to be biologically successful. This meant that the species had to reproduce in sufficient numbers and raise the offspring to a stage of independence. In modern terms this would mean a lifespan of about thirty. The limits of human lifespan, even in the primeval, is several times this age. The presence of elders in the clan provided the group with the advantage of having individuals who could impart the wisdom 'gained from experience.'" The learning we've referenced throughout this book focuses on one's experience being of such a nature or significance as to call one to retain material that's either been experienced before, or is new.

"In a number of primitive cultures there is evidence that individuals too old or ill to contribute work effort were cared for by the group. We can imagine that this was accomplished through demonstration and with species development also through an oral tradition."

CREATIVE COGNITION: INNOVATION AND ACTIVE ENGAGEMENT IN LEARNING AND TEACHING

"Ages prior to the development of modern neuroscience we engaged in successful education. *Successful educators have always engaged their students in 'active learning.'* From the earliest of times physicians have learned their vocation from apprenticeships. Modern medicine is taught the same way just as are all trades requiring skill. The skills and knowledge are imparted through engaged physical activity under the direction of a master.

High level skills from medicine to carpentry to performing arts are mastered by repetition or innovation obviously training the required pathways.

"The concept that learning is exclusive to use of one's modalities is outdated. These are the portals or means to engage the development of neural pathways. To these portals must be added the active engagement to stimulate development of the pathways.

"Since the dawn of humans we recognize there has been a development of culture and accumulation of acquired knowledge. We learned how to hunt and gather, we developed farming, trades, crafts and industries. Our intellectual capacities enabled the development of art, music, literature, and science. Our collective and individual knowledge base is increased by deduction and observation. Successful methods of teaching were rewarded with continued use and development."

THE IBR AND RECENT NEUROSCIENCE

Reading the explanations of neuroscience it's good to realize that only recently has neuroscience caught up with developed training protocols. Now we have greater understanding of neural pathways, the plasticity of neural function, and the ways in which pathways are formed. With this understanding we can revisit our classical learning procedures and make them more effective, as with the use of the IM and its strategy of the IBR requiring the application of neuroplasticity and the design and creation of interactive instructional resources. This is accomplished by effective pathways that develop when the subject is engaged, alert, motivated (see chapters 7 and 11) and able to focus.

Dr. Sasken states that "The subject should also be free of distraction and conflicts. Repetition strengthens the pathways, as do[es] exposure to new concepts. The way to master a difficult [process] is to practice. Learning processes are influenced by atmosphere and attitude. The subjects engaged in learning should be placed in the most conducive environment and in the best frame of mind. A belligerent or disruptive subject will not be apt to form strong pathways."

OTHER REALITIES OF NEUROPLASTICITY

Did you know that the principles of neuroplasticity may be applied to rehabilitation? They can be! Brain function may be lost or impaired as a result of disease or injury. Current methods of rehabilitation have been enhanced by the application of advances in neuroscience directly through the understanding of neuroplasticity. Therapy has incorporated the effort to produce new neural *pathways* with the goal of replacing the ones lost. Features of the therapy include repetitive use of new pathways with as much positive reinforcement as can be obtained. Similar positive pathway production may be applied to control of emotions and "talent development," as evidenced in use of interactive instructional resources, in short, applying the IM for learning and teaching.

PRINCIPLES OF NEUROPLASTICITY

Principles of neuroplasticity may be applied to general childhood and adolescent education, as well as those seeking advanced degrees. The goals entail establishing well-formed pathways. These pathways are established when they are associated with other pathways to form large "interconnected" networks. An educator must establish the most conducive environment for learning. "The student must be engaged." The idea of using interactive learning and teaching methods coupled with the design and creation of an IBR align nicely with the teaching-learning "engagement" theory and practice.

"Also, the idea of having learning presented in a manner that includes varied ways of interaction to best formulate memories and retention of material without the specific IBR is operational. The IM precedes the IBR, as portions of the latter may be used as easily as the entire project. This may involve a little thinking out-of-the box, but the neuroplasticity certainly allows for that.

"Interaction with peers and mentors establish successful pathways. This amounts to approaching the subject from as many associated pathways as possible, creating new defenses and raising new questions. One of the strongest ways to cement a pathway of the brain is to teach the subject to others. Teaching and learning activities establish a large array of interconnected networks that foster neuroplasticity and are, quite evidently, the subject matter of this book" (Sasken, 2014).

MINDFULNESS AND CREATIVITY

Overview:

This section of the chapter commences with a connection between the brain-mind and mindfulness to the beginning of this chapter's topic of neuroplasticity. Then, philosophy professor Michael Russo addresses the definition of mindfulness as being attentiveness. An experiment connecting mindfulness to creative expression is presented. Mindful introspection and creative expression precede the closing Journal and/or Discussion Questions.

CHAPTER SECTION CONNECTIONS

You've just read a section relating how your brain is plastic, moveable as it were. Now in order to further comprehend the importance of one's brain, it is related that "the brain is the center of the nervous system and close to the primary sensory apparatus of vision, hearing, balance, taste, and smell. The brain is extremely complex and is seen as the main controller and determiner. The brain is the center of thought and the organ that perceives sensory impulses and regulates motor impulses. So, the brain effects and affects our thoughts and feelings.

"The mind includes seeing it as the aspect of intellect and consciousness experienced as combination of thought, perception, memory, emotion, will and imagination, including all unconscious cognitive processes" (Schwartz and Begley, 2003). Focusing on the last sentence, it is the mind and brain, working in conjunction with one another, that allow for memory to be realized with our feelings and creativity recognized through use of one's imagination. The act of one's "conscious will" joins the neuroplasticity of the brain to the mind and most definitely mindfulness.

MINDFULNESS DEFINITION

Professor Michael Russo addresses the topic of one's being mindful when it comes to creativity. What is meant by this, he explains, is to focus one's thinking on the subject at hand. He relates "For those not familiar with the concept, mindfulness practice is also known as insight meditation. This meditation allows for a person to be aware of their creativity and the processes used to incorporate it into actions taken to imagine, formulate ideas and produce a final product."

MINDFULNESS AND ATTENTION

Schiering calls attention to chapter 5 of this book where memory is described as the result of three consecutive actions. The first is attention: "Attention: The ability to focus on a specific stimulus without being distracted. The second area of memory acquisition involves orientation and the third decision-making and problem-solving."

Russo relates, "When one pays attention his/her relation to things changes. You see more and you see more deeply. You may start seeing an intrinsic order and connectedness between things that were not apparent before." Schiering explains that this deals with orientation and leads to decision-making, which are the final steps in memory acquisition and application.

"By paying attention, you literally become more awake. It is an emerging from the usual ways in which we all tend to see things and do things mechanically, without full awareness. . . . This [experience] leads directly to new ways of seeing and being in your life because the present moment, whenever it is recognized and honored, reveals a very special and magical power: *it is the only time any of us ever has*. . . . It is the only time we have to perceive, to learn, to act, or to change.

"Through the practice of mindfulness, subjects of mindful attention, no matter how mundane they might appear at first glance, are intensified in their rich particularity and vivified (literally "brought to life") before the imagination, which leads to creativity." This has been illustrated in chapter 2 with the two graphic organizers on 1) Linear Creative Processes, and 2) Reciprocal Creative Processes. "Through the power of mindfulness, students have been given the experiential content that they were missing that becomes the fodder for creative production."

FROM MINDFUL EXAMINATION TO CREATIVE EXPRESSION: AN EXPERIMENT

According to Professor Russo, "With the basic practice of mindful awareness, a person, place, thing or experience can become a subject of finite exploration. To illustrate this point, we ask students to look around their homes and try to find some ordinary, seemingly boring, object to bring into class. In fact, we tell them, the more boring the object, the better. When the time comes for this follow-up exercise, the classroom is filled with a wide assortment of rusty tools, office supplies, articles of clothing, and the like.

"Each student is instructed to sit with his or her object of choice for a significant period of time, examining it in all its rich complexity. *It's only after this long and arduous process of becoming profoundly attentive with the object of investigation that the hands-on process of creating takes place.*

"At this point, students might be guided to express their creative visions in a specific medium of the teacher's choice. In our program, the first step in this process has traditionally involved shooting a series of photographs of the object in various settings and lighting situations. The camera in this context becomes an extension of the process of mindful awareness, allowing the student to continue to deeply study their object.

"Students can also be asked to reflect upon what medium might best enable them to convey the depth of the subject they have chosen and then be invited to engage in some sort of creative activity using the medium of their choice. I'm often amazed at how incredibly innovative children and adolescents can be when they are given control of both the subject and the mode of creative expression. Just as objects of mindful study are virtually unlimited, so too are the possible forms that creative expression can take, once educators in particular get beyond their own limited, and often biased, perspective on what are 'appropriate' and 'inappropriate' vehicles for creative expression."

MINDFUL-INTROSPECTION AND CREATIVE EXPRESSION

Russo continues, providing more mature students with the opportunity to get in touch with the content of their thoughts and emotions is a powerful experience indeed. The practice of mindfulness is applied to strong emotional-feeling states like anger, fear, or desire, or those mentioned in chapter 11's *Reciprocal Feeling Phases*. It's related there that students learn to observe these emotional-feeling states as they reveal themselves, without adding additional mental content and without judging them as either good or bad, but impacting their creativity expression. The practice of observing these feeling states and treating them with some degree of objective detachment can be an extremely liberating experience. Still, it should be noted, that some students find "mindful introspection" too intense, which is the reason why this practice should be used judiciously.

Russo states, "What I have found in my teaching experience is that *when students are able to sit with strong thoughts and emotions using the techniques of mindfulness practice, a world of creative content comes pouring out of them, greatly enriching their creative expression.* This should hardly be surprising, since great artists are usually deeply introspective individuals. Provided students are able to handle the strong emotions that can surface during this process, *I and my colleagues in the Philosophy have found that the process of 'mindful-introspection' can be a source of tremendous inspiration for the individual creator."*

MINDFULNESS: THINKING INSIDE MY HEAD

Picking-up on Russo's mindfulness narrative, I (Schiering) recently had a conversation with a colleague in middle-America on this topic. In past conversations we'd discussed how some people talk to think and others think to talk. Neither is better than the other, just a fact of how things are. Chapter 2 relates Linear and Reciprocal Creative Cognition Processes and in those one might consider the idea of creativity being a mindful exercise.

The thing is that thinking may be seen as talking inside one's head (Million, 2015). If doing this too loudly then unclear mindfulness would be the result. Subsequently, the practice of mindfulness becomes necessary for lucidity regarding being creative, or for that matter comprehending the possibilities of one's creative cognition.

JOURNAL AND/OR DISCUSSION QUESTIONS

1. How would you define neuroplasticity?
2. How does the IBR and/or creative cognition relate to neuroplasticity?
3. How would you describe "mindfulness" in relation to creative cognition and/or creativity?
4. How does mindfulness equate with the "attention" section of memory?
5. What is the connection between mindful-examination, creative expression, and mindful-introspection?
6. Are you one who thinks to talk or talks to think? How do you suppose that either of these might influence one's creative cognition?

FOURTEEN

IBR Pages and IBR Use as an Assessment Instrument

CHAPTER OVERVIEW

This chapter provides the contents of the IBR for a review of a specified piece of literature and a thematic unit of study. Then, how the IBR may be used as an assessment/evaluation instrument is given specific attention with a rubric and a detailed accompanying narrative. This is followed by the IBR and/or portions of it as an alternative means of assessment. There is one closing question.

A REVIEW OF LITERATURE IBR

Materials:

For the IBR that reviews of piece of literature, you'll need a binder (3–4 inches), page protectors, laminate, markers, construction paper, continuity tester, index cards, cardstock paper, 12-inch ruler, masking tape, aluminum foil, Top-lid box, and brass fasteners.

General Directions

This IBR is designed to review a piece of literature, and the major requirements include: An "About the Author" page, story summary, invitation page, five interactive pages with one for each major discipline. While you may have more than five and include sedentary pages, the main requirement is at least five tactile and/or kinesthetic pages. What follows is the sequence for making this type of IBR:

1. Select a piece of literature that's either a children's picture book or chapter book. The latter is recommended for grades two through twelve.
2. Read the book, and, using Post-it Notes or regular note paper, earmark the sections of the story you want represented in your IBR.
3. Using the Internet and available resource books, research the author and create an Author page that gives information about the books this author has written and important facts about his or her life.
4. Again, using the Internet or your own awareness of the book's storyline, create a Summary of the Story page.
5. Write an *Invitation to Play-the-Pages of* the IBR that welcomes learners to engage in the activities you create.
6. Create a minimum of five interactive pages that require tactile and/or kinesthetic involvement. You may have pages that require more sedentary involvement, such as making an audiotape or doing a Crossword Puzzle, but there should be five definite get-up-and-move pages.
7. The interactive pages need to be in each of the five major disciplines of reading, math, science, social studies, and English language arts.
8. You may have a creative page where you design something new that is in the format of an educational game. This may be a board, wall, or floor game or one that requires movement, or a role-play activity, a puppet theater with puppets, or making of a quilt, or a specific drawing that is possibly three-dimensional, such as a diorama.
9. Decide which activities are going to be represented for each discipline and plan out your IBR.
10. All activities need a title. Try to make this title appealing.
11. Number each page in the IBR.
12. Create a Table of Contents.
13. Make the interactive/game pages using your own ideas or those presented in chapters 15 and 16.
14. Title each page of the IBR.
15. Create a Chart that lists the activities and corresponding cognitive and metacognitive skills you think are used when playing the page.
16. Put the pages in page protectors, or laminate them for multiple use, and place in the binder.
17. On the back side of each activity page, you might have encouragement statements, or information related to the book, and/or an example of how the page would look if not already self-corrective.

18. Have a *Congratulations Certificate* at the close of the IBR. You may want to include a *Your Comment Page* where learners may express their opinions about the IBR (Schiering, 1996).

THEMATIC UNIT IBR

Materials:

"For the IBR that addresses a unit of study you'll need a binder (3–4 inches), page protectors, laminate, markers, construction paper, continuity tester, index cards, cardstock paper, 12-inch ruler, masking tape, aluminum foil, Top-lid box, and brass fasteners.

General Directions

This IBR is designed to address a specific area of the grade-level curriculum. This may be something like ecosystems, or body systems, such as the skeletal, respiratory, nervous, and circulatory systems. Or your unit of study may be on feelings, character development, life cycles of various animals, planets in our Solar System, the Earth, oceans or continents, explorers, or a period of history, such as the time of the pioneers. The major requirements include: a title page, an invitation to "play the pages" page, an overview of the topic page, and a minimum of five interactive pages with one for each major discipline. While you may have more than five and include sedentary pages, the main requirement is at least five tactile and/or kinesthetic pages. What follows is the sequence for making this type of IBR:

1. Select a topic that you are either interested in studying or, in a classroom, that is part of the grade-level curriculum.
2. Using first- and second-hand resources, such as someone's addressing the topic from first-hand knowledge; using the Internet as a research guide, or gathering information from books on the topic, take notes (audio or handwritten) on the topic and include these in a Topic Overview page.
3. When using a book for information use Post-it Notes or regular note paper, earmark the important points you want represented in your IBR.
4. Discuss this with others in your group, or, if in a partnership, discuss your findings with your partner. Try to stay on topic.
5. Beginning construction of the IBR includes an outside cover page and inside title page for the binder. Then, write an *Invitation to Play-the-Pages of* the IBR that welcomes learners to engage in the activities you create. Remember that all pages need to be self-cor-

rective, or show an example on the flip-side of the activity and its instruction page.

6. All activities need a title. Try to make this title appealing. An example would be "Math Mania" and then state the IBR topic.
7. There are to be a minimum of five interactive pages that require tactile and/or kinesthetic involvement. You may have pages that require more sedentary involvement, such as making an audiotape or doing a Word Search or Word Jumble or even a Maze, but there should be five definite get-up-and-move pages.
8. The interactive pages need to be in each of the five major disciplines of reading, math, science, social studies, and English language arts.
9. You may have a creative page where you design something new that is in the format of an educational game. This page may be a board, wall, or floor game, or creating a map where cardinal directions are in-play. You may choose to have directions for a role-play activity, puppet-theater with puppets, or making of a quilt out of large baggies with drawings on paper inserts, and colorful duct tape to bind the quilt together, or a specific drawing that is possibly three-dimensional, or making of a diorama that would be engaging and a point for discussion of the topic being addressed.
10. Activity pages: other suggestions may include Flip-Chute, Pic-A-Dot, Wrap Around, Electro-Board, graphic organizers that require Velcro match. Most importantly, use your own imagination to design and then create pages for self-actualizing. See chapters 15 and 16 for other ideas.
11. Decide which activities are going to be represented for each discipline, and plan out your IBR.
12. Number and title each page in the IBR.
13. Create a Table of Contents.
14. Create a Chart that lists the activities and corresponding cognitive and metacognitive skills you think are used when playing the page (see figure 10.4).
15. Put the pages in page protectors, or laminate them for multiple use, and place in the binder.
16. On the back side of each activity page, you might have encouragement statements, or information related to the book, and/or an example of how the page would look in case you've not developed an self-corrective page.
17. Have a *Congratulations Certificate* at the close of the IBR. You may want to include a *Your Comment Page* where learners may express their opinions about the IBR" (Schiering, 1996).

THE IBR AS A MEANS OF ASSESSMENT

Ah, assessment and/or evaluation of this making of an Interactive Book Report is three-fold.

1. First there's the assessing of the pages themselves. Are they interactive? Does the page address the literature review and/or the topic of a unit of study? Is creativity demonstrated and if so, how?
2. Next, there's the use of the IBR as a means to demonstrate comprehension. In this instance, rather than giving a test with multiple choice or fill-in-the-blank questions, the designer and creator of the IBR demonstrates understanding by use of his or her imagination in addressing the topic with pages that are educational games; pages to be played. Success in making the pages serves as a key factor in an ability to relate the content and concepts through individual imagination and design.
3. Then, the IBR may be used as a means of evaluation when one is playing the pages. Is the player able to successfully play-the-page? If so, comprehension is realized. If not, then an additional review or playing-of-pages may be necessary. This form of evaluation is done through observation, as opposed to writing or a formal test. Coming up is a comprehensive evaluation of an IBR. Please note how thorough the evaluation is.

"I understand that this may seem overwhelming; however, feedback is an integral part of the IM/IBR process. You can use a checklist, anecdotal notes, or Likert scale. YOU will decide the level and type of feedback you wish to give. Remember: Feedback is a gift!!! Eventually this will be an ongoing process.

"After receiving feedback the learner can go back and amend their project (allow the feedback to become a positive opportunity for their growth in their creative development rather than critique or criticism, which can be viewed as negative). Additionally, as YOU become more comfortable with evaluation, your ability to provide commentary will evolve and you may find yourself explaining why something is well done and, if incorrect, make a suggestion for improvement rather than criticizing the error. 'You get more with sugar than you do with salt' (After, 1953), Momma always said." (Marino, 2014).

COMMENTARY: GENERAL EVALUATION ABOUT THE IBR: DESIGN, LAYOUT, CREATIVITY, ATTENTION TO GOOD GRAMMAR, AND OVERALL IMPRESSION OF THE PAGES: PROFESSOR'S NARRATIVE

CRITERIA	3	2	1
Title Page	Complete and well designed with book title, author, IBR author, and theme addressed in an appealing manner for student learner. Recommended grade noted.	Mostly complete with only one or two elements from previous listing (3) missing	Relatively incomplete with a minimal listing of the required title page information being supplied.
Thinking Phases	A chart or graphic representation, which has the Thinking Phases, and corresponding terms within the Phases attributed to each activity. This is for T.C. awareness and attention to the cognitive and meta-cognitive skills to be developed by playing that particular page.	A chart or graphic representation, which has the Thinking Phases, and some corresponding terms within the Phases attributed to some activities. This addresses T.C. awareness of cognitive and meta-cognitive skills to be developed by playing that particular page.	A representation, but not a graphic or chart-style one that has some of the Thinking Phases, and a few corresponding terms within those Phases. The T.C. does not demonstrate awareness of cognitive and meta-cognitive skills to be developed by playing that particular page.
Author Review/Study	A complete review of the life of the author of the selected piece of children's literature with titles of other books written, and the theme, as well as year of publication of the selected book. All author awards, if applicable, are mentioned. The author's style of writing and general plot, theme, scope and sequence of the selected book should be mentioned., along with your reaction to the book.	A partial review of the life of the author of the selected piece of children's literature with partial listing of titles of other books written, and the theme, as well as year of publication of the selected book given. Some author awards, if applicable, are mentioned. There's a limited mentioning of story plot, theme, scope and sequence, and the IBR creator's reaction.	A minimal review of the life of the author of the selected piece of children's literature with minimal listing of other written pieces, theme, year of publication of the selected book given. No mention of author awards, although one or more may have been received. There's a grossly incomplete mentioning of story plot, theme, scope and sequence, and the IBR creator's reaction.
Story Summary	A complete review of the plot, characters, theme, setting, mood, events, problem and solution of the book.	A partial review of the plot, characters, theme, setting, mood, events, problem and solution of the book.	A minimal reviewof the plot, characters, theme, setting, mood, events, problem and solution of the book.

Figure 14.1. IBR Assessment Rubric with Commentary (*Source*: Schiering, 2003a.)

Dear Nancy,
Without a doubt this is one of the most creative, imaginative, cognitively sound, and student-learner friendly IBRs I have ever had the opportunity to review. From the attractive cover page to the binding with the penguins, to the back page with the reproduction of information from Scholastic Inc., this IBR is superlative! The cover and aforementioned additions really invite the children to wonder about what's inside and subsequently, open the IBR.

Inside you have a copy of the book, as well as the game pieces for the excellent floor game you created, which resembles the game of Monopoly. Right away one sees the detail and imaginative ideas you

Welcome Page	Inviting with interest.	Somewhat inviting.	Not inviting.
Reading Interactive Page(s)	Obvious multi-modality applications for playing the page. Attractive design with good color contrast and clear and concise directions for playing the page, as it relates to reading.	Not clear as to what the interaction involves and/or minimal interaction. Not attractive or readable, due to font or background colors. Directions unclear.	No tactile or kinesthetic involvement and little or no interaction with only reading of the page. Directions for playing the page not given or unclear.
ELA Interactive Page(s)	Obvious multi-modality applications for playing the page. Attractive design with good color contrast and clear and concise directions for playing the page.	Not clear as ELA or to what the interaction involves and/or minimal interaction. Not attractive or readable, due to font or background colors. Directions unclear.	Not clear as to main subject area being addressed. No tactile or kinesthetic involvement and little or no interaction with only reading of the page. Directions for playing the page not given or unclear.
Social Studies Interactive Page(s)	Obvious Social Studies multi-modality applications for playing the page. Attractive design with good color contrast and clear and concise directions for playing the page.	Not clear as to what the content area is or that there's interaction, and/or minimal interaction. Not attractive or readable, due to font or background colors. Directions on how to play the page are unclear.	No reference to content area, tactile or kinesthetic involvement, and little or no interaction with only reading of the page. Directions for playing the page not given or unclear.
Math Interactive Page(s)	Obvious multi-modality Mathematics applications for playing the page. Attractive design with good color contrast and clear and concise directions for playing the page.	Not clear as to content area, or what the interaction involves, and/or minimal interaction. Not attractive or readable, due to font or background colors. Directions unclear.	No tactile or kinesthetic Math involvement with little or no interaction needed for playing the page, and only reading of the page. Directions for playing the page not given or unclear.
Science Interactive Page(s)	Obvious Science multi-modality applications for playing the page. Attractive design with good color contrast and clear and concise directions for playing the page.	Not clear as to Science content, or what the interaction involves and/or minimal interaction. Not attractive or readable, due to font or background colors. Directions unclear.	No Science tactile or kinesthetic involvement and little or no interaction with only reading of the page. Directions for playing the page not given.
Creative Page(s)	Demonstrates innovative ideas, creativity and theme of book or extended theme application. Attractive design and use of color contrast with clear directions for playing the page.	Demonstrates minimal innovative ideas, creativity and theme of the book, or extended theme application. Somewhat attractive design and use of color contrast with clear directions for playing the page.	No innovative ideas, creativity and theme of book or extended theme application. The design of the page is confusing and detracts from the overall appearance of the page. Poor color contrast, and directions for playing the page.

Figure 14.2. IBR Assessment Rubric with Commentary (*Source*: Schiering, 2003a.)

have incorporated for children's active engagements in learning. Now, having related that, I shall begin the review/evaluation of this fine piece of work. But, here's a forewarning that the superlatives shall be repetitive.

1. The inside cover page is terrific with the bold font and the pictures of the penguins.
2. The Table of Contents is very attractive with the red font on the vibrant gold background insert. Then, the flip-side with the book cover repeated and notation of the Newbery Honor clearly present serves to remind the player-of-the-pages about the specialness of this book.
3. The Author's page needs the "s" taken away from the word "Author." That written, this page reads exceptionally well-constructed with a good deal of pertinent information about the original author and then his wife, who finished writing the book for him.
4. This page with the Reciprocal Thinking Phases is aesthetically beautifully configured. It also addresses the cognitive and metacognitive skills employed when an individual or partners are playing the pages in a finite manner. You need to add "self-actualizing" to the "Monopoly" floor game, but other than that this page is exemplary!
5. I LOVE the phrase "adventure in learning," which you used on the Welcome to the page players to the IBR you created! The verbiage you employed explains that there are supplies provided to play-the-pages, and you've a nice formidable invitation to engage the students in this project of learning-through-play!
6. The Story Summary is superlatively written with a good deal of detailed information,
7. The first activity with the writing of a letter to one's favorite character in the book is innovative and addresses ELA skills. The sample letter you provided is good. (Suggestion: When you provide a sample in ELA for a letter, please remember that there need to be four sentences for a *complete* paragraph). Then, the supply pouch and instructions to put their letter in the mailbox folder is excellent! The folder idea is clever and the "U.S. Mail" with the flag being in the "up" position is just ingenious! For a writing activity, you have managed to have interaction.
8. The "Pic-A-Dot" activity is again superlative. The direction page #19 explains the story extension through this activity being the introduction of facts about penguins to be found on a fact sheet page. The transference to the interactive, tactual of the P-A-D is really exemplary! You've a good amount of facts, and the actual holder for the cards is so attractive that everyone in class, including me, was "oohing" and "ahhing!" You are artistically gifted and this

adds to the attractiveness of your IBR! Just a magnificent entry to your IBR!

9. Could an Electro-Board be more adorable? No! This entry in your IBR is excellent. And, I so hope you'll share this IBR with other teachers and children, prior to actual use in your own classroom. It's wonderful! Also, I'd certainly like you to come and share your IBR again, next semester, with EDU.506A teacher-candidates.
10. The *Magnificent "Penguin Flip-Chute."* I have run out of superlatives, I'm sorry to relate. However, being repetitive, *this F.C. is extraordinary* (I'd like to keep it for display, but you've a future wider audience for this), and the information on page #33 is well written. Here you provide pertinent material about testing one's knowledge of possibly new vocabulary words that were in this story. You provide explicit directions on how to use the F.C. and offer a "Good Luck" thought.
11. The picture on the reverse side is good. And, the pouch with the laminated F.C. cards is excellent. The words you selected are also very good with perfect definitions and the children being able to use the definition first and guessing the word or vice versa being applicable.
12. The Wrap Around with characters' names in the story being matched with their roles in the story is good. Also, the page is attractively designed. And, for that matter, *each page entered in this IBR is lovely and inviting with good color contrast, placement of titles and information, as well as illustrative work.*
13. Nice encouragement pages!
14. Janie and Bill's Jigsaw is excellent with the cutout pieces providing good tactile and kinesthetic involvement, depending on where the children choose to put the pieces together—on desk or floor. In any event this activity is a good idea and this one, along with all the others, have been addressed well on the Thinking Phases Chart.
15. Clever—"Penguin Mask-erade!" *Truly, you are innovative, imaginative, and creative in the pages you've configured and especially this one!* The supply pouch you provided is thoughtful and the template with directions really lets the children be involved in this creation through their own imagination application. (That "Penguin" circle you made is precious!)
16. Task Cards on the different species of penguins is an excellent idea for story extension. Then the actual cards with the pictures of the penguins is not just attractive and invitational in their design, but highly informative with a good idea of penguin awareness and knowledge to be gained.
17. The Floor Monopoly Game/Creative Page: What can one say? It's all of this: magnificent, attractive in design, has superlative color contrast, is inviting, provides exemplary use of all modalities, looks

beautiful, causes one to want to play the game immediately—as observed by your classmates reaction, and is erudite with cognitive and metacognitive skills addressed in a finite and erudite manner!

18. The Congratulations page and accompanying certificates are excellent! Color design and contrast with different fonts and placement of items on pages is excellent. The added Reference section is also excellent, as is your entire IBR!

THE IBR AS AN ALTERNATIVE MEANS OF ASSESSMENT

A learner may make one or a few of the interactive resources for the purpose of demonstrating knowledge of a specified topic. Making Flip-Chute cards for vocabulary, creating a Pic-A-Dot for story or theme comprehension questions, or any of those interactive instructional resources presented in the next two chapters may be designed and configured. There's proof of knowing the material when the educational game/learning tool is made and/or played. The IBR replaces the traditional and conventional means of testing to ascertain what is and isn't known. In so doing the IBR is engaging and evaluative of learner's complete comprehension and serves as an alternative means of assessment.

JOURNAL AND/OR DISCUSSION QUESTION

1. Do you envision this creative learning and teaching experience helping students develop their creative cognition? Why or why not? How is the IBR an alternative assessment?

FIFTEEN

Differentiated Instruction and Activities for the IBR Pages

CHAPTER OVERVIEW

This chapter and the next one are devoted to two things. The first is types of differentiated instruction and how to apply these in the classroom setting. The second is actual suggestions for pages of the IBR with explanations and design of these. Included are varied types of graphic organizers. All of the "figures" in this chapter have been configured by this book's author. The chapter closes with Journal and/or Discussion Questions.

TWO SCHOOLS OF THOUGHT

Why we teach what we do and how this is done are two areas for consideration when addressing differentiated instruction. Let's think about this: Should we teach all lessons the same way? Why or why not?

You may have experienced, during your kindergarten through college years, instructional strategies that focused on telling you what was to be done and how to do it. Or, the second idea is that you were given information on what was to be learned and were provided latitude on the implementation. Those are two schools of thought on teaching. They're diametrically opposed to one another. Whether we should teach all lessons the same way focuses on whether we think all students learn the same way. If you think this point is not the case, then differentiated instruction is what would be utilized for classroom teaching. Using the IM in conjunction with the IBR or portions of the latter are examples of differentiating instruction addressing those mentioned in this chapter.

THE IM AND IBR: DIFFERENTIATED INSTRUCTION

You're asked to focus now on the concept that, if all children do not dress alike or look the same, we may surmise that they learn differently from one another. At the most basic level, some would prefer listening to a teacher explain something, while others would want to see a demonstration, be able to touch (tactile) it, or be kinesthetically (whole-body) involved. Varying the instructional modalities or use of students' perceptual preferences is important. You might not teach the same topic with lessons repeating the material in each perceptual preference. However, you might vary lessons by using different modalities for different content material.

Some learners may be best served with auditory presentations, while others call for involvement tactually, kinesthetically, or visually. Modality preferences are one form of differentiating instruction. Others are those that consider the pace at which students work best, their ability level, varied kinds of instruction, interest areas, needs, learning-styles, and finally, scaffolding or tier practices. These are presented below and on the following pages with examples of each differentiation provided.

IBR and Five Types of Differentiated Instruction:

As you read this next section, ask yourself which of the differentiated instructional strategies you prefer, and then try to explain to yourself, through examples given, how these apply to everyday learning.

Within the confines of the IM and IBR are many different types of instruction. While up to this point this book has finitely emphasized interactive instructional resources, creativity, educational gaming for self-efficacy, and empowering of the learners, it is time now to convey information about *how* the IM and IBR address Learning Pace, Learning Ability Level, Kinds of Instruction, Student Interests, and Student Needs.

Learning by Pace *and the IM & IBR:*

Clearly, the first of these listed involves the time-on-task that best accommodates learners. While some learners need a good deal of time to complete an assignment, others may require less time, or a small extension of time in order to address the material presented. Your IM lessons need to take this time element into consideration by providing some students the opportunity to work for longer, shorter, or intermediate periods of time on the same assignment, or construction of an IBR interactive page. Of course, the IM, addressing creativity and interaction, automatically allows for variations in time on task.

Pace Example:

The four different types of sentences—declarative, interrogative, exclamatory, and imperative—have been assigned making and/or using Task Cards. Those who work at a slow pace will be allotted twenty to forty minutes to complete the making or playing of this interactive IM differentiation-of-instruction game. Those who are able to complete work quickly or at a medium speed will be given fifteen to thirty minutes, respectively.

Learning by Ability Level *and the IM & IBR:*

This Ability Level differentiation refers to the general expectation of student performance and competency at a given grade and/or age. Student-learners may function at what has been determined as above, at, or below grade level. More specifically achievement level may vary from one discipline to another so that grade or age level is acceptable, but content within a subject area may differ. Scores on standardized tests are often the determining factor for what is considered "on-level" and what is above or below it.

Ability Level Example:

The students have come up with the idea of an acrostic poem for their IBR on the topic of Seasons of the Year and Storms. An illustration of the word selected is required. Those who are adept at thinking of different words to use in this type of poem would use a word like "snowstorms." Those who were less adept would have a word of shorter length, such as "sledding." Those with the least ability to construct an acrostic poem might be asked to use the word "snow." The IM is evident in the creativity of the acrostic poem and drawing. The IBR page has student learners imagining and then inventing drawing so anyone doing the page will be involved in its creation.

Learning by Kinds of Instruction *and the IM & IBR:*

The type of instructional techniques or methods one uses is what is meant by kinds of instruction. Passive recipients of knowledge would be diametrically opposed to the instructional strategy where students are actively engaged in the process of acquiring information which is representative of the IM.

The Socratic, Behaviorist, Experientialist, and Constructivist methods are a few of the ones practiced in schools. Learning through discussion, examples, types of questions (convergent and divergent), inductive or deductive reasoning, as well as emotional components are considered when addressing varied kinds of instruction. So is lecturing.

The IM and its accompanying IBR exemplify "kinds of instruction." These are demonstrated by accommodations for learning style preferences and/or processing styles, partnerships or small-group work, as well as student involvement in making interactive IBR pages. Another kind of instruction referenced by Tomlinson (2000) as being flexible is having collaborative groups of learners, or whole class instruction, with varied products where choices as to how a student may evidence what has been learned are realized.

Kinds of Instruction Example:

The students have been assigned to conduct research on community helpers for later reporting to the class. Some would use the now-popular Internet media to gather this information. Others might seek an interview with a community helper, and some might use their experiential past encounters with someone practicing this job. Still others may watch a video that provides information, or simply read the textbook and take notes on important points for information gathering and later reporting.

Reporting styles would also vary in accordance with the kind of instruction to be utilized when disseminating information. Some might use PowerPoint slides in their IBR to show what's been learned, while others create an educational game or an entire IBR. Those who prefer lecturing might have a page in their IBR and ask the page player to dress as a character and recite something from his or her experience. This would be disseminating information to the class as if representative of a story character or time period or topic/subject being discussed.

Still others may ask students to contribute their experiences with community helpers to add to a presentation or create illustrations with commentary, while others conduct a role-play scenario of a community helper practicing his or her job, or telling of a real-life experience related to these persons. Creating and playing a board game or floor game would bring about kinesthetic instruction. Involvement in the use of graphic organizers, such as cause and effect or Electro-Boards and Task Cards would also call for active involvement in learning as a Kind of Instruction.

Utilizing Learners' Interests and the IM & IBR:

This section refers to the areas where students are focused, because of intentness, concern, curiosity, importance, consequence, and variations of thinking or feeling regarding learning fields. Some learners may want to gain information about sports, while others are not even mildly concerned. Subsequently, the topic of the IBR being constructed might rely on this factor. The IM is addressed through student interests being demonstrated as part of one's creative process when imagining and later self-actuating.

Simultaneously, one may have curiosity about how to get from one place to another while others are simply interested in another taking care of that circumstance. Map making, cardinal directions, map legends, and making up one's own land form could each be a social studies IBR portion. Interests are emotionally and/or cognitively based. They might involve using varied kinds of instruction, which correspond to modality preferences, or they may have an interest in construction of materials to facilitate their learning.

Learners' Interests Example:

The teacher suggests that students create a chart to examine the similarities and differences between two characters in a selected piece of literature. Some students may be interested in 1) creating a Velcro-match graphic organizer/Venn diagram to illustrate these and others may choose, as with kinds of instructional reporting, 2) to conduct a mock interview, or 3) make an audiotape, 4) configure slides for a presentation, or 5) make a mobile, 6) conduct a scripted role-play, or 7) use excerpts from the book's dialogue to show where the characters are in agreement or disagreement with today's standards; a debate would be addressed with instructions on how to conduct one.

LEARNERS' NEEDS AND THE IM & IBR

This point is the subjective and/or objective evaluation component regarding instruction. Since the IM and IBR are creativity-based and allow for flexibility, meeting learners' needs is incumbent in this methodology and project/performance-based learning strategy.

Some needs are obvious, such as in a specific adaptation, as in the hearing-impaired student requiring an amplification system in the classroom. Others are not as apparent. Student needs vary as much as individuals themselves at any given time. Emotional components, assessment tools, achievement in one area and not in another, students' sense of security, and stress factors are all considered as being indicative of learners' needs. Knowing your students' likes and dislikes is very important for this differentiated type of instruction.

Determining, through subjectivity, the needs of a student is feeling-based (see chapter 11). Determining the needs of a student through objectivity is based on a comparison and contrast of a student's performance, as in results on an assessment. Most importantly, learners' needs should be met by the teacher's emphasizing the students' areas of strength and confidence.

Learners' Needs Example:

The teacher notes that several students in the classroom have hearing impairments. As a story is orally presented, these students may have a copy of the story to read silently. Visually impaired learners would have an audiotape of the story as backup. If a lesson focused on the use of writing notes where fine motor skills were employed and the students had difficulty with this process, the teacher might have assistance provided when these skills were necessary. Emotional or special needs (see chapter 8), such as Dyslexia, ADHD, or decoding areas of difficulty may well call for sand writing, structuring a lesson with notations on how the lesson is to be implemented, and using a whole-language approach to providing information. The IM fully addresses students' needs with its flexibility and accommodations for innovation and creativity being at the forefront. The IBR interactive pages may be designed with a learner's needs taken into consideration and allow for making an activity in accordance with what the student is capable of doing.

OVERVIEW OF IM AND IBR: DIFFERENTIATED INSTRUCTION

Overall, the use of differentiated instruction strategies—which are represented in the IM and IBR—fosters the chance to interact, as well as to work individually, for taking in information so it is pertinent, germane, and significant to arrange and plan for the learning situation so it meets the student's needs.

The IM and IBR are differentiated instruction, because at the foundation, the methodology and strategy realizes that all persons do not learn the same material in the same way. Yet, there are other reasons for using this IBR reporting technique. A student's life experiences are taken into account with social and societal realities, belief and value systems, as well as the Cognitive Collective. This realization of life experiences happens regularly inside and outside of school; through reflection on these, we become aware that differentiated instruction explores and allows for choices to be made about what material is presented and how it's presented.

How, you may further question, is differentiated instruction a connection to the IM and IBR? As Bogner stated (1990b), "Structuring the content of learning so that it is useful and applicable to the learner's present situation is vital. This is best facilitated with the use of differentiated instructional strategies."

Over fifty years ago, Dewey addressed the idea of the relevancy of reforming education to make it something to which students could relate when he stated: "If I were asked to name the most needed of all reforms in the spirit of education, I should say 'cease conceiving of education as mere preparation for later life and make of it the full meaning of the present' . . . An activity which does not have worth enough to be carried on for its own sake cannot be very effective preparation for something else" (John Dewey, 1945, in *Self Realization as the Moral Ideal*, as explained by Bogner, 1990b, EW, 4: p. 50).

As stated in chapter 2 of *Teaching and Learning: A Model for Academic and Social Cognition* (Schiering, Bogner, & Buli-Holmberg, 2011), Dewey's philosophy of education is such that it refers to Experientialism . . . learning through experience. This is not very different from what has been practiced over the past several decades with the Constructivist theory being utilized in schools. This is where learners construct meaning from real-life experiences.

In alignment with both of these educators' statements, Dewey (1937) and Bogner (1990a) relate that all too often education is separated from learners' experiences because of the types of teaching that are implemented in the classroom. In separating or "divorcing content from the learner's present experience, the teacher minimizes the content's impact on learning."

It is more difficult to form connections when the content is removed from current experience. In a similar vein, Dewey (1933/1986), as also cited in *How We Think* (LW, 8: pp. 141–150) within Bogner's writing in 1990, (pp. 129–130), relates, "By removing content from applicability to the present, the teacher negates an important motivation for learning. If the content is immediately useful, then the motivation to learn the facts and information is extremely high. Conversely, if the only motivation is a grade or a possible usage of the material, then the motivation to learn will be much less. Furthermore, there's a suggestion that choosing content that is useful and applicable to the learner is important."

Along with all these aforementioned reasons for using differentiated instruction is that of providing students with the opportunity to think about how they best learn. This task is accomplished by using strategies that provide new learning techniques or former ones that have been modified. Not all students learn when information is given to them in a lecture format—talking at them. Yet, many teachers use this method, exclusively, especially in the high school and college settings. A few means of using differentiated instructional strategies are presented in the remainder of this chapter with respect to varied and interconnected modalities being utilized.

IBR INTERACTIVE INSTRUCTIONAL STRATEGIES

The use of graphic organizers (G.O.) to promote student-learners' decision-making, problem-solving, story creation and review, sequencing, as well as character personality analysis, and comprehension of cause and effect relationships is presented. Why? This point is answered simply with the notion that creating these organizers addresses beginning cognition as much as critical thinking and the metacognitive processes that involve creative cognition. At the same time, the topics of these organizers provide an interdisciplinary opportunity to arrange thinking sequentially or simultaneously for comprehension.

Graphic organizers are designed to create visual stimuli for those constructing it or reading it. Generally, they serve as a means for recording known information, as well as speculative responses to specific categories represented within or on the organizer.

A popular way of making the following graphic organizers interactive is to have Velcro pieces with the appropriate information able to be placed in the proper section on the graphic organizer.

Graphic organizers foster the use of creativity, reflection, conversation, risk taking, initial decision-making, synthesizing of material, prioritizing, and self-actuating to form solid reasoning for present-time implementation. Additionally, applying this newly gained information for later subtle and informed addressing of life experiences is plausible. This point would be the case whether the learners are in a social or academic setting. However, most importantly, activities which are designed to develop, apply, and implement effective teaching are those which adhere to the needs of learners through this differentiated strategy.

Assignment	Requirements	Purpose and Relevancy
Create Graphic Organizers (GO) that address: 1. Story Maps, 2. Sequence of Events, 3. Cause and Effect, 4. Character Analysis, 5. Decision Making.	1. Use 36"x24" poster-board, oak-tag, foam-core, or card stock paper. 2. Design and create these five- different types of graphic organizers. 3. Have boxed sections bordered, use theme related decorations, and good color contrast for all sections, as well as dark and large print on light color backgrounds. 4. Provide the appropriate information in written format for an animated oral presentation.	Graphic organizers utilize varied organizational designs, allow for developing creativity, linking thoughts and feelings of characters, and connecting disciplines. They assist in goal setting, developing theme or concept comprehension, as well as cognitive / meta-cognitive skills. Common social realities, individual and whole-group belief and values, being a reflective practitioner, and providing attention to social literacy through performance-based work when these are shared in class are realized. Design of graphic organizers allows for application of creative cognition.

Figure 15.1. A Chart for Lesson Purpose: Graphic Organizers (G.O.) (*Source*: M. Schiering, 1976.)

IBR PAGE: STORY MAP

The Story Map graphic organizer addresses a piece of literature's six story elements. These are the Character(s), Setting(s), Mood(s), Events, Problem(s) and Solution(s). Each one is addressed in a separate section of the organizer with connecting lines to depict the linkages of elements in a story. Each one may be placed on a Velcro strip for putting in the correct section on a Story Map Board.

- The first section is Story Characters and should include the name of each character, as well as a personality trait and/or to whom the character is related or serves as protagonist or antagonist.
- The Setting relates to where the story took place and at what time period. This could be present day, in the past, or future.
- The Mood section of the graphic organizer relates the different feelings evoked by the reader of the story and/or those thought to be intended by the author when specific events occurred in the story.
- The Events section relates, in chronological order, the key situations in the story.
- The Problem and Solution sections relate what the main character(s) had to consider as causing dismay, conflict, and/or confusion in that an action needed to be taken to alleviate the situation, which led to a culminating circumstance that resulted in solving this problem and the subsequent end of the story.
- Overall, depending on the story theme, the students will learn about new situations that address thinking and feelings in social, work, or academic situations. Along with an opportunity to reflect on what he or she might have done in a similar situation, the Story Map provides opportunities for analysis and critiquing.
- Interestingly, the Story Map may be used for creating a story as much as reviewing one. In this instance, the six elements are provided to give writing guidance and organization of thoughts, ideas, opinions, judgments, and feelings. This type of graphic organizer provides one with making links from the characters to the setting, moods, and events/rising and descending actions, which lead to the climax of the story/situation and result in a solution to a posed problem. *(All the figures in this book, previous to this chapter and on the following pages in this chapter and the next one, have been created by the author (Schiering).*

IBR PAGE: SEQUENCE OF EVENTS GRAPHIC ORGANIZER

The Sequence of Events graphic organizer is designed to have four or more events of the story listed in their order of occurrence. The main focus of this graphic organizer is to place, in order, from beginning to

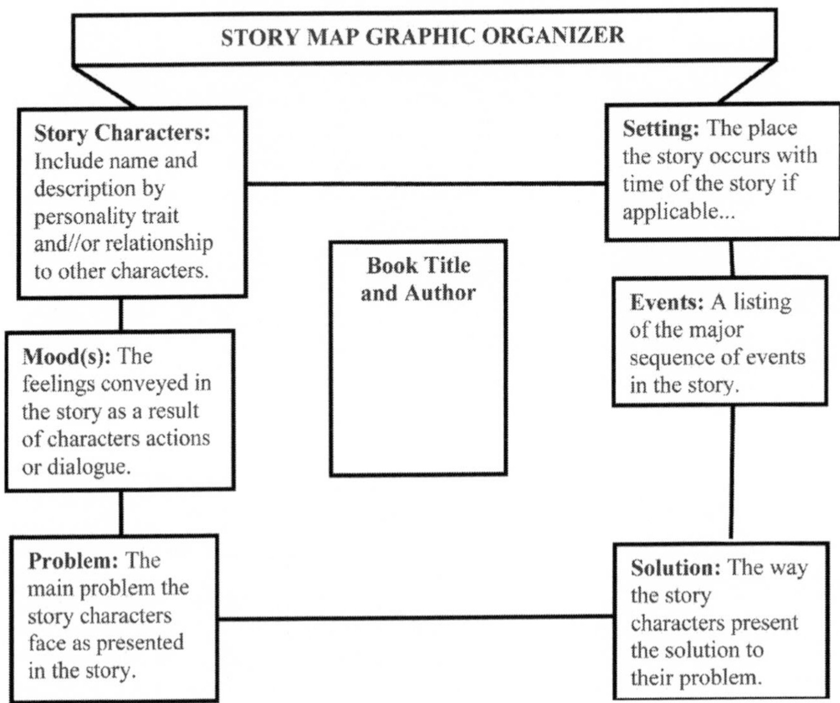

Figure 15.2. Story Map Graphic Organizer

end, what events occurred that were of particular relevance in the story. This may be done as a floor game with sentence strips and illustrations placed on the floor in order of when each occurred in the story. Sentence strips should be numbered. The primary purpose is to illustrate the connection of one story's situational-event leading to another one.

IBR PAGE: CAUSE AND EFFECT G.O.

Cause and effect relationships are represented on this next graphic organizer. The requirements involve relating an action or decision to the effect it has on either the character(s) of a story, other events, or the relationship of individuals in a real-life situation. The Cause and Effect graphic organizer presents singular actions or dialogue with a short narrative that has singular, dual, or multiple effects. These may be emotional effects or those that change one's beliefs or values. Then again, the relationship between the cause and effect may result in no immediate changes, but bring about the future, through reflection, modifications in actions or words spoken. These will result in other causes and effects.

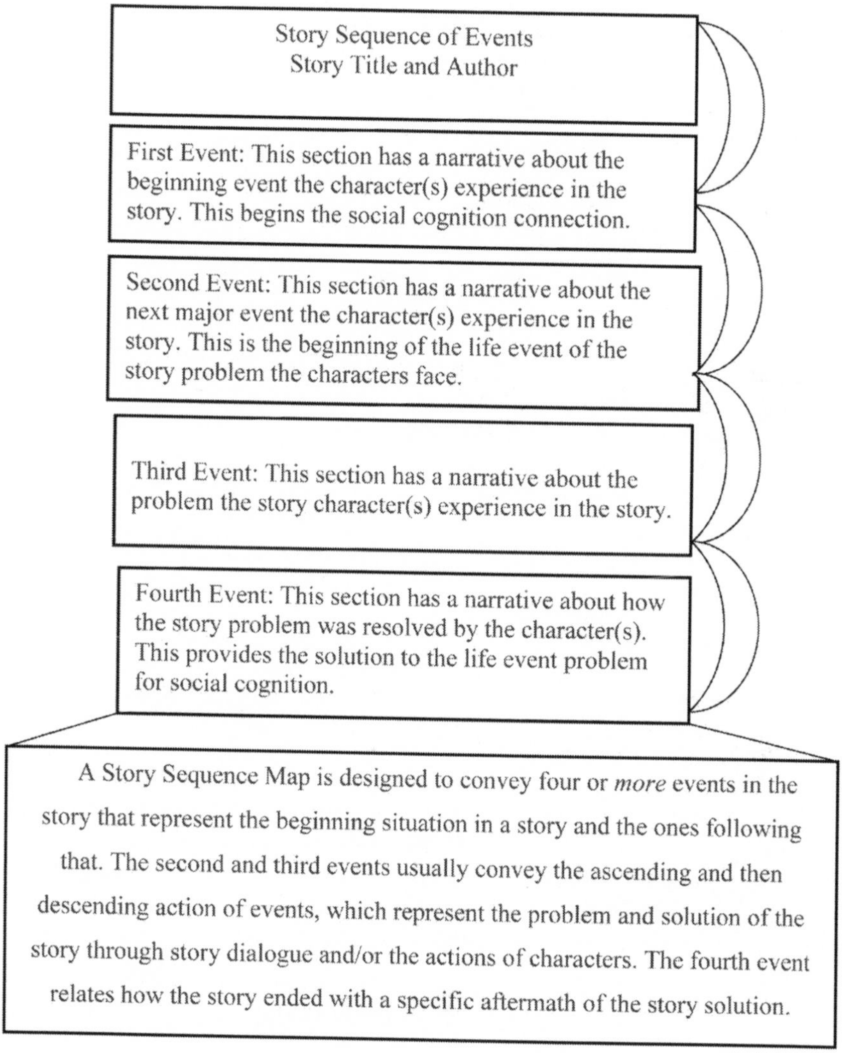

Story Sequence of Events
Story Title and Author

First Event: This section has a narrative about the beginning event the character(s) experience in the story. This begins the social cognition connection.

Second Event: This section has a narrative about the next major event the character(s) experience in the story. This is the beginning of the life event of the story problem the characters face.

Third Event: This section has a narrative about the problem the story character(s) experience in the story.

Fourth Event: This section has a narrative about how the story problem was resolved by the character(s). This provides the solution to the life event problem for social cognition.

A Story Sequence Map is designed to convey four or *more* events in the story that represent the beginning situation in a story and the ones following that. The second and third events usually convey the ascending and then descending action of events, which represent the problem and solution of the story through story dialogue and/or the actions of characters. The fourth event relates how the story ended with a specific aftermath of the story solution.

Figure 15.3. Sequence of Events Graphic Organizer

This type of graphic organizer visually displays the chain of events that brought about a story's problem and solution, or extended the problem with no solution, or resulted in simply a series of events that impacted on one another to cause new feelings, thoughts, ideas, opinions, or judgments to emerge.

One of the most significant components and purposes of this type of graphic organizer is that it provides an opportunity to make connections to real-life situations—common social and societal realities. To make this activity interactive, it is suggested that the causes and effects be written on cutouts and then placed on a Cause and Effect Board with connecting lines also being cut out and placed as connectors.

IBR PAGE: CHARACTER ANALYSIS G.O.

Each character of a story or person in our lives has a specific role which forms the overall content theme of the story/our social reality with that person. The personality traits of each character or person are supported by events that occurred or dialogue that took place at specific times in the story or real-life occurrence. The Character Analysis Graphic Organizer has at the top or center section the character to be addressed. Then a list of four personality traits and information that supports these is given. This may be with events or dialogue that has been provided either from the book or personal circumstances, depending of the character's place of origin: story or real-life experience.

While there are often several character traits, there may be more than one to support each one selected. One character trait is placed in a box and connected to one or several situations that verify that trait being present in the represented story character/person in our life or the book's depiction of that character. As with the previous graphic organizer, it is suggested that information be put on cutouts and Velcroed or taped to the graphic organizer in the appropriate fashion. This graphic organizer, as with the others may be done on a magnetic board with the pieces to be attached being smaller magnet shapes.

The purpose of this type of graphic organizer is to involve the learner in reflection, analysis of discourse, evaluation of personality traits, making connections between actions and/or characters' or supporting characters' expressed thoughts and feelings, as well as to recognize, realize, compare, and contrast while synthesizing.

IBR PAGE: DECISION-MAKING GRAPHIC ORGANIZER

From the time we're little and exploring things around us, we're involved in making decisions. However, our reflection on this process reveals that our decisions are most often limited to two things. The decision-making pattern is imposed upon by parents and society in general. Examples would be that we can wear sandals or sneakers, a green shirt or white one, go to visit a relative or friend, play one particular computer game or another, and the list could continue.

What's been established is a pattern of having two choices. This pattern carries over to the beginning and ensuing school years where the two choices may not be present at all, because of teacher- or school-imposed rules and regulations. Or there are also teacher schedules that

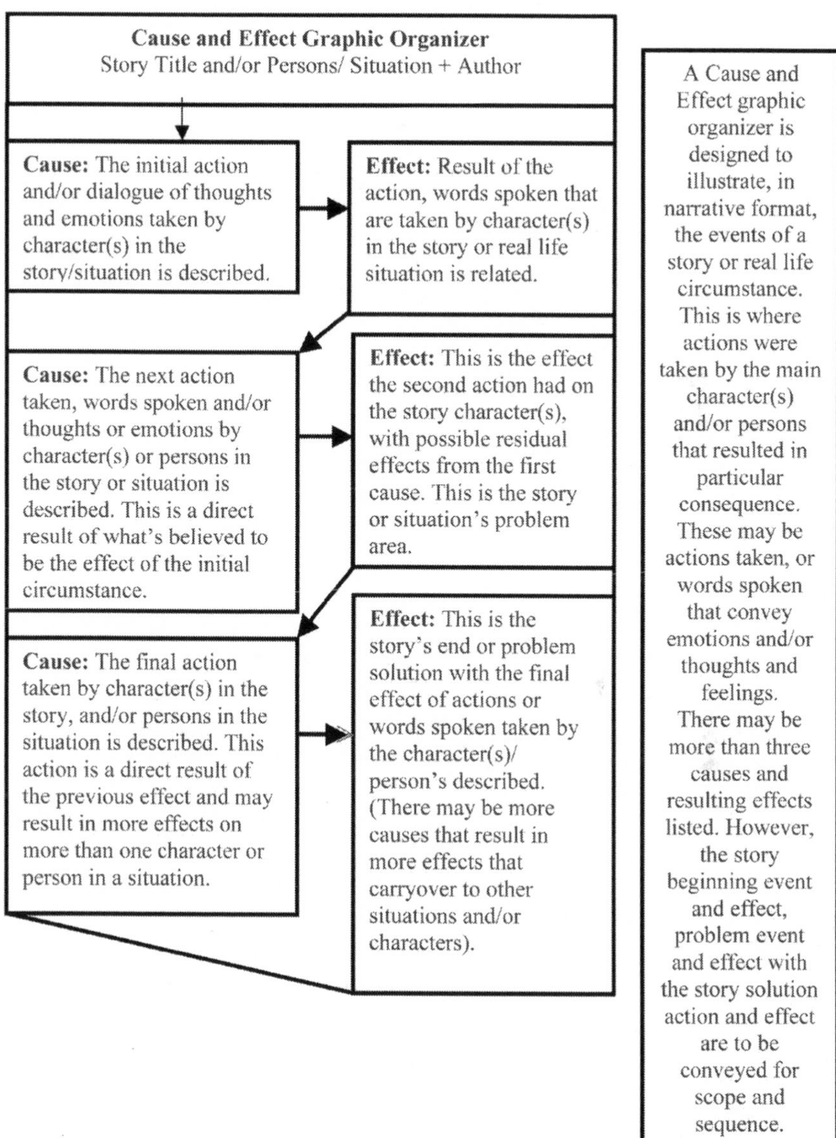

Figure 15.4. Cause and Effect G.O.

relate exactly what's to be done at a given time on a given day in a particular manner. However, differentiated instruction through this upcoming graphic organizer eradicates that structure.

Frequently provided for us are the materials with which we'll work, whether we'll work alone or with another/others, the amount of time to

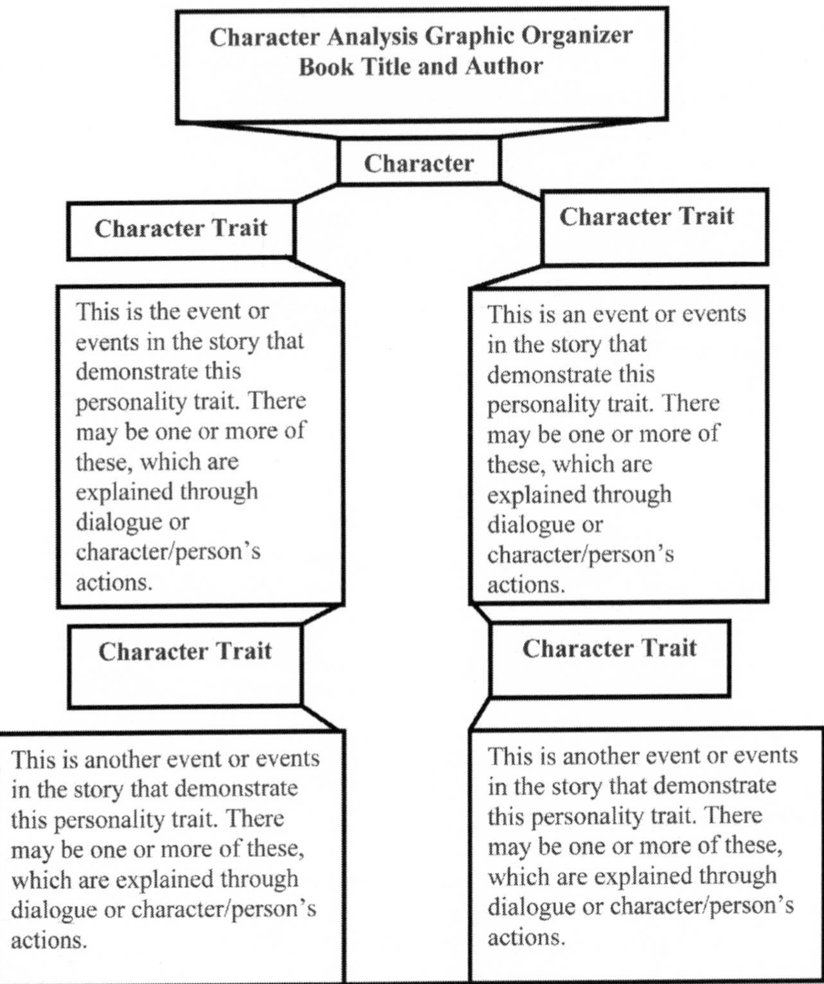

Figure 15.5. Character Analysis Graphic Organizer

do this assignment, where this work will take place, and the specifications that lock it into a designed configuration. With this process, the ability to make decisions becomes clouded. In fact, we suggest that an *inability* to make decisions becomes apparent.

The Decision Making graphic organizer requires three or more choices to be posed with three possible positive and negative outcomes imagined for each one. These lead to a final decision, with reasons for this decision. A line is drawn from this choice to the Final Decision box.

This graphic organizer directs one to realize multiple possibilities for solutions to problems or everyday situations that require thinking and feelings being evidenced. And the situations are those that revolve around the external factors of our lives such as academics, economics, and politics. These external factors influence our lives and are the places where we come to develop our beliefs and values, as a result of our nuclear family's influence, as well as those values of our common social and societal realities.

At the onset, the purpose of this type of graphic organizer is to recognize the steps taken for one to make a decision within a piece of literature or personal circumstance. The problem and solution are related to those instances. The use of critical thinking is evident. Further analysis of the decision-making process is heightened when analyzing *why* a particular decision was formulated. All learners benefit from seeing this process's scope and sequence by examining their own thinking and feelings as they prepare to make decisions. Applied comprehension is evident with cognitive awareness leading to self-actualization, the highest level of metacognition.

To make this activity interactive, it is suggested that the graphic organizer be done on a foam-core board as an attachment to the IBR. For an "in" IBR page one might use Velcro tabs or magnetic ones on a magnetic board.

DIFFERENTIATED INSTRUCTION: TRI-FOLD BOARDS

Tri-fold Boards serve as an interactive vehicle where material involving a piece of literature or thematic unit topic may be newly presented and/or reviewed.

Particularly, the Tri-fold Board's purpose is designed to develop student's cognitive and metacognitive skills through game playing. An example of a Tri-fold Board would be to have a Story Map Graphic Organizer in the board's center section. Then the side flaps may have Task Cards, Pic-A-Dots, and other games mentioned earlier and presented fully later in this chapter. Activities are presented on the board, which adhere to a student's use of precise thinking skills. Using the Reciprocal Thinking Phases, ask yourself this question, "What cognitive and/or metacognitive skills are being used by the student when playing each of the interactive instructional resources on the Tri-fold Board?" How do the center and/or sides of the Tri-fold Board address organization, sequencing, or any of the Beginning Awareness, Critical and Creative Thinking Skills, or Metacognitive Processes form the Reciprocal Thinking Phases?

Please note that the Tri-fold Board is an attachment to the IBR involving the IM.

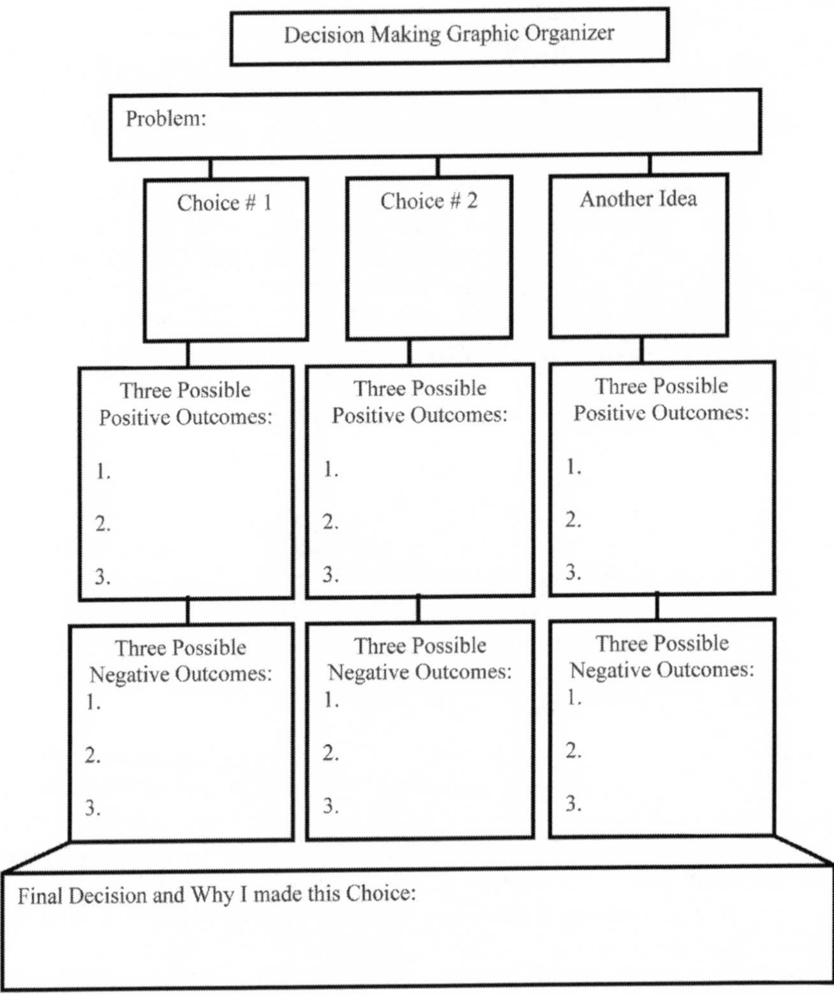

Figure 15.6. IBR Decision-Making G.O.

STEPS FOR CREATING A TRI-FOLD BOARD

Step One: Select a white or dark color Tri-fold Board. The board color is important as you want to be sure you have good color contrast. This means that, if the board is dark blue, you should use light color borders and/or sections having internal sections with white and then dark print.

Step Two: Decide on the piece of literature or discipline to be addressed. Have the center of the board providing information about the main point of the literature or, if a specific discipline, the vocabulary or key concepts of that unit of study. For example, if the unit to be ad-

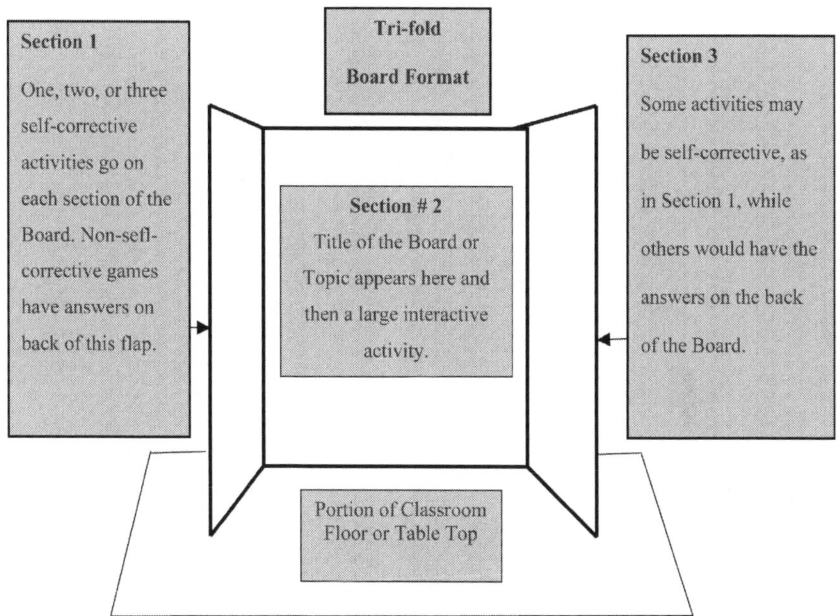

Figure 15.7. Interactive Tri-fold Board: A Way to Utilize the IBRM, or an IBR Outside-Activity for an IBR

dressed is about the "weather" topic, then the center section would represent different types of weather with appropriate labeling. If, however, a piece of literature was selected for the Tri-fold Board, then the center section may have characters' pictures with names and personality traits for matching. The important factor is that the center section is the largest and would contain information about the main points of the unit of study or selected literature.

Step Three: Select interactive instructional resources to enhance student-learners' conceptualization of the content in a piece of literature or specific discipline. Construct these so one, two, or three, depending on the size of the item selected, are on each section of the board. Place an explanatory and instruction piece on each section of the board that addresses the discipline being referenced and the actions to be taken to play this interactive resource. On the back of the board, list the cognitive and/or metacognitive skills that are being developed for each activity. And, if the activity is not self-corrective, then place the answers taped to the board's back section for those activities. The decision-making graphic organizer is an excellent representative of the IM and portions of an IBR with respect to the designing and construction of creative interactive instructional resources being in-play . . . learning-through-play!

JOURNAL AND/OR DISCUSSION QUESTIONS

1. What are the five ways to differentiate instruction mentioned in this chapter?
2. Which of the five ways to differentiate do you think you're most likely to use for yourself or others' learning? Why?
3. What are two graphic organizer activities in this chapter you think may foster learning?
4. Why do you think these two decided-upon activities would foster learning?

SIXTEEN

Differentiated Instruction with More Activities

CHAPTER OVERVIEW

This chapter provides evidence of differentiated instruction with six interactive instructional resources and corresponding thinking skills developed when using these activities for learning-through-play. There is an overview of chapters 15 and 16 along with a few chapter questions.

OVERVIEW OF IBR GRAPHIC ORGANIZERS AND INTERACTIVE INSTRUCTIONAL RESOURCES

Chapters 15 and 17 cover a good number of ways to differentiate instruction with the use of graphic organizers and interactive instructional resources. Each serves a purpose to address students' needs by varying instruction through the use of interactive instructional resources, or educational games. Are there more, you may ask, and the answer would be, "Certainly!" Just as importantly, there are others you'll discover, even ones you invent as you learn and teach.

What has been attempted in these two chapters is exposing you to different instructional methods by taking into consideration that students do not learn in the same way and do benefit from active involvement in learning. From these chapters, it's hoped you are refining your comprehension of new ways to teach a lesson, and/or concretizing those of which you were already aware for self-learning. Teaching is an art, a craft that encompasses learning. How we learn for best retention is done, as this and other chapters of this book explain, by having individuals involved in their learning experience.

INTERACTIVE INSTRUCTIONAL RESOURCES: USES, MATERIALS, AND CONSTRUCTION DIRECTIONS

The resources presented in this topic section have come to be justifiably associated with those in Dunn and Dunn texts on learning styles perceptual preferences, beginning in 1978. However, as stated earlier in this book, these educational games have been around since before that time.

The directions for these resources of the Flip Chute, Pic-A-Dot, Wrap Around, Task Cards, Electro-Board, and Floor Game have been taken from the book Dunn and Dunn's book *Practical Approaches to Individualizing Staff Development for Adults*, chapter 14 (Schiering & Taylor, 1998).

Flip Chute (F.C.): Uses:

This is one of the most often used and beneficial self-corrective interactive resources for tactile learners. This particular learning game is designed to assist students to glean information by placing a question/answer card in the top slot and receiving an answer in the bottom one, as the card flips over going through the chute.

The student has control of this device. The learner determines when to let go of the card, as the answer is said to oneself and the card goes through the chute. A pile of correct answer cards is made, as well as one of incorrect answers, with the latter being revisited until mastery is achieved. This learning device is appropriate for all age/grade levels. College students have been successful in learning foreign language vocabulary, while elementary students have found the F.C. instrumental in learning their multiplication tables.

Suggestions for the F.C. cards with answers on the flip side include vocabulary with definitions, fraction picture like one quarter of a pie on one side and the fraction (1/4) stated on the reverse side. Another use is identifying characters and their quotations, cause and effect, and even fill-in-the-blank for vocabulary or sentence structure, synonyms and antonyms, or parts of speech. Another idea is to have a picture on the front/top side of the card with the word on the flip side. Or, one might have consonant blends on one side with the word "clown" and the "cl" letters underlined with a picture of a clown on the flip side of the card. Figure 16.1 is an illustration of the Flip-Chute.

Flip-Chute and F.C. Cards: Materials:

Half-gallon milk or juice container, two 5x8-inch index cards, 1-inch wide masking tape, ten 2x2.5-inch cut index cards, razor cutter and/or X-ACTO Knife or box cutter, scissors and 12-inch ruler, and contact paper and thematic stickers for container decoration.

Flip-Chute and Flip-Chute Card Construction Directions:

1. Pull open the top of the milk or juice container.
2. Cut the side fold of the top portion down to the top of the container.
3. On the front face measure down from the top one-and-a-half inches and then two-and-a-half inches and draw a horizontal line that is one-quarter inch in from each side.
4. Cut out that opening with the box cutter (razor knife or X-ACTO Knife), and repeat the same procedure at the bottom on the container.
5. Using your 5x8 index cards, measure one six-and-a-half inches long by three-and-a-half inches wide, and using the other card, measure seven-and-a-half inches long by three-and-a-half inches wide, and then cut out these pieces.
6. Score the longer card half an inch up from the bottom and the shorter card half an inch up from the bottom and half an inch down from the top.
7. Insert the smaller strip into the lower opening, and attach it with masking tape to the upper part of the lower opening and lower part of the upper opening. It should form the letter "c" backwards, if one is looking at it from the side.
8. Insert the longer strip with the scored part going over the lower part of the bottom opening and taping this. The upper portion of the strip is taped to the back of the container. At this point, you now have the chutes in place.
9. Using one of the two-and-a-half-inch cutouts, put a notch in the upper right corner and write on the card a math equation, such as 2 x 2; now turn the card upside down so the notch appears in the lower right corner, and write the answer to the equation.
10. Place the Flip-Chute card into the upper slot of the Flip-Chute. This step is done by having the equation showing with the notch in the upper right corner of the card. The card will flip over once it's placed into the upper opening/chute, and the answer to the equation will appear in the bottom slot of the Flip-Chute. Make as many cards as you choose, and have students make these in any discipline. With each student having his or her own set of cards and Flip-Chute, each may switch cards with a classmate to learn new material or review previously presented topics. Laminating the Flip-Chute Cards is recommended as they'll last longer than those not laminated.

Activity: Flip-Chute: This is a "question-in" and "answer-out" activity. An empty and dry one-half gallon milk container is used with a- top-and-bottom-slot, which is interiorly connected with two pieces of card-stock paper. This forms the chute.

The student places a right-side notched Flip-Chute card having a question, quote, math problem on the top side of the card and the answer on the reverse side, written upside down, into the top slot. The answer comes out of the bottom slot. This activity is self-regulatory, as the student says the answer mentally and then decides when to release the card to discover the answer. The activity is also self-corrective.

Applied Thinking Skills: Acknowledging, recognizing, realizing, inferring, recognizing, initial-deciding, recalling, inventing, generalizing, recalling, and self-actuating.

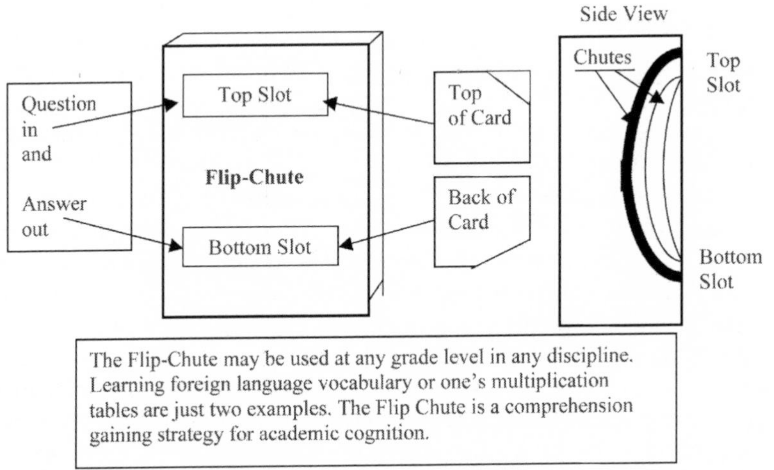

Figure 16.1. The Flip-Chute

Pic-A-Dot: Uses:

This is a multiple choice type of interactive self-corrective learning tool. A question or problem is posed, and then three answers are available. A pointed object, such as a pen or golf tee, is placed in the opening of the selected answer. If the card slides out, then the answer is correct; if not, then another try is deemed necessary for this self-corrective tactile game. The same types of uses as were mentioned for the Flip-Chute apply to this interactive resource with the difference mainly being the concept of three possible answers and students' having to make a choice regarding the correct one.

Figure 16.2 in the same chapter provides additional visual information about the Pic-A-Dot. Laminating the Pic-A-Dot Cards is recommended.

Pic-A-Dot Holder and Cards: Materials:

One 2-pocket folder, fifteen 5x8 index cards, a one-hole hole-puncher, masking tape, 12-inch ruler, and scissors.

Pic-A-Dot Holder and Pic-A-Dot Cards: Construction Directions

1. Using a 2-pocket folder, cut this in half, vertically, down the center.
2. Choose one half of the folder, and place the other half off to the side.
3. Addressing the pocket, use your ruler to measure and mark half an inch in from each side and two-and-a-half inches down from the top of the pocket. Cut out this "U" shape section (see photos for visuals of areas to be cut out).
4. From the bottom of the pocket, measure and mark upward one inch and two inches and half an inch in from each side. Cut out this rectangle.
5. On the bottom strip of the pocket, punch one hole on the left, middle, and right side.
6. Place one 5x8 inch index card in the pocket. Trace the top opening outline, and each of the hole-punch circles. Remove the index card from the pocket and punch the holes out. But, for where you will place the correct answer, punch the hole out all the way to the bottom of the card (this is the Pic-A-Dot Holder).
7. Place the index card back in the folder. In the outlined open space at the top, write a question. Example: The boy had four apples that cost one dollar each. He bought two more for one dollar each. How much did he spend on apples in all?
8. Just above the hole-punch areas write three answers. Example: $3.50—$5.00—$6.00
9. Insert the golf tee and/or pen point into the hole that has the correct answer and pull the top of the card. If it easily slides out, then the correct answer has been selected.
10. Make as many Pic-A-Dot cards as you choose and have students make these in any discipline. With each student having his own Pic-A-Dot holder and cards, he may switch cards with a classmate to learn new material or review previously presented topics.
11. Fold the top of the pocket folder down over the P-A-D and secure it with a Velcro tab to hold the P-A-D cards in place and form a completed Pic-A-Dot Holder for these.

Activity: Pick-A-Dot: This activity requires learners to make a 'correct answer selection'. A Pic-A-Dot Holder is configured to contain approximately five-to-twenty laminated question cards. Two to three possible answers are written on the bottom of the card with three holes punched into it that align with those on the Pic-A-Dot Holder. The correct answer hole is punched all the way to the bottom. The card is inserted into the Holder. Using a pen, the student places it in the Dot which is thought to be the correct answer. Then the card is pulled from the top, and if it pulls out, the correct answer has been selected.

Applied Thinking Skills: Recognizing, realizing, predicting, risk-taking, initial and advanced deciding, problem-solving, analyzing, comparing, evaluating, recalling, reflecting, self-actuating.

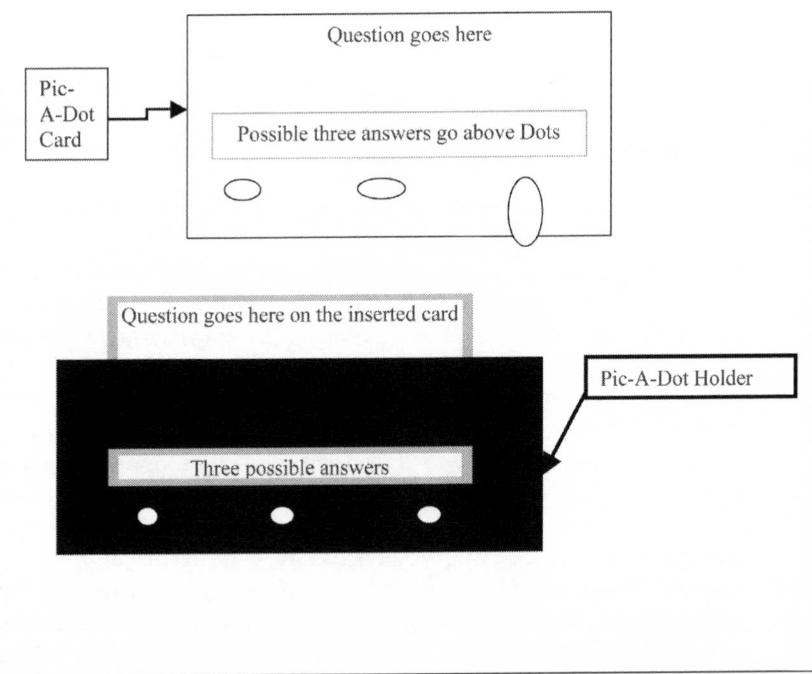

Figure 16.2. Pic-A-Dot

Wrap Around: Uses:

This tactile/kinesthetic self-corrective device is a matching game with questions on the left side of a paper and answers on the right side. However, answers are not placed directly across from the questions or statements. The size of the paper may vary. This interactive resource may be used for vocabulary with definitions and for matching characters with their statements/quotes.

It may also address identifying parts of speech, noun-verb agreement, singular and plural verb forms, math equations and answers, word problems involving multiple computation skills, word opposites, colloquiums, different language/English vocabulary words, and the ideas mentioned for the preceding interactive resource. An illustrated picture of the Wrap Around is in chapter 16, figure 16.3. (Laminating the Wrap Around allows for years of use by making it more durable.)

Wrap Around: Materials:

One piece of card-stock paper (8 1/2 x 11); scissors; 12-inch ruler; contrasting paper; colored yarn, string, or ribbon; and a dark-colored Magic Marker.

Wrap-Around: Construction Directions:

1. Using the 12-inch ruler, create a 1-inch margin around the card-stock paper.
2. Place a topic title on the top margin, such as "English/Spanish Wrap Around."
3. Select the vocabulary, or other criteria for the right left-hand side and make a notch on the outside edge next to this word.
4. Select the vocabulary word definition, or the same word in another language, or other criteria for the right side "answer." Be sure the match is not directly across from the word or what you have on the left side.
5. Notch the card stock paper on the outside edge of the right side (see photos 7 and 9 for a visual of this).
6. Placing a hole at the top center of the card-stock paper, string a three-and-a-half foot piece of yarn through this and knot at one end.
7. Swing the yarn in back of the board and into the first notch.
8. Put the yarn into the notch on the right side that provides the answer/match for the first notch on the left side. Swing the yarn around back, and go to the second notch on the left side, as the process is repeated.
9. When finished, trace the back of the card stock where the yarn appears. Use a marker or pen to do this. Now, undo the wrap.
10. The students wrap the yarn beginning with the first left notch, to the correct answer on the right side until the Wrap Around is completely wrapped. This is a self-corrective activity because the student turns the Wrap Around over and checks to see if the marked lines match where the yarn is located.

Activity: Math Wrap-Around: Using laminated card-stock paper, yarn, and a hole-punch, design the paper with quotations on the left side and the person's name on the right side. Punch half a hole by each listed item on both sides of the paper. Use the yarn to match the quotes with the persons. Then, on the reverse side draw a line under the yarn. When the students turn the paper over, they'll see if their lines match those presented. Answer should not be directly opposite of questions. This is a self-correcting activity for cognitive skill development.

Applied Thinking Skills: Recalling, reflecting, classifying, comparing and contrasting, initial and advanced deciding, problem solving, organizing, sequencing, evaluating, and self-actuating.

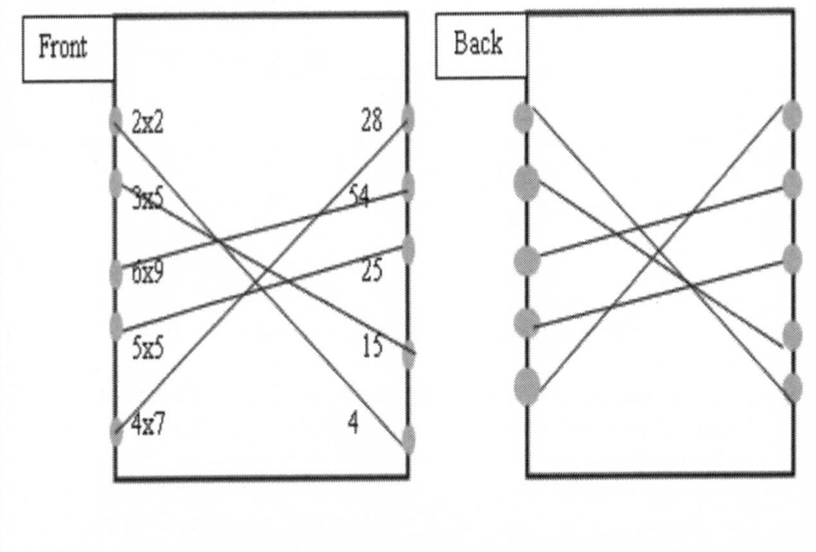

Figure 16.3. Math Wrap Around

Task Cards: Uses:

This puzzle piece self-corrective game calls for a shape-match only, as the print on the cards is the same, as well as the color of the cards. These either form a rectangle or some geometric shape, or some irregular configuration representing the theme of the topic being addressed. The reason for the shape match only is to direct the student to rely not on print format or font, or color of the cards, but rather completing the puzzle shape.

The identification of information with the left side having a partial statement and the right side having the completion of this statement is realized when the puzzle pieces are put together. Or, one side of the card may have a picture and words to identify it on the matching side. And yet another idea is to have a math problem on one side and the answer on the other part. Additionally, there may be a word on one side and the opposite of it on the other, or a quotation and who said it on the opposite side. Also, Task Cards need not be put in a left-right pattern shape match, but top-bottom, if desired.

Furthermore, the Task Cards may form a timeline if the top portion has an illustration of an event and the bottom shape matches the date. If more explanation is needed, then one might have a three-way shape match with the top piece's being the event, the bottom left being the date, and the bottom right shape being the description of the event. Chapter 16 has an illustration of two-sided Task Cards in figure 16.4. (Task Cards may be laminated before the cut is made. Lamination allows for extended length-of-time use of this game).

Task Card: Materials:

One-half of a two-pocket folder; a package of 5x8-inch blank index cards or color card-stock paper, 5x8-inch size; and scissors (regular or pinking scissors shapes).

Task Card Holder and Task Card: Construction Directions:

1. The Task Card holder uses half of a two-pocket folder. The Task Cards are placed in the folder in nonmatching style. The top of the folder is folded down to cover the pocket and decorated with the topic of the cards represented. An example would be a Task Card Holder having different color geometric shapes for cards that had geometric shapes on one side and the name of this shape on the other side.
2. Take ten 5x8-inch index cards and cut them in half using different shapes. Examples may be seen in chapter 16. Further explanation of this process would include cutting one card straight up the center, the next one would have a diagonal cut, and the remaining ones a combination of these cuts, as well as/or half-circle shapes.
3. Task Cards may also be done in whole shapes that match a theme of the topic being addressed. For example, Task Cards for vocabulary about the book *Charlotte's Web* might be in the shape of Wilbur the pig who is the main character, or Arable's barn. Then, the shape would be cut in half, as explained in "2" above.

4. In random order, place the Task Cards in the Pocket Folder, and then invite students to take these pieces out and match the cards by shape.

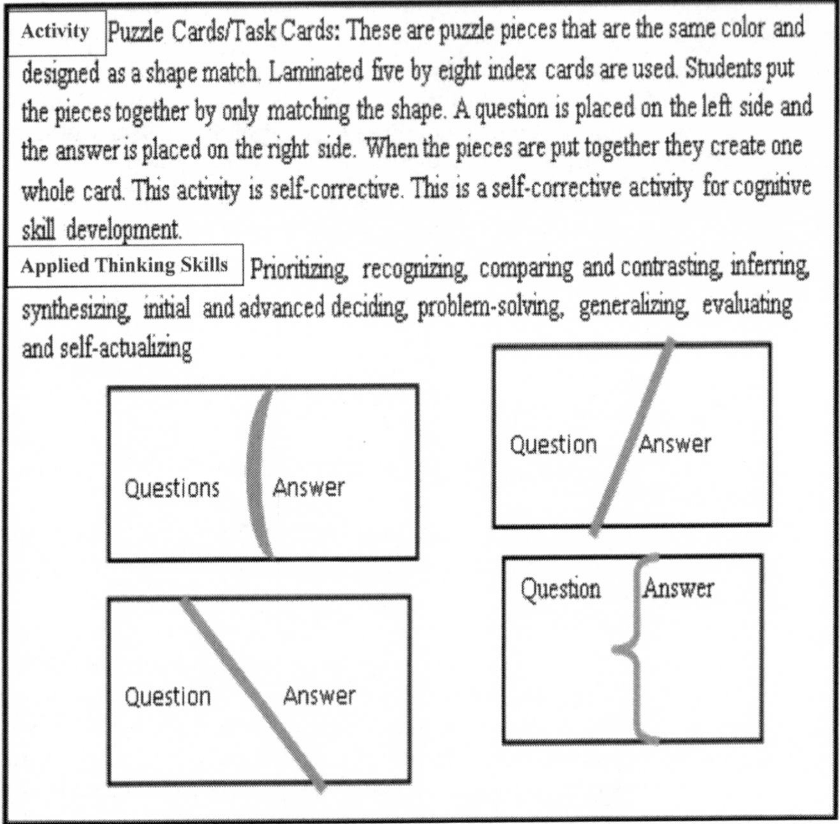

Figure 16.4. Task Cards

Electro-Board: Uses:

This is a very popular self-corrective tactile and/or kinesthetic interactive instructional resource. It's kinesthetic when it's made poster-board size. One of the most interesting things is that this interactive instructional resource does not have a specified order for the match that's to be created. The connection between the question, such as a vocabulary word and its definition, may be anywhere on the Electro-Board.

Naming parts of an object, such as a flower, house, car, or animal, may have the part listed on the bottom of the board and a drawing of the object on the top portion. The student uses a Light-Type Continuity Tester and places one end on the question and the other on the thought-to-be answer. If the light glows, the correct answer has been selected, and if not then it's time to try again.

Such things as math problems in addition, subtraction, multiplication, division, and word format, vocabulary and definitions, or English words matching with objects of foreign language words of the same object, Spanish or any other language/English vocabulary, identification of systems such as respiratory, circulatory, or sequence of events, as well as life cycle of the butterfly, frog, or stages of human development might be topics for the Electro-Board. Figure 16.5 in chapter 16 provides an illustration of the Electro-Board.

Electro-Board: Materials:

Poster board; colored markers; aluminum foil; hole-punch three-quarter-inch masking tape; continuity tester; and scissors.

Electro-Board: Construction Directions:

1. Begin with two pieces of poster board of exactly the same size and shape.
2. Section the left side of the Electro-Board to correspond to the number of questions you will be asking. Section the right side similarly for the answers.
3. Using the hole-punch, make one hole at the point where each question will appear on the left side of the poster board, or randomly. Corresponding holes should be placed where the answers will appear.
4. Print the questions and answers on the poster board next to the punched holes. If you desire, a brass fastener may be placed in the punched holes with the wings on the reverse side opened fully. Answers should not be directly across from the questions.
5. Turn the poster board over. Place a one-quarter-inch-wide strip of aluminum foil in a line, connecting a question with the correct answer. The foil should begin at the hole for the question and end at the hole for the answer. Cover the foil strip with a three-quarter-inch strip of masking tape so that there is no foil (brass fastener) exposed.
6. Using a Light-Style Continuity Tester, purchased in a hardware or automotive store, check the circuit by touching the aluminum foil hole and/or the brass fastener with the clip and the pointed end of the Continuity Tester on the question and then the thought-to-be answer on the Electro-Board.

Activity Electro-board: This is a learning tool that requires an electrical connection made with brass fasteners and masking-tape covered aluminum foil on the back of the card-stock paper Electro-board. On the front of the Board, there are only the brass fasteners beside the questions and the answers. On the back, these are opened winged sections but covered by the masking tape. The back of the board is covered with another sheet of card-stock paper, after the board has been made, so students may not see these connections. The student, using a "light" producing Continuity Tester, then places the pointed tip of it on the question and the other end, which is a clip, on the answer. If the light lights-up, the answer is correct. If the light does not show, then the answer is incorrect and the student tries again to find the answer. This is a self-correcting activity for cognitive development.

Applied Thinking Skills Classifying, recognizing, initial deciding, critiquing, comparing and contrasting, inventing, predicting, synthesizing, organizing, advanced problem-solving, and self-actuating.

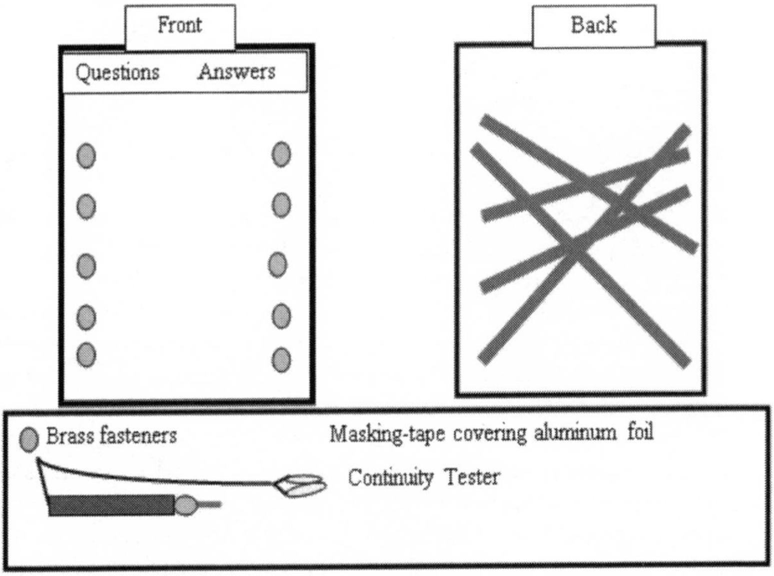

Front

Questions Answers

Back

Brass fasteners

Masking-tape covering aluminum foil

Continuity Tester

Figure 16.5. Electro-Board

Floor Game: Uses:

This primarily kinesthetic, but also tactile, visual, and auditory, interactive instructional resource usually requires two to six players and is used to identify, recognize, compare and contrast. A shower curtain liner with Magic Marker–denoted areas is used to create a picture of an object or general shape with question/answer cards being used for moving from one place to another on the floor game.

The students would best be advised to remove their shoes to protect the liner during multiple uses. Interestingly, the Floor Game may be designed to represent a sequence of events, time line, character similarities and differences from a story in Venn diagram style, parts-of-speech identification columns, matching game, cause and effect, or who said that, to name a few.

Basically, a question is asked which is read from a question card. Then, a correct answer allows the student to move to a particular space on the floor. An incorrect answer means remaining in the same place as another game participant tries his or her luck/knowledge. Question/answer cards may be laminated for extended durability. Figure 16.6 in chapter 16 is an illustration of the Floor Game.

Floor Game: Materials:

Shower curtain liner; package of different colored markers; twenty 5x8-inch index cards for questions and answers.

Floor Game: Construction Directions:

1. Place a shower curtain liner on the floor. The liner should be of a solid light color.
2. Design the liner to match the topic of the game. For example, see chapter 16, figure 16.8. Another example might be to create three columns with them headed respectively, "Nouns, Verbs, and Adjectives." Then, have a pile of 5x8 index cards with either an example of a noun, verb, or adjective on one side, and the part of speech on the other side. Students select a card, place it in the correct column, and check to see if this is correct by turning the card over.

   There are many ways to design a Floor Game, and another idea is to have photographs of story characters Velcroed to the liner. These would be from a selected piece of literature. Then, have bubbles leading from a character's face. The student is read a question card that has a quotation from the character. The student goes to the bubble to designate who said that.
3. The first person to answer all the questions correctly is the winner of the game. A player may move from one place to another on the Floor Game, or place identifying objects in appropriate spaces on the Game Board, or identify parts of an object by standing on that space.

Activity: Floor Game: This activity is a subject/discipline specific designed shower-curtain liner, which is placed on the floor. Students remove their shoes to play this tactile and kinesthetic game moving sequentially form one numbered shape to the next one. This is a partnership, or small group activity. A series of question cards are made with the answer on the reverse side. Two to four persons may play this game. A correct answer to the question provides the move from one space to another. The design of the shower curtain should be attractive and inviting. Content may or not be theme based as it builds comprehension skills.
This game may also be used as a wall game with a bean-bag used for tossing at the spaces and questions addressed in accordance with the numbered space. If a throw is on target, the player looses his/her turn and the next player goes.

Applied Thinking Skills: Recognizing, classifying, comparing and contrasting, prioritizing, communicating, inferring, predicting, generalizing, initial and advanced deciding, active listening, initial and advanced problem-solving, tolerating, recalling, reflecting, and self-actuating.

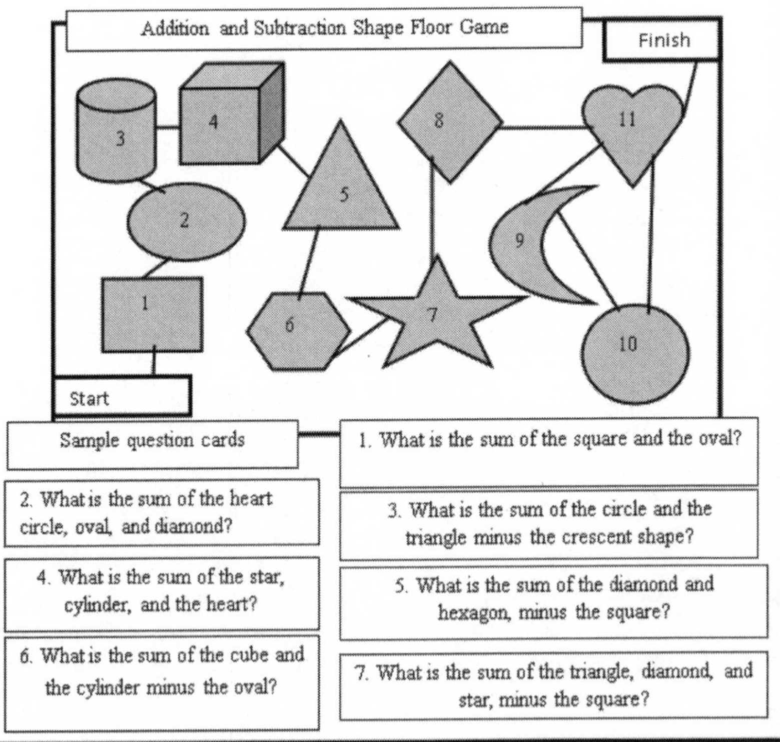

Figure 16.6. Floor Game

JOURNAL AND/OR DISCUSSION QUESTIONS

1. What are eight types of interactive instructional resources, and how might each of these be used in a classroom?
2. What are five reasons that convey interactive instruction as being important?

SEVENTEEN

Three Topics Including Effects and Affects of IM and IBR

CHAPTER OVERVIEW

This chapter addresses interactive activities and the thinking skills utilized when learning-through-playing the pages of an IBR. The chapter is divided into four "Topic" areas. The first is

Topic One: This section has a listing of each of the Reciprocal Thinking Phases Skills with interactive activities adhering to each phase when making the page or playing it. This section also has nineteen activities with corresponding thinking skills from all three phases that are either developed or applied by using them.

Topic Two: This section addresses Team Learning, Circle of Knowledge, and Creative Cognition Writing with a definition and example of how to do each one.

Topic Three: This section supplies the probable effects/consequences and affects/emotional impact of the IM and IBR interactive instructional resource activities on learners.

With that written, try not to skip to the end of the chapter, but have a look at the ideas presented for bringing learners and teachers together for a common purpose, that of learning and teaching using creative cognition via interactive instructional resources.

TOPIC ONE: COGNITIVE SKILLS AND LIST OF ACTIVITIES TO DEVELOP THESE SKILLS

Star (*) areas are associated with Dunn and Dunn Learning Styles.

PHASE ONE

Cognitive Skills:

Basic Awareness and Acknowledging: *Recognizing, Realizing, Classifying, Comparing, and Contrasting.*

Activities to Develop Cognitive Skills:

Audiotape, Slide Show, SMART Board Activity, Velcro-match game, Character Map, Cause and Effect Map, Flip-Chute, Overhead Transparencies, Storytelling, Venn Diagram, Character Maps, Comparison of Preferences Category Chart, SMART Board Activity for Comparing and Contrasting, *Task Cards, Wrap Around, *Pic-A-Dot, and *Electro-Board, *Team Learning with Create section of poems, dioramas, mobiles, window design, figures of papier-mâché or Paris Craft.

PHASE TWO

Cognitive Skills:

Critical and Creative Thinking Skills: *Prioritizing, Communicating, Inferring, Active Listening, Inventing, Predicting, Generalizing, Sequencing, Initial Deciding, and Initial Problem-Solving.*

Activities to Develop Cognitive Skills:

Problem and Solution Map, Listing of Favorites Cart, Hula Hoop Venn Diagram, Audiotape of Book or Activity, *Circle of Knowledge on Songs, Things related to a topic such as Animals, Things in an Ecosystem, Bones in the Body, or Different Types of Plants, *Programmed Learning Sequence Book, *Contract Activity Package, *Multisensory Instructional Package, Tri-fold Boards, Small-Group Techniques, Three-Dimensional Graphs, Dioramas, Role-Play, and *Team Learning, Designing and Creating Computer Game.

PHASE THREE

Cognitive Skills:

Metacognitive Processes: *Evaluating, Organizing, Critiquing, Collaborating, Tolerating, Advanced Deciding, Risk-Taking, Analyzing, Synthesizing, Advanced Problem-Solving, Recalling, Reflecting, and Self-Actualizing.*

Activities to Develop Cognitive Skills:

Velcro Match, Anecdotes, Storytelling, *Team Learning, Role-Play, Floor Game on Parts of a Flower, Car Parts, Figure of Baseball Field or any sport playing field layout, Graphic Organizers of Character Map, Sequence of Events, Decision-Making, *Circle of Knowledge, Brainstorming on Grade-Level Curriculum Topics Chart, and three-dimensional Crossword, or Word Jumble or, Word Search and regular Puzzles showing a scene or perhaps map of the United States or the world, and a Travel Brochure or Poster Advertisement, Button Candy for Braille Writing, Slide Show on Educational Gaming or topic of one's choice within the grade-level curriculum, Three-Dimensional Geo-Board.

Eighteen Activities and Corresponding Cognitive and Metacognitive Skills from All Reciprocal Thinking Phases Story Map Graphic Organizer:

Classifying, Reflecting, Analyzing, Organizing, Classifying, Comparing and Contrasting, Prioritizing, Sequencing, Synthesizing, Recalling, Reflecting, and Self-Actualizing.

1. Sequence Mapping: *Organizing, prioritizing, deciding, classifying, comparing and contrasting, generalizing, sequencing, initial deciding, initial problem-solving, analyzing, and self-actualizing.*
2. Flip-Chute: *Recognizing, realizing, initial deciding, recalling, reflecting, risk-taking, inventing, generalizing, initial and advanced deciding, and self-actualizing.*
3. Electro-Board: *Classifying, deciding, comparing and contrasting, inventing, organizing, synthesizing, initial and advanced deciding, initial and advanced problem-solving, risk-taking, predicting, synthesizing, recalling, and self-actualizing.*
4. Pic-A-Dot: *Realizing, recognizing, classifying, comparing and contrasting, organizing, initial and advanced deciding, predicting, risk-taking, reflecting, prioritizing, analyzing, and self-actualizing.*
5. Task Cards: *Prioritizing, comparing and contrasting, inferring, synthesizing, recalling, initial and advanced deciding, problem-solving, and self-actualizing.*
6. Who Said That: Matching Characters and Quotes: *Recognizing, realizing, recalling, reflecting, comparing and contrasting, classifying, predicting, communicating, initial and advanced deciding and problem-solving, analyzing, and self-actualizing.*
7. Math Word Problems: *Realizing, recognizing, recalling, reflecting, prioritizing, initial and advanced deciding with problem-solving, inventing, reflecting, synthesizing, comparing and contrasting, and self-actualizing.*
8. Cause and Effect: *Recognizing, classifying, analyzing, critiquing, deciding, initial and advanced deciding with problem-solving, inventing, re-*

calling, realizing, and advanced problem- solving with deciding, analyzing, risk-taking, evaluating, and self-actualizing.

9. Word Search: *Deciding, generalizing, acknowledging, comparing and contrasting, recognizing, generalizing, initial and advanced deciding, organizing, critiquing, sequencing, predicting, analyzing, evaluating, and self-actualizing.*
10. Wrap Around: *Classifying, deciding, comparing and contrasting, inventing, organizing, synthesizing, initial and advanced deciding, initial and advanced problem-solving, risk-taking, predicting, synthesizing, recalling, and self-actualizing.*
11. Food Pyramid: *Classifying, comparing, organizing, advanced and initial problem-solving, contrasting, generalizing, inventing, and self-actualizing.*
12. Role-play: *Classifying, deciding, communicating, active listening, organizing, initial and advanced problem-solving, critiquing, evaluating, inferring, tolerating, organizing, and self-actuating.*
13. Fill in the Blank: *Inventing, evaluating, synthesizing, organizing, recalling, prioritizing, and self-actuating.*
14. Team-Learning: *Collaborating, communicating, active listening, comparing, inferring, contrasting, predicting, initial and advanced deciding and problem-solving, and self-actualizing.*
15. Circle of Knowledge: *Collaborating, communicating, active listening, tolerating, recalling, reflecting, critiquing, evaluating, risk-taking, comparing and contrasting, recognizing, and self-actualizing.*
16. Floor Game: *Inventing, communicating, tolerating, organizing, reflecting, synthesizing, generalizing, initial and advanced deciding, and self-actualizing.*
17. Self-Designed Pages: *Inventing, comparing, risk-taking, inferring, collaborating, and in many cases all of the cognitive skills are utilized.*
18. Essay, Letters, Creative Writing: *Problem-solving, deciding, inferring, generalizing, organizing, predicting, sequencing, generalizing, communicating, prioritizing, synthesizing, recalling, reflecting, and self-actualizing.*

TOPIC TWO: TEAM LEARNING, CIRCLE OF KNOWLEDGE, AND CREATIVE WRITING: DEFINITION AND EXAMPLES

Team Learning:

This is a small-group activity where students read a selected literature passage and then answer questions about this passage. The questions are designed to address all three types of comprehension (literal, applied, and implied). An additional component is added with directions for students to *create* one of the following: a poem, interactive resource, drawing, role-play, or inventive means of conveying the synthesized information from the read paragraphs of the selected passage.

EXAMPLE: TEAM LEARNING: BENJAMIN FRANKLIN

Directions:

Record the names of your group members above the passage to be read. Then, read the paragraphs about Benjamin Franklin aloud in your group. One person may read, or you may take turns reading the information. Underline or mark in some fashion the areas you think are most important, as the reading occurs.

When the reading is complete, answer the questions presented. Do this in a collaborative manner. Be sure everyone in the group agrees that the answers are correct. Then, the last portion of this Team Learning is to work together to create something that presents the information from the paragraphs, or a portion of that, in a manner that represents your group's interest. We will go over the answers to questions in a whole-class format, and then each group will present their "creative" portion of the Team Learning.

(Team Learning Exercise: Schiering, 2010)
Benjamin Franklin: Inventor, Scientist, and Leader
(Synthesized material from: *Time Magazine: Benjamin Franklin: An Illustrated History of His Life and Times*, 2010)
Names of Team Learning Members:

____

A STORY ABOUT BENJAMIN FRANKLIN

Benjamin Franklin was a founding father of the United States. He was a scientist and inventor, and his accomplishments made him a famous American of his time. He was also a diplomat with achievements as a key figure for an alliance with France and the American victory in the Revolutionary War. He was known to be an easygoing person and one who could associate easily with everyone.

Benjamin was born in 1706 in Boston, Massachusetts. He was the fifteenth child by his father's two successive wives. They all lived in a modest house on Boston's Milk Street until he was six. It was then that the family moved to a larger place in the same town. Ben was an athletic boy and a profound swimmer at a time when this sport was unusual. In his memoirs, he recalled a time when he was flying his kite by a mill pond when he decided to go swimming. He took the kite in hand and let it pull him around by wind power while he floated all the way across the pond—today we call this activity wind-sailing.

Ben had little formal schooling but was in the famed Boston Latin School for a year and then received tutoring in arithmetic and writing. His formal education was over by the time he was ten years of age. Nonetheless, he had a thirst for knowledge, was curious, and definitely had intellectual gifts. Additionally, Ben was continually reading books and scripture, and he had a love for learning. He was exposed to all sorts of reading material as he was apprenticed to his brother James' printing business when Benjamin was twelve. Ben began writing poetry and was permitted to publish his own work.

Five years into the apprenticeship, Ben moved to Philadelphia to serve as a printer's assistant. In 1732, he published the first edition of *Poor Richard's Almanac,* and five years after that he was appointed as the Philadelphia postmaster. Benjamin Franklin's contributions to the colonies include his becoming their postmaster for some thirty-five years following his apprenticeship to his brother.

Some major accomplishments of Benjamin Franklin include his flying a kite with his son William in 1752 and experimenting by linking lighting to electricity; proposing a plan to join the colonies together when in 1754 the French and Indian War began; inventing in 1762 the glass harmonica, a musical instrument; being elected to the Second Continental Congress in 1775 and proposing the first Article of Confederation; helping draft the Declaration of Independence in 1776; signing treaties of alliance, amity, and commerce with France in 1778; and in 1782, with John Adams and John Jay, negotiating a peace treaty with Britain.

Franklin died in 1790 at the age of 84, and in his lifetime witnessed the first manned balloon flight and was instrumental in the establishment of the great compromise with the creation of a United States House of Representatives and Senate. For a man from humble beginnings, he contributed widely to the ideas held by our present government with freedom and representation of the people in a democracy.

QUESTIONS FOR TEAM LEARNING

1. In what year and century was Ben Franklin born?
2. What do you suppose is meant by the term "founding father" of the United States and what events established Ben's being this?
3. What type of person was Ben Franklin?
4. In what year did Benjamin Franklin become an apprentice to his brother James and what was this apprenticeship?
5. How did being an apprentice to James Franklin help Benjamin with respect to reading and writing?
6. What were two interests of Ben during his childhood?

7. Benjamin Franklin went to work when he was twelve years of age. How do you think you'd feel about doing that today? (Your answers may vary, but record them all).
8. What were three major accomplishments, during the life of Benjamin Franklin, in which he was directly involved?
9. How does the schooling you experience differ from that of Ben Franklin's? List five differences at a minimum.
10. This is the creative portion of Team Learning. Select one (1) of the following to present to the class. You will have approximately forty minutes to complete this portion of the Team Learning.

a. Create a poem (acrostic, rhyming, or free verse) that states at least five accomplishments of Ben Franklin.
b. Illustrate five things for which Benjamin Franklin is noted. You may do this by making a cartoon, mural, or storyboard.
c. Using the computer, create five slides depicting important events in Ben Franklin's life.
d. Write and present a scripted role-play about two important events in the life of Ben Franklin.
e. Create a Comparison Chart of Ben's life between ages six and twelve and your own life during those years. There need to be at least five events mentioned.
f. Create a Travel Brochure or poster to entice people to visit the newly formed Benjamin Franklin History Museum. Highlight important events in his life, and feel free to conduct further research about Franklin, using the Internet.
g. Create a song with a minimum of five stanzas about the accomplishments of Ben Franklin.

Circle of Knowledge:

This is a small-group activity with three to four groups competing in a timed response situation (see "Example" below). The scoring of correct answers is recorded on chart paper or a board. Each group provides answers to a basic question and receives one point for each correct answer. However, if one group provides an answer that another group has on its list, but has not given it, that answer may not be repeated.

If a group is concerned that an incorrect response has been given, then this group may challenge that answer. If the group cannot provide substantial verification for its answer, then the point is given to the challenging group. If it can provide the information, then that group receives the point without penalty to the challenging group. The group with the most points is declared the winner of the Circle of Knowledge activity.

Example:

In one minute, make a list of all the words you can think of that relate to ecosystems.

Possible Responses: Environments, ecosystems, succession, climax and pioneer stages of succession, forests, inanimate objects, living objects, plants, animals, mammals, predator, prey, plains, niche, and habitat.

Do you want to have some fun with an adolescent or adult group using Circle of Knowledge? Ask them to name as many songs as possible with a female's name in it. Follow the directions for scoring points as stated under "Circle of Knowledge."

CREATIVE COGNITION WRITING

There are many sources for having creative writing. In the IBR, two that come readily to mind are from a study I was conducting in 2013 and then a fifth grade group of students from 1998. In the former group ecosystems and sustainability were being addressed. A study in chapter 20 has detail on this. The idea was to think of and write a story about an already existing object and how it could be reused. Working in small-group format, alone, or partnerships, many stories emerged with the interactive part being a three- or one-dimensional picture of the original object and how it was modified to be used again. One student wrote about a tree that needed cutting down as the area was being reforested where it lived. Writing from the tree's perspective long after being removed from the forest, the tree was relatively happy that it had been put to good use in the following ways:

a. Parts of me became pencils for school children to use each day.
b. Parts of me were made into lumber to build a house.
c. My leaves were used for mulch.
d. My branches were made into a dining room table.

The above creative writing was orally presented in class and photos, or in some cases the actual (a and c) recycled objects were shown as the stories were orally presented. Other ideas were given for how to reuse, recycle, or renew. The classroom community was encouraged to share what other things the tree might become. "You could say that some of the tree became the paper you used to write your story," one learner responded. Overall, new ideas for being creative emerged.

The other aforementioned idea for creative writing was done in my fifth grade class many years ago. I brought in pictures of flowers and the students wrote what their day was like from the perspective of the flower. Then, taking pipe cleaners, construction paper, glue, and clear tape, the students rolled the green paper into a tube, made four cuts at the bottom and splayed these out so the "flower stem" could stand. Next, each person made his or her own flower petals, using the flower book we had to make different kinds of flowers. The flowers were put together on a round table as they made an *artificial flower garden*. The table was put outside the classroom so when walkers-by passed our room, we had a lovely display of a nature scene. Looking back I'm inclined to say that the recycled tree from the previous story in this chapter section could have provided the paper for the flower construction.

The idea of using photographs serves as a creative writing stimulant as the students write about what is in the picture or from the imagined perspective of some object in the picture. This calls for all of the Reciprocal Thinking skills from each phase to be used in the story.

Challenge:

Now, here's your chance to try this idea. Take a picture from any you may have and write a made-up story about the people in the picture or the situation you think occurred. Include the setting and then, if time allows, create the setting in a diorama and/or make puppet characters or role-play the story with a friend or two. If you've a classroom of students, have them do this Challenge.

Decision-Making Poster-Board:

The Decision-Making Organizer Poster-Board was first used by Schiering in the mid- to late 1980s at the fifth and then sixth grade levels in the North Rockland Central School district in Stony Point, New York. Since the year 2000, it has been used in EDU.506A at Molloy College, and this board has been one of the assignments for the teacher-candidate's later student-learner instruction and implementation in the K–6 classroom. However, many teacher-candidates have commented on how this decision-making process has assisted them in problem-solving long after the course assignment has been completed. Also mentioned is the opportunity to be involved in *creative cognition* in designing the board with the choice sections providing a chance to decorate the board addressing a specific theme relating to the topic of the decision.

Decision-Making Poster-Board Graphic Organizer: Uses:

This activity is a large graphic organizer and allows for individuals at any age to apply the reciprocity of thinking in the process of decision-making. This phase two and three cognitive/metacognitive skill activity, with initial and advanced types, provides students the opportunity first to learn how to make a decision and then to experience it unconsciously as it becomes part of their daily routine. The graphic organizers were originally used during the 1980s in Schiering's elementary and then middle school classrooms and it later became a mainstay in many teachers' high school English and Social Studies classes and some Molloy College Division of Education courses.

Sharing these boards in a classroom setting provides for social literacy with awareness of the problems that cause one concern. Also, means for comprehension of possible ways to solve problems, should they arise, in another person's experience—now or in the future—allow for academic and social cognition on a variety of topics.

The first step of this decision-making process requires recognizing that a problem exists that needs a decision to be made for a solution to be put in place. Next is awareness that there are more than two solutions to the problem. Then, there's the realization of the decision-making process taking in all of the cognitive and metacognitive skills on the Reciprocal Thinking Phases Chart, as well as more thoughts, ideas, opinions, judgments, and feelings on the topic being evidenced.

As explained in the decision-making section of chapter 15, individuals are used to realizing and/or imagining only two possible choices for a solution to a decision. Subsequently, when one is teaching the process of the Decision-Making Graphic Organizer, it is suggested that students confer in a collaborative fashion with classmates and/or adults to receive suggestions beyond these two possible choices.

This idea of more than one choice also applies to the sections under each choice where there are three possible negative and three possible positive outcomes for each projected choice. The final decision will take these into consideration and weigh the positives and negatives in personal reflection before stating the final decision and why this one was selected. In chapter 15, figure 15.6 is an illustration of this interactive activity.

Decision-Making Organizer: Materials

Poster-board measuring approximately three-and-a-half inches high and two-and-a-half inches across (this may be smaller or larger as desired); colored construction paper; various colored markers; stickers or other forms of decoration. These are for the purpose of connecting the board's topic in an illustrative fashion to the theme of the board.

Decision-Making Poster-Board Organizer: Construction Directions:

1. At the top center of the board, place a rectangle and in the left corner the word "Problem;" Then, using large font or neat large hand-printing, state the problem with some detailed sentences.
2. Border this section so there is a color contrast with the color of the Board.

3. Under the Problem section, have three boxes labeled "Choice #1," "Choice #2," and "Choice #3." There may be more choices, but a minimum of three is required.
4. Under each "Choice" section, make two bordered boxes, again for color contrast. One box is under the other. In the top box, place the words, "Possible Negative Outcomes." In the other one write, "Possible Positive Outcomes."
5. Then, in these boxes, in large font or large hand-print, first list a minimum of three possibilities of negative outcomes of this "Choice," and then a minimum of three possible positives that may result from this "Choice" idea.
6. At the bottom of the poster-board, place a rectangle and write the words in the far left corner, "Final Decision and Why." Using large font or large neat hand-printing, state the final decision and why this has been made, in your opinion.
7. Decorate the board so it connects with the theme or provides a good color contrast with the background color of the poster-board.

TOPIC THREE: EFFECTS AND AFFECTS OF IM AND IBR

The purpose for this section regards how, as you have read this chapter, ideas might come to you about creativity being 1) personally empowering, 2) a means for building community, 3) a tool for knowing about one's character, and/or 4) helpful in creating if not concretizing friendships. The overall effect and affect of the IM and IBR touch on an individual's and a group's emotional security. The four numbered items most likely result in stabilizing one's view of himself or herself to the point of being an individual who, through self-actualization, realizes self-reliance as well.

EFFECTS

First, let's take a moment and examine the definition of this word, "effect." You've probably heard it often enough in relation to the word "cause." An example might be that a person jumped-up when the book fell on the floor and made a loud sound. The cause of the jumping-up was the loud sound the book made when falling on the floor. The effect was the jumping-up of the person when this happened. In order for there to be an "effect" on a situation or someone, there needs to be an understanding of the means to realize a *consequence or achievement*, or to *make something happen*, as to *bring it into being*.

An example would be: The *effect/result* of the IM caused learners to realize their creativity was part of their ability to imagine and invent. The *effect* of their imagining and inventing resulted in bringing into being pages of the IBR for learning-through-playing. Another *effect* of the IM and IBR is that others learned when playing the pages of the book and retained information simultaneously. The *effect* of the method and strategy, together, made an *impression* on all who experienced it. This was formidable and became part of their life-long learning.

Overall, the effect of the experience was that memory was utilized through reflection and recalling, which are part of the metacognitive processes. The interconnection of one's reciprocity of thinking and encountering the IM and IBR may well determine the significance of the learning situation's being most positive when one is engaged in it.

AFFECT

There's much to be related about the *affect* of the IM and IBR. This word "affect" means the emotional impact of something on oneself. When referring to the emotional impact of this method and strategy, the first thing that comes to mind is realizing the magnitude and differences of feelings about one's own creativity abilities as evidenced in the IBRs I've seen over the past twenty-plus years. What comes to your mind when you think of the affect of the IM and IBR? Share your thoughts with another or others.

Learners, and we're all learners, are affected by circumstances encountered each day. Some cause more of a reaction than others, but regardless of this, the reaction results in knowing about ourselves or those experiencing our response. Let's say you're using the IM to design and then create an IBR. If one is working with another few persons on this project, there needs to be cooperation and collaboration. If not, then the work doesn't get done, unless one is working alone. Regardless, when the accomplishment of using the IM way of learning and teaching is realized along with the making of an IBR, the participants have been immersed in conversation. By having this continual or ongoing communicating of ideas, thoughts, opinions, and even feelings about the project, there comes a comprehension of who one is as a learner and possibly a teacher as well.

Definitely, there is an overall sense of self-worth and empowerment when experiencing the method and strategy of this book. Individuals come to know that each one is capable of giving to others only that which one has for him or herself. With the use of the IM and IBR these affective–emotional impact qualities include, but are not exclusive to having for oneself and others *respect, caring, trustworthiness, fairness, kindness,* and being *responsible.*

JOURNAL AND/OR DISCUSSION QUESTIONS

1. What are the four topics of this chapter?
2. Which educational game was your favorite and why?
3. How would you explain Team Learning and Circle of Knowledge?
4. What is meant by something having an "effect" on a situation?
5. What is meant by something or someone having an "affect" on another or a situation?
6. What is one *effect* and one *affect* of the IM and IBR as explained in this chapter?

III

Part Three

EIGHTEEN

The Proof of the Pudding

IM and IBR in Action

Patricia Mason, PhD | Lucia Sapienza

CHAPTER OVERVIEW

This chapter presents the actual narratives of two teachers from two different schools and their experience with using either the IM, IBR, or both in their classrooms: The method and the strategy. Material from chapters 18, 19, and 20, along with teacher candidate and grade-school students presentations of IBRs may be found at www.creative cognition4U.com.

INTRODUCTION AND NARRATIVE OF DR. PATRICIA MASON

Pat is a professor at Molloy College in Rockville Centre, New York, and for many years her area of expertise has been working with teacher-candidates to assist them in instructional techniques for special needs student-learners.

Pat relates, "The potential of class assignments, I have found, is often lost in a time when efforts are measured by grades. However, teacher-candidates enrolled in a strategy course were able to experience the significance of their assignment while gaining confidence in their ability to make learning relevant. They also discovered learning's being rewarding for groups of young students with emotional and behavioral difficulties. The academic support offered by using the IM made a lasting impression on both the children and their respective teachers. Interactive learning tools were created by graduate teacher-candidates as part of their course requirements. The Cognitive Collective of Schiering was evident in this semester-long teaching and learning journey and is presented in this Case Study that follows:"

Students with emotional and behavioral difficulties are often prevented from experiencing learning in an enjoyable and rewarding manner. Their impulsive behavior often prevents teachers from being more than merely disciplinarians. Often, a punitive environment further stifles the creativity of teachers and discourages any belief that interactive instruction could improve the learning-teaching relationship.

One teacher was waging a battle to fight off the negativity and self-defeating attitude of teaching students who many had already "written-off" in a very negative environment. While teacher-candidates may read about educational inequity, they often fail to appreciate its ramification without seeing the face of a struggling and disappointed student. For this one semester-long course, teacher-candidates gained understanding through interactions with student-learners, as well as collaborations with classmates using the methodology of the IBR and creating not a book, but interactive instructional resources to assist the children in learning.

The student-learners were from a self-contained urban class of thirteen classified emotionally and behaviorally disadvantaged students. They were, socioculturally, African American in an inner-city school community, while the graduate students were Caucasian and enrolled in a suburban college and living in surrounding areas. The experiences of these two groups couldn't have been more diverse.

Although many of the graduate students attended public schools, they were continually surprised if not overwhelmed with the description of this urban school. Furthermore, many had read about the absences of the extras needed to make schools supportive to students, and they were surprised as they learned how much the teacher needed to provide to enhance the learning experiences of this class in a community less than thirty miles away.

The elementary school teacher had high expectations for her students as well as herself, and she was firm in her approach, using a variety of tones and facial expressions to accompany her reminders to attend to learning activities in what was to be a well-managed environment. Her comments were about raising their academic skills, a perceived normal desire. She saw her students' capabilities but also their disappointment when unsuccessful—which was often the root of their acting-out behaviors. Her dedication initially inspired the project offered to the suburban graduate students.

The teacher-candidates had taken Integrated Reading and ELA in the Diverse and Inclusion classroom with Dr. Schiering. It was here they learned of the IM and IBR. The purpose of the strategy course I was teaching was to develop techniques that would build academic and content skills, especially for students with disabilities. Content knowledge and creativity are expected as course activities and assignments are completed.

Previously, as teacher-candidates would present their work to the class, there was a somewhat false sense of accomplishment, as the students presented their projects to their peers or submitted projects to the instructor for grading. The "false sense" is established because no one actually gets to see the interactive projects in the practice of engaging the student-learners. Teacher-candidates, before this semester's project, did not get to observe students' enhancing their learning or developing mastery of thinking skill identification when learning-through-playing the interactive resources, because they are not actually with the students.

PROCEDURE

The classroom teacher was observed teaching a literacy lesson on writing a friendly letter. The students had read *Flat Stanley* and seemingly enjoyed the idea of writing a letter and mailing it to a friend. The class came up with the idea to write letters to friends, but it was noted that all "friends" were in the same building. The result of this observation was that teacher-candidates were requested to support this letter writing assignment and paired with a student-learner with whom they would communicate three times during the semester.

The teacher-candidates initiated the pen pal tasks with a friendly and personal letter to the student-learners. The letter was introductory, leaving the students ample opportunities to ask questions and share similarly relevant information. Both classes were ecstatic to receive their individual letter. The younger students had a mountain of questions that arose from reading their letter, and they quickly asked their teacher for a time and support to write back to their pen pals.

The T.C.s felt good about doing this assignment, and they were rather surprised with the honesty and gratitude conveyed in the student-learner letters.

The second correspondence from the young students clearly expressed their difficulty and disappointment in their recall of math facts. They related that everybody was worried about the math and no one knew math facts. This view was supported by many of the letters written. After the T.C.s shared their letters and compared comments, they reflected on the course readings regarding the IM, IBR, and learning-style perceptual preferences, a technique which was also part of the previous and present course. The result was that the teacher-candidates volunteered to create interactive instructional resources for an IBR on math facts. These educational games were well received by the student learners. Each student learner received an individual "gift" with a letter attached explaining the directions with encouraging comments. Each pen pal letter suggested that the students take turns sharing the learning-through-play games so that the class would all master their math facts for the upcoming exams.

After the second letter, both groups were curious about their partners. Pictures were taken of school buildings, classrooms, and students at work. A video recording was forwarded to the teacher-candidates by the classroom teacher of the students using their interactive instructional resources, now put in an IBR. Directions on how to make the games were given to the student-learners upon their request. This was because the class didn't want to give up their "game," but wanted to make ones for the class next door.

RESULTS OF IM, IBR, AND LEARNING-THROUGH-PLAY

1. Student learners wrote in one of their pen pal letters that this was the best way to study math because it was fun to use the game each morning.
2. Both groups felt connected to one another through the videos, letters, pictures, and artifacts;
3. The final letters were bittersweet because the project was completed. Nonetheless the teacher-candidates realized and saw the possibilities of their efforts with a group of struggling students while the younger pen pals had grown in skill and confidence.
4. Letters increased in length and quality;
5. The teacher-candidates were touched by the gratitude the student learners showed in their writing and invitations to visit the school. One student wrote: "Just take the A train and we'll meet you at the train station and walk you to the school."
6. The T.C.s commented that it was their familiarity with the IBR activities that made it an automatic response to consider interactive instructional resources in response to the students' comments in their initial letters about having difficulty with math facts.
7. The design of the personalized interactive instructional resources motivated the young students to practice, review, and master skills in an enjoyable and engaging manner.
8. The gifts of the educational games used in an IBR became the magic Genie for the emotionally and behaviorally challenged students' teacher. This was because the individualization almost instantaneously changed her classroom climate. Students' focus and attention increased as they wanted to complete other lessons to get to the *playing* part;
9. Student learners were anxious to write their teacher-candidate pen pal to tell how well they were doing.

10. The student-learners didn't want to disappoint their pen pal and they were empowered by their success with the IM."

DR. MASON'S IM AND IBR: ADDITIONAL COMMENTS

The joining of information teacher-candidates had in a previous class was successfully put to use in a practical manner. This information helped to increase college collegiality for the participants. The methodology and IBR itself challenged the realities of all participants. External factors that are generally used to explain away student and teacher failure or disconnect, such as poor academics, poverty, low expectations, irrelevant curriculum were all challenged by the success of the two groups of students who connected and wanted to learn and put pedagogy into practice to support student-learners.

Dr. Mason quotes Schiering (2011); "Common social and societal realities experienced in all settings impact on the individual and whole group's beliefs and value systems." The experience of the semester hopefully made a long-lasting impression as the relationship with pen pals developed the student-learners' creativity, use of their imaginations for making interactive instructional resources, and inventing ways for them to learn outside of those given to them. "Researching theory and writing a paper about it is one thing," states Mason, "discussing learning ideas, sharing thoughts, having interaction with students with experiential and project- and performance-based learning is quite another." When learning is a process supported by the teacher, the affective domain is realized.

The teacher-candidates' interaction with their pen pals gave them an opportunity to reflect on the efficacy of their partners, as well as themselves. The comments in the children's letters suggested that learning was difficult and that many times the students felt sad and alone in their struggle to learn. The teacher-candidates were able to articulate the need to motivate, but equally important, they now got a glimpse of how students feel about themselves and how that shapes how they attempt new things and how the IM and IBR helped them achieve success. This success was achieved by bypassing a roadblock to their previous learning experience, as they now were fully engaged by *learning-through-playing* the games dealing with math. Perhaps most important is that, as the teacher-candidates became engaged in this project their comments revealed that they felt that they learned as much about the humanity of education as their partner student learned about skills and strategies.

(One further comment is that the cooperation between Professors Mason and Schiering enhanced the reflective practitioner experience of the teacher-candidates. This happened simultaneously with helping the student-learners achieve success that may well last throughout their lives.)

INTRODUCTION AND NARRATIVE OF LUCIA SAPIENZA

Lucia is presently a second grade teacher at PS 153, Maspeth Elementary School, Queens, New York. She's been teaching for ten years and in the early 2000s she made an IBR in EDU.506A: Integrated Reading and ELA for the Diverse Learner in the Inclusion Classroom.

Lucia explains, "I created an IBR on the book *The Lion, the Witch, and the Wardrobe* by C. S. Lewis. And, I used this when I taught fourth grade. The students were so involved with the process of playing-the-pages and eager to move onto the next activity, that I was amazed. What I thought was most great is that groups of students work on different activities at one time and use their imaginations to create. I put my IBR on a castle platform and this intrigued the students' interest as well. Then, I created a learning center using some of the activities in the IBR, and these were put on a Tri-fold Board. So, you could come up to the Board and take off an activity to play at your desk. I included an art lesson.

"This art lesson had the students in my room creating characters from the book out of clay (in the book characters are turned to stone). All these activities made the students more involved in the book. Their comprehension was 'over the top,' and even questions and discussions they had were at a high level. Once the projects were completed, students were given certificates of completion where they were able to escape the wardrobe. Doing this IBR with my fourth graders really opened my eyes on how creativity produces higher learning through the students' being involved in the creative process, using their imaginations, and inventing while realizing what they are thinking. The last of these is because we knew what activities developed which thinking skills.

"Another IBR created was based on the book *Miss Spider's Tea Party* by David Kirk. After doing a read aloud, asking and answering a few comprehension questions, students were directed to the *Miss Spider's Tea Party* Tri-fold Board. This Board housed all the activities students would complete based on the book. At first we worked on the Shower of Adjectives, where students chose a character from the book and wrote adjectives to describe that character. This was done in partnerships, and adjectives were hung from the umbrella points as shown in figure 18.1."

"As the students had an understanding of adjectives, they were given a blank drawing of a picture frame. In this frame they drew a self-portrait and wrote descriptive words about themselves around the edges of the frame. Those who finished early worked together to complete the activity on the Tri-fold Board of matching rhyming words by matching the tea bag with the tea cup. This activity was self-assessed because of the color and font of the correct matches. Another activity was making an Electro-Board where students matched parts of insects and arachnids to the correct labeling of them. The students loved doing this match with a continuity tester, a light lit up when the correct match was made. So, I used

Figure 18.1. Interactive Tri-fold Board

the Tri-fold Board as an application of the IM and then the IBR for two different books as a review of the literature.

"As an elementary school teacher, I have come to realize that creativity motivates my students to be involved in their learning. Even though I must follow curriculum, I can do this in a creative way and find that when I do my lessons interestingly, students retain the material throughout the year. Some other things I noticed about this interactive method are that there are problem-solving, decision-making, and a lot of cooperation when making activities and even playing them. The self-correction makes their mistakes private, and that privacy makes students less hesitant to try again for the correct answer."

JOURNAL AND/OR DISCUSSION QUESTIONS

1. What are your thoughts about Dr. Mason's college teacher-candidates' work with special needs students?
2. What are your thoughts about Lucia Sapienzia's work with student learners?

NINETEEN

The Proof of the Pudding

Continued

Jennifer Botte | Amanda Lockwood |
Audra Cerruto, PhD | Rickey Moroney

OVERVIEW

This chapter presents the narratives of four teachers from three different schools and their experience with using either the IM, IBR, or both in their classrooms: The method and the strategy. The chapter closes with a few journaling and/or discussion questions.

INTRODUCTION AND NARRATIVE OF JENNIFER BOTTE

Jennifer is a fifth grade teacher of gifted students at PS 188 in Queens, New York. Having been in EDU.506A in 2004, Jennifer used the IM and IBR with her student-learners addressing the topic of *Body Systems*. Showing through modeling varied interactive instructional resources and providing her students time to conduct research addressing this mode of instruction, Jennifer practiced the idea of "Creativity will set you free" (A. Balt, 2009).

Jennifer writes, "As a teacher, I find it completely natural to make connections to my own education, including elementary, high school, and college experiences. I find myself drawing on these memories often. I remember what it was like to sit at 'my desk' and be the listener instead of the facilitator of learning; the feeling of paying attention and not wanting to miss a word—of wanting to impress the teacher with my understanding and grasp of content. But what I remember most was my excitement of wanting to be there. We had fun! We did projects and experiments! We were CREATIVE!

"As I look out at my own sea of eager eyes, I realize their experiences are very different from my own. Not so much in content, as fifth graders will be learning about context clues and improper fractions til the end of time! It's the WAY they are learning that is so different. I had ample opportunities to be creative, often on a daily basis. We were eager to be successful, but not by the stigma of *tests* and being *held-over.* These kids in front of me are under PRESSURE! It's 'how much content can be squeezed into a day'?! I began to feel uncomfortable that they would not be given the gift of excitement towards school that I had. And that's what creativity is . . . a gift. This is a gift that can be shown and recognized. My thinking is that we are all creative.

"Creativity is inspirational! That feeling you get when your ears perk up to really listen attentively, eyes widen, and you can't keep your mind still. It fills you up until you let it out—like a volcano erupting or a shaken can of soda! It needs to find a way out and that's often forcefully! Creativity is also contagious. I remember going to one of my high school's musicals to watch a few friends perform. They belted out songs and overflowed with, what I can only describe as, happiness! That was creativity. That was inspiration. I am not a performer. I am not a singer. Watching my friends on stage did not make me want to get up and join them. But, it did make me want to go home and paint. And draw. And take pictures. And make collages. I felt a pull, a drive to be expressive in MY way. That's why I know creativity is contagious. And that's why I knew I needed to give my students the 'creativity bug'!

"Now, some people are born with a great deal of creativity. It's like it is woven into each strand of their DNA. They are the kids/people who need to draw pictures in the margins of their notebooks while they listen to you go on about converting fractions to decimals. Others need to be given opportunities to be creative, to realize how it feels. To be shown how to turn it on for him or herself. These were my students. Thirty-one gifted fifth graders who were so consumed with grades and test preparedness . . . who needed an outlet. And I knew exactly what I was going to do!

"Now don't misunderstand me, it's not like I didn't weave project-based learning into my classroom. But I started to rethink how I structured the projects I assigned. I had enjoyed giving projects as alternatives to a final test on a unit, or as an enrichment activity. But I always gave tight parameters . . . create *this* or *that,* use *this* material, make it *this* size. I decided to think of projects as 'skeletons' where students must fill in all the necessary parts to make it come alive! I provided the support frame, which is my job as a teacher. But by giving learners full access to everything else, I hoped [that] would spark a new insurgence of excitement for everyone!

"The *Interactive Book Report* was the perfect conduit to tapping into creativity. I had such a wonderful experience putting together my own during my Graduate Studies at Molloy College.

"I began by showing my students my own book. I explained to them that this was a project that would take TIME! I walked them through each activity, showed them how everything came together. They were COMPLETELY overwhelmed! I assured them that they would be given a ton of class time where I would be here to help with whatever they needed. And I didn't set a due date right away. I wanted to see how their progression went before making those types of decisions. These kids are always under so much pressure with test dates and application deadlines. I wanted this to be a rewarding experience for them, one they would be proud of for a long time to come.

"Because of the timing of the assignment, towards the end of the year, I was afforded a bit of luxury when it came to what content on which the IBRs would focus. I eventually decided on the *Body Systems* because we had already finished our science curriculum and the children had expressed interest in learning about them as an enrichment activity. In keeping with the notion of a positive experience for the children, I allowed them to give me a list of three classmates they would like to work with and two systems that were of the greatest interest to them. It surprisingly didn't take much time to set up my groups and assign each group a body system.

"I took it slow at first. We were just coming on a week-long vacation, so the only assignment I gave them was to become an expert on your system. I encouraged them to visit the library, go online and learn about what they were going to be responsible for. (As an added bit of intrigue, I explained to the kids that at the end of the production of the IBRs, they would be presenting them to the class and ultimately 'teaching' their classmates about their body system . . . something they LOVED to do.) Vacation came to an end and the kids returned to class, body system library books in hand, and were eager to begin!

"I showed them my IBR again, but in a different way. I showed them the 'back-end' of production . . . how all the activities were created. I showed them the materials I used for all the activities and how each one was put together. (They were most fond of the Electro-Board and the Pick-A-Dot.) And then they were off and running, so to speak!

"I gave them several weeks of class time to work on the projects, but quickly learned that students were getting together over the weekend to continue working. Not only was this an educational assignment, it was turning into a social one as well! Students were also taking the books home each night to share with their parents what they were doing!

They were proud of what they originally thought would never be accomplished.

"I also noticed each morning students would show up with 'pieces' for their IBRs they had worked on at home. There was a sense of responsibility group members took on—making sure to accomplish whatever was expected of them so as not to let anyone down. As a teacher this was amazing to see! And all of this was under the guise of a creative project.

"I eventually set a due date when I could see the light at the end of the tunnel for most of the groups. I had them present their Body System IBRs to the class, as well as to Dr. and Mr. Schiering, whom they were all very excited to meet. It was difficult, but I convinced them to let me hold onto them for future classes to learn from. That is what is so great about these projects—they will be there for others to learn from, like interactive textbooks, but better!

"In winding-down the project with my class, I had them complete an evaluation of the experience. It was an incredible positive and empowering experience for them. They were able to do something none of them thought they could do. And it was done amazingly well! I am incredibly proud of the work my class did. I'm even more proud that I was able to give them this creative gift. I know it will remain with them, and hopefully inspire them to keep 'creating.'"

The following are ideas by Jennifer Botte's learners (regarding a Body System IBR that the students created and were not part of the graphic organizers or listing of other interactive resources provided in chapters 15 and 16):

1. Muscular System [1–5] Writing an illustrated story from the perspective of a body's muscle.
2. Filling-in a body-diagram with Velcro tab names of muscles.
3. Completing the Statement Velcro match (example: Your ________help extend your legs.)
4. Crossword Puzzle.
5. Muscle Jeopardy.
6. Immune System [6–7] Stratego Game with flags/Asthma and Bomb/AIDS game pieces. The purpose of this game is to show how the body attacks the illness. Who wins depends on the cleverness of the players and the employed strategy.
7. Chess Immune System/Bacteria and Virus (example: king piece = brain for immune System and AIDS for Bacteria/Virus).
8. Respiratory System [8–12] R.S. Maze: find your way through the lungs to help with victims of asthma.
9. Multiple Choice "History of Lungs" Electro-board.
10. Respiratory System T-shirt design and construction using a paper cutout.

11. Airway Board Game, which refers to the passage of air in the lungs.
12. Lung Bingo, which uses vocabulary associated with the Respiratory System.
13. Circulatory System [13–19] Circulate Your Heart's News: A letter.
14. I Heart You Just the Way You Are: Illustrate and Match Heart Parts.
15. "Functions of the Heart Velcro-Match" game.
16. A Record Sheet for taking your pulse rate at "rest" and "work" times.
17. Make a Mummy using papier mâché.
18. Wheel of Fortune Circulatory System.
19. Skeletal System [20–25].
20. Design Skull Candy: Celebrating Day of the Dead in Mexico.
21. Velcro Skeletal Bone Match.
22. Search for the Bones/Word-search.
23. Decision-making Board (example: would you rather have another hand or foot?).
24. Bone Marrow Color Game,.
25. Make a Body "Using Geometrical Shapes," Endocrine System [25–29]: Welcome to the Endocrine Book of Knowledge.
26. Endocrine Poem Creation.
27. Make Your Own Gland.
28. Create a Hormone.
29. Endocrine Word Scramble.

It should be noted that each game comes with directions so page players may be successful when attempting the activity. In Mrs. Botte's evaluation, *The Body System Interactive Report Evaluation* really helped the learners hone-in on what was important. This had short answer questions of:

What was your favorite part about this project? Please be specific.
Of which activity you created are you most proud and why?
How effective/productive was the collaboration between all of our group members?
What part of the project was your least favorite and why?
If you could change anything about your project, what would it be?
Do you think this project is an effective way for students to learn about the systems of the body? Why? How?
What other subjects or assignments could you see this type of project (IBR) work for best learning? (You're invited to check-out the IBR website to see videos of the fifth graders presenting their IBRs.)

INTRODUCTION AND NARRATIVE OF AMANDA LOCKWOOD

The IM was practiced by me when I made a *Word Family Board* for teaching phonics to my student preschoolers. I wanted them to discover word families like the "at, op, an" ones. The idea was to have them recognize that each of them belonged to a family and words could too. There were different members of a family, but the family name was like the ones mentioned previously in this paragraph. So, there could be a cat in the "at" family, a mop in the "op" family, and a pan in the "an" family. In our 506A class at Molloy, we divided into partnerships to research, create an information packet and tri-fold brochure, and then give a demonstration lesson on a reading method. Dr. Schiering explained how difficult phonics can be for some children, having to sequence and connect letters and sounds. However, she said, "When you make the connection to a family, you have an identification place for the children and that makes it personal."

On both outside flaps of the Tri-fold Board are pictures of things that belong in the word family houses of "en, in, sh, un, and at." Pictures of such things that'd be the house members include: the number 10, a top, cop, bin, fish, as well as the alphabet letters. In the middle there's the

Figure 19.1. Word Family House (Lockwood, 2012)

Word Family House, which is a drawing of a house and the name of the family on the roof. A blank space in front of the family name is left for students to Velcro the letter that makes a word and that word is the family member. There's also a space for the picture of that family member. Or, for my Board, I had the pictures go on the bottom of the house at the front doormat. I used creativity and creative cognition in the overall design of the board and, of course, when making this activity by drawing the house and adding detail to the windows, the bushes, and/or chimney.

The reaction of the students when first seeing the *Word Family Board* was amazing as they said, "Wow, who made that, Ms. Lockwood?" When they discovered it was me they commented on how I put a lot of work into the board, how it was awesome and beautiful. They wanted to use it right away. Even my older students saw the creativity and work I put into it. I think some of them may be proud of me by being creative and using it in my teaching. This opens up a whole other world for these students. Most of the time students only get excited by using technology an iPad or SMART Board.

Designing and constructing this Tri-fold Board required the use of technology, but then took a step back, because after it was completed no technology was needed to "play" with it. It is just as interactive as a SMART Board, even more so, because the students can physically touch, remove and replace the letters and pictures, and move them around to different locations instead of moving pictures on a board. The Tri-fold is three-dimensional! The students love the interaction of coming up to the Tri-fold Board, which is kinesthetic involvement, and then tactile involvement when making a decision about which letter goes where, and which picture represents that family member.

As a child I was very creative or I always tried to be; I remember that I could not draw beautiful pictures, as I wasn't born with that natural talent. I have always appreciated and sometimes felt jealous of people who were born with the ability to draw anything, easily. I think that with some things I may be a perfectionist, which might hinder my creativity by thinking my work is inferior, or I am not good enough. In elementary school my favorite special subject was art. I loved going and creating something new, because I found "Creative Cognition" to be very RELAXING for me!

Maybe because of my reaction to creativity, I want my students to appreciate it or find it enjoyable. I think it can be a huge help in learning. I'm an English Second Language teacher and with students creating something without words I find it comforts them, because the language barrier is not in art. Also, when creating worksheets, PowerPoints, or SMART Board lessons for my students, I always include some graphic or animation to help get their brains stimulated.

As for the IBR, it was a big project when I was in college and it challenged me. I thought about designing pages and making the pages attractive with borders that were colorful. I stretched my thinking to be imaginative and inventive. Some things I kept just as I had them and some things I changed. What really matters is that I grew from this experience in realizing that there are many ways to do a project and I know this because I saw so many of my classmates' IBRs and they were all different.

I don't mean different because they used a different book, but different because of the way the pages were to be played and the overall design. Creativity takes many forms and I think it's important to let children use their imaginations to develop their thinking skills and be part of something instead of apart from it" (A. Lockwood, 2014).

INTRODUCTION AND NARRATIVE FOR AUDRA CERRUTO AND RICKEY MORONEY

As reported by Dr. Cerruto: "At the time of this project with special needs students, there were two teachers most involved. These included myself, a professor at Molloy College with expertise in special education, and daytime parochial school teacher and nighttime adjunct instructor, Rickey Moroney. Molloy College professor Marjorie Schiering enthusiastically volunteered her time and expertise in the area of learning-style theory and use of interactive instructional resources to facilitate this project. The IM was put into use with the iPad apps presented to a small class of student-learners experiencing instruction that met their learning needs.

"Both of us, the lead educators in this project, considered the iPad project to be 'hands-on,' because student-learners had never used the computer in the manner of this program's design and implementation. And, in fact, students involved had their hands on the iPad, manipulating the programs selected for them. It was believed that later, this introduction to the technology teaching tool would lead to student-learners creating educational games on the iPad, as familiarity with this technology became more prevalent. The response of the students to be[ing] involved with this instructional tool was most favorable. New meant exciting!"

As Dr. Cerruto explains further, "Our project was titled *APPy Together: A Collaborative Technology Initiative,* and involved the Division of Education at Molloy College and a Catholic school not far from Molloy (St. Agnes Cathedral School). The report on successes and challenges of this iPad project follow:

> The introduction of the use of the iPad in educational settings, as an innovative tool to address the individual needs of diverse student-learners, has inspired one graduate special education class to modify the nature of its syllabus. In the Fall 2011 term, the course EDU.572: *Strategies and Methods for Diverse Learners,* incorporated the iPad to re-

search educational apps as a cutting-edge technological device to promote teaching and learning.

In order for this project to be meaningful, the graduate students teamed up with fourth grade students at St. Agnes Cathedral School to identify apps based on each youngster's needs, interests, and preferences which included the tactile modality.

The preliminary results of this collaborative project suggest that the student-learners who used the iPad apps that were individually selected for them, based on their personal learning-style preferences and academic strengths and weaknesses demonstrated growth in the areas of 1) social-emotional and 2) academic functioning. The elementary students appeared to feel 3) more self-confident in and out of the classroom setting facilitating their willingness to be 4) open-minded to new learning experiences.

The teacher candidates at Molloy College benefited from this experience by connecting 1) theory practice strategies and 2) IM to remediate academic skills, doing this through the use of 3) innovative technology resources. It was believed that these teacher-candidates would have a competitive edge in the job market because of their experience with the uses of interactive technology, a component of the IM and possible strategy or page of an IBR at some point, with an iPad in a classroom setting to teach their students.

The collaboration between the College and St. Agnes Cathedral School has provided participants the opportunity to engage in community service learning experiences while promoting teaching and learning, based on this learning tool. The potential for this technology's later leading into creation of interactive instructional resources was evident. Designing educational games using technology relied on the student-learners' comfort with this initial project. In the long run, the experience provided them with information to use at a future date for innovative, creative applications of interactive and self-corrective work.

Overall, the iPad has proven to be an effective tool to unlock the challenges teachers face in an increasingly demanding field and the potential achievement of diverse learners that encourages classroom application of the IM.

Benefits for teacher-candidates:

They connect educational theories to teaching practices;

Apply cutting-edge technology to teaching practices;

Identify meaningful teaching and learning strategies and interventions to actual students with disabilities;

Practice individualizing learning experiences and assessments, as well as evaluating results to assist classroom teachers and resource room specialists, and to help students reach their educational goals;

Collaborate as a team with the wider learning community" (Cerruto, 2014).

JOURNAL AND/OR DISCUSSION QUESTIONS

1. What are some thoughts you have about the IBRs made by Jennifer Botte's students?
2. What are your thoughts and opinions about the Tri-fold "Word Family" Board of Amanda Lockwood's student learners? Why do you suppose the students were so involved with this phonics-based interactive instructional resource?
3. What is your reaction to the use of interactive technology in the classroom? Why do you think that Dr. Cerruto and teacher Rickey Moroney were so successful with their student-learners?

TWENTY

The Summation

A Research Study Involving the IM and IBR: Ecosystems and Sustainability

CHAPTER OVERVIEW

This chapter completes this book and is about a study conducted using the IM and IBR in four schools. Three of the schools were in the New York area and the fourth one was in Sweden. The participants were one class of third grade students and three of fifth graders. The learners' teachers' experience in the field of education ranged from six to just under twenty years. The level of cooperation between schools was exceptional as the preconstruction ideas of IBRs were shared and then the actual created IBR activities were either shared or exchanged within and between schools. But, rather than encapsulate the essence of this chapter, you are invited to read the process in the following pages and then use the IM and IBR for yourself or to influence learners and teachers you know.

THE INTERACTIVE BOOK REPORT (IBR): LEARNING THROUGH "PLAY" AND "STYLE"

Author: Marjorie S. Schiering (Professor: Molloy College, Rockville Centre, New York)

Contributors: Audra Cerruto (Special Needs School Psychologist in New York City)

Tara Benton (Teacher at a New York City Special Needs School)

Elizabeth McGovern (Teacher at Our Lady of Victory Parochial School, United States)
Heidi Heilmann (Teacher at Our Lady of Victory Parochial School, United States)
Erin McCarthy (Teacher at Thiells Elementary Public School, United States)
Ann Hultman Jakobsson (Teacher at Edboskolan Kvartettvägen 5–7, Sweden)

Abstract:

This paper is a direct result of the LEGO Corporation's Children's Division giving a grant to Molloy College's Dr. Marjorie Schiering. This grant was for providing materials necessary for teaching children to teach themselves about ecosystems and sustainability. This teaching and learning experience was done with students making and using *The Interactive Book Report Method (IM) and Interactive Book Report (IBR)* (Schiering, 1995; 2003).

A method is "how" something is done. In this case the IM is a creatively interactive means of learning and/or teaching. The IM's approach involves a student or students who learn by inventing, imagining, and being innovative for the purpose of being creative, sharing ideas, exchanging visions, and engaging participants in the process of information retention through self-actualization: *learning-through-playing*.

The accompanying IBR of the IM is an interactive set of educational games/instructional resources put together in a binder designed to address either a selected piece of literature or a thematic unit of study in any discipline. Aims of this paper include informing the readership of the procedures employed in four classrooms (three in the United States and one in Europe) and the student's attitudes about learning using the idea of "learning-through-playing" or "playing-to-learn." Tactile/kinesthetic instructional resources, as well as visual and auditory skills, were used and ultimately related to learning and one's processing style preferences.

All of the instructional tools were designed to develop a student's imagination for product-, performance-, and evidence-based learning resulting in creativity, student engagement, and empowerment for self-efficacy by knowing what cognitive and metacognitive skills are in use when learning, collaborating, and communicating.

A qualitative attitudinal questionnaire was utilized to realize how students felt about creating and then using the educational games as a learning methodology and strategy. The study involved three schools that varied in type of population and locations in the New York area and one school in mid-Sweden. Participants in each addressed the IBR teaching and learning method, which was implemented as a creative instrument and then instructional process in grades three and five. Learners in each class were visited weekly for several hours from January through mid-June, 2013 by the author of this article.

The major relevance of this paper synthesizes the introduction to the IM and IBR, and uses them to actively engage students in learning for optimum retention of material. Later the relevance is for other educators and student-learners to incorporate this method into their instructional techniques once they realize the positive significance of using "play" and "style" to learn. Each activity for the IBR was addressed with respect to what cognitive and metacognitive skills were developed when making and then playing the educational game/interactive instructional resource with reference to *The Reciprocal Thinking Phases: Cognition and Metacognition* (Schiering, 1999; 2011 pp. 110–114 & 211–217). (See figure 10.1 herein.)

Key Words: IBR, cognition, educational games, interactive

1. INTRODUCTION: "IBR" HISTORY, RATIONALE, GOALS, AND PAGES

History:

"The first experience with The Interactive Book Report took place in the mid-1990s in a fifth grade classroom at Stony Point Elementary School in Rockland County, New York. It came attached to a *philosophy of education* that became known as *A Model for Academic and Social Cognition* (Schiering, 2003; Schiering, Bogner, & Buli-Holmberg, 2011, p. 56). This model addressed knowing students based on Common Social/Societal Realities, their Belief and Value Systems stemming from the *Cognitive Collective*/Thinking and Feelings, external factors of religion or lack thereof, economics, academics, and politics effecting education (Schiering, 2003; 2011).

These four external factors move inwardly and outwardly to influence a person's behaviors and life goals through reflection on experiences we've had. "When the components of this Model are put together with concern for those we teach, there's an understanding that prevails regarding who one is as a teacher and learner and who our students are as well" (Schiering, 2011).

Dunn and Dunn, in their Learning Style Model (1992), referred to its being important to realize the varied ways students learn. Certainly, one of the variations was with respect to perceptual preferences, as well as room design, working alone or with others, and the physiology of learning operatives. After combining the components of "style" with knowing "who" one is as a learner, the idea of the Interactive Book Report came into being as a self-corrective method of teaching any discipline through review of a piece of literature or as an introduction and/or review of a thematic unit topic. Additionally, the idea of how we first learn was addressed in the IBR's development.

Rationale:

Considering the rationale for this project, it's what this author/presenter said when discussing the IBR with her teacher-candidates: "The first way we learn as babies and children is through play (gaming) which can be and often is creative and imaginative. Let's play house, school, nurse, or teacher.

"These activities are also preparing and equipping us for future life experiences. When you create something you take hold of that work as belonging to you. This makes the learning that takes place more authentic and a learning experience that the learner takes with him (remembers and incorporates into his life) going forward.

"This IBR book is something that's *natural* when realizing we learn through play by addressing 'style' preferences of learners, regardless of their age or grade levels. And, these play and style experiences we have impact us by causing formation of memories. We retain what impressed us! Being involved and engaged in something helps us to recall it. Consider the IBR at the 'cutting-edge' of project- and performance-based teaching and learning to promote thinking and overall creative cognition. The IBR may also be used for alternative means of assessment and overall evaluation-of-instruction" (Schiering, 1995; 1998).

Goals:

Each of the schools in the Ecosystem and Sustainability discovery-of-the-means of sustainability, "regarding our world's environments project, had similar but not exactly the same components for reaching the IBR learning goals. These goals involved the making of educational games and developing, as well as identifying, cognitive skills when playing the pages of the IBR. The ultimate goal of the completed IBRs is their being slated for exchange between schools involved in this project, and for sharing within schools with respect to 'going green.'"

In all, seventy-four students were involved in the project. (In addition to the making of IBRs the New York special needs and parochial schools' students, working in small-group format, created posters on the topic of recycling. These were entered in the NYS Department of Environmental Conservation Poster Contest at the end of May, 2013. The students' work was so innovative that the aforementioned department created a new category for posters called "Interactive Posters." The students took first, second, third, and honorable mention in this new category. There were approximately 2,000 entrants in the poster contest in all. An award luncheon was held in Cooperstown, New York in November of 2013. The students who won the Interactive Poster category attended this event and received statewide recognition for their creativity as their work, and also posters made by students in the special needs school, was put on display).

The IBR method has relevance for educators, trainers, and practitioners of educational gaming. It has relevance regarding learning-style perceptual preferences (auditory, visual, tactile, and/or kinesthetic) in that the techniques adhere to learners being able to teach themselves by creating hands-on self-corrective educational games. Additionally, there are social contexts being implemented by working in small groups or partnerships in accordance with components of *A Model for Academic and Social Cognition* (Schiering, 2003; Schiering, Bogner, & Buli-Holmberg, 2011).

Pages:

The IBR is a set of educational games placed in a binder. This is one that usually has four-inch rings and the educational games are in pouches, page protectors inside the binder, or are laminated. Following a decorative cover page that represents the topic or theme of the IBR, the first inside page has a Table of Contents. Then, there's a Welcome page that invites the students to "play" the pages. This is followed by the Reciprocal Thinking Chart's Cognitive Skill Identification Page (Schiering, 2003b). This page has the learners identifying the cognitive or metacognitive skills utilized when playing a page.

Next, the interactive pages for a thematic unit have a minimum of five educational games with a title and explanation of how the specific activity is played. For this Theme IBR: interactive instructional resources relating to reading, English Language Arts (reading, writing, listening, or speaking activity), social studies, math, and science are provided along with two more "creative pages." A closing page thanking the students for playing-the-pages is oftentimes accompanied by a congratulatory "certificate of completion."

2. METHODOLOGY

School One: Psychologist, Dr. Audra Cerruto, and Teacher, Tara Benton:

The first school to begin the project was a special needs school in New York City. This school also services the surrounding area. School psychologist Dr. Audra Cerruto and third grade teacher Tara Benton's students participated in this IBR method. Additionally, they applied what they learned about educational gaming and style to create three posters for the Department of Environmental Conservation's Recycle Contest.

"From my perspective as the school's psychologist, I found that, in the midst of this tenuous time for teaching and learning with an increasing emphasis on testing, test preparation, and implementing unproven academic standards, my colleagues and I question the impact on our students. Will our students be able to sustain their enthusiasm for learning despite the hours spent confined to learning and performing within the limitations of the testing movement?

"As a school that services students with a hearing loss that is severe enough to impact adversely the development of language and the learning process, we are challenged to make every learning experience meaningful. By striving to make learning useful, it is our hope that students will internalize and apply the information to build a rewarding life. So, will state tests capture the dynamic process of learning that is occurring in our classrooms each day, month, and year? Are there other tools available to demonstrate the complex teaching and learning process that brings into the individual application of what's presented and retention of it?"

THE CHALLENGE

The first challenges were to build prior knowledge, to develop vocabulary skills, to apply information to personal experiences, and to act on student knowledge in meaningful ways. But how does one do these things with children whose sensory limitations may have affected their experiences and exposure to content that their "typically" functioning peers may have learned vicariously through their personal and educational experiences so easily? The concept of recycling is everywhere, but what do the blue and green containers actually mean?

In order to teach the concept and value of recycling and sustainability to these young children, a dynamic approach that envelops their senses, and captures their curiosity and enthusiasm for learning was utilized. As a result, hands-on learning with tactile and kinesthetic instructional resources, known as "educational games" was employed throughout this study; "style" was evidenced.

SEQUENCE OF ACTIVITIES

1. Initially, the programmed learning sequence book *Ecosystems: Now, There's a Niche for You* (Schiering, 1996) served as the introduction to the aforementioned topic. Several IBRs were shown and educational games, made by teacher-candidates in EDU.506A (Integrated ELA and Reading) at Molloy College were there for these stu-

dent-learners to "play." The first topic to be introduced was ecosystems. Vocabulary words were extensive for the second, third, and fourth grade students who are hearing impaired.

2. As a result of having so much vocabulary, the use of interactive puzzles/Task Cards relating to varied "environments" were created with the students. Vibrant illustrations were used to portray the ecosystem. This vocabulary was infused into the day-to-day discussions in the classroom, posted on the "word wall," practiced and applied in a science journal, and "played" with through games. Mastery of the vocabulary words was not the goal. Rather, the application of the concept of sustainability and the importance of recycling for our environment were the focus, which was reinforced through the use of authentic literature.
3. The class listened to *Something from Nothing* (Gilman, 1993). This picture book relates how a grandfather makes his grandson a blanket and then, when it's "tattered and torn," sequentially, makes seven, each time smaller, pieces of clothing for the child to wear. When there was nothing left of the original fabric, it was discovered that there was enough "material," content wise, to write a story about this process of recycling and reusing the original blanket.

   Each student drew a design on a piece of construction paper and created a paper-blanket to transform, using scissors, into the clothing items in the book. This hands-on experiential task provided the students with the opportunity to see the dynamic and creative process of sustainability of the paper-blanket representing the real blanket in the story.
4. The next step in this study found the teachers placing recyclable items around the respective classrooms. The student learners, then dressed in teacher-provided white shirts, which served as "labcoats," went on an "Ecologist" scavenger hunt. Finding the "hidden" items around the classroom, the children in each class made a list of these objects and discussed how every one of them might be reduced, recycled, and/or renewed. Their ideas were charted. The concept of the 3Rs was applied to real objects in their world. This activity involved the students' physical and mental participation.
5. Tara Benton, these special needs children's teacher, created an interactive SMART Board activity on the topic of what materials could be recycled based on whether they were biodegradable or nonbiodegradable. After she introduced these terms, there was a slide with a pile of dirt where there were scattered, such items as an aluminum soda and plastic bottle, piece of paper, plastic bag, metal thermos, toothpick, glass pitcher, and other items.
6. When the child went up to the board, he or she would say, before touching the item, whether it was biodegradable or not. If the item

disappeared upon touching it, the student knew it was biodegradable and wouldn't be recycled. But, if the item went around in circles, it was not biodegradable and would be able to be reused in some fashion. Students made a list of how these items may be used again. (Tara Benton shared her SMART Board activity with the other schools doing this project.)

7. Additionally, as all of the aforementioned activities took place, there was a science notebook maintained on how three items put in plastic tubs filled with dirt would respond over time. One tub had paper in it and the other two a piece of apple and a hearing-aid battery, respectively. The children drew pictures of the objects when first put into the soil and then at weekly intervals for the duration of the IBR project. The goal was to realize how the first two items were biodegradable, but the last one maintained its shape and size with all internal components not affected.
8. Thoroughly understanding the basic concepts of the 3Rs, the students developed interactive activities to promote mastery. A class of six students created Flip-Chutes and Pic-A-Dot cards for each other. They also made Task Cards. Interestingly, students "played" interactively with the materials. Then, the students designed their own posters based on the topic of the 3Rs for the aforementioned Environmental Conservation contest. They were encouraged to incorporate the interactive activities into their posters. Once again, the students created educational gaming materials, applying their knowledge in different and creative ways, on a poster board that took on new dimensions.
9. The flat board took on a three-dimensional aspect when the students built educational games, complete with manipulatives, into the board. The importance of the message regarding the 3Rs took on a new scope when the audience, usually passive observers, now played interactive games to learn about sustainability. Following the making of posters, the students began the process of creating an *IBR on Ecosystems and Sustainability.*

School Two: Beth McGovern and Heidi Heilmann:

Our Lady of Victory School on Long Island, New York was the second school to become involved in the LEGO grant Ecosystem and Sustainability endeavor. The fifth grade teachers Beth McGovern (science and math) and Heidi Heilmann (ELA and social studies) are veteran teachers. Considering the grade level the students have had more experiences than the third graders in the other three schools. Like the other students in this project they were extremely enthusiastic about the creation of educational games. They were all for discussion about how things should be done and celebrating a sharing of ideas and became engrossed in "creative cognition" (Schiering, 2012).

The student-learners in these fifth grade classes worked primarily in small-group format. They were the first to do creative writing by imagining themselves as a metal, glass, plastic, or paper recyclable item. This creative writing assignment included possibly giving the item a personal name, like "Tom," and then explaining how he or she was used on an everyday basis. The writing sequence that followed was to relate how this item was, at some point, discarded, and what happened next, later, then, and lastly. They then role-played this story as it was read to the class.

One student group wrote how the reused/recycled item was a milk container in a refrigerator in a store. Bought by a young girl's mother, the milk container in the story was named Ruth. She was used on cereal each morning for a few days. Then, the girl's mother went to "throw out the empty cardboard half-gallon milk container" when the girl stopped her by saying, "Wait, don't throw that out, my teacher said that if you clean this out, thoroughly, that it can be used for a project we're doing tomorrow. We're making Flip-Chutes." The mother responded, "What's that?" The girl answered, "Oh, it's an educational game and we make openings in the top and bottom and then chutes for cards to be put in the top slot.

"The card has a question on it like a math problem. And, when the card comes out the bottom opening the answer appears. Wait til we make it, and I'll bring it home to show you. Actually, you don't have to wait to see what it looks like, because here's a picture of a Flip-Chute." (The student then produced a picture perfectly drawn of the recycled milk container as a Flip-Chute.)

Ms. Heilmann related that she thought the students' writing overall was amazing, and both teachers complimented everyone on their creative stories. One student wrote by herself about the recycled item's being a Christmas tree and being decorated in the house for this holiday. Then, the tree was taken to a shredder to be used as mulch for plants. The story's end was especially loved with this thought of the tree, "I may not be used now for the purpose I was intended, but I'm helping our environment, and that's a good thing."

The teacher, Beth McGovern, commented about being truly impressed with the high level of collaboration the students have had during the times we've met. "They are really 'getting along' and sharing ideas and acting on them so well. I am really impressed with their creativity and use of imagination. And, I think they are going to use these educational games for a long time to come; beyond this year. And, some of the children who have had difficulty sharing ideas, well, I'm looking at one right now who is really producing work when previously there was little involvement or effort. It's really nice to see them participating so much."

School Three: Erin McCarthy:

"At Thiells Elementary School in Rockland County, New York, my third grade class followed the same procedures as the *second school* in this article. This was with respect to the introduction to ecosystems, laminating the Task Cards they created, doing creative writing as if a recyclable object from that object's point of view, sharing the stories, going on an Ecologist Scavenger Hunt, doing teacher Tara Benton's SMART Board activity, making posters, and sharing ideas about how sustainability and the 3Rs work for people in their school and surrounding area.

"The third graders exhibited high interest each Friday when Dr. Schiering came to visit the class and instruct on ecosystems and educational games with 'style' in the mix. The educational games that my students have been working on with Dr. S have been beneficial for various reasons. The use of these educational games has helped many of my struggling learners feel successful. These games are a great way for students to see curriculum material in a new or different way. It also helps to make the facts or information more meaningful and exciting to them. This in turn helps the students to retain the information. In addition, many of the games require the students to be creative by using their imaginations. All of this gets the students excited about learning.

"The games that they have made are also tools that the students will be able to carry over into other subjects and curriculum areas. I can see many opportunities for the students to create games to practice their math facts or a game based around a story we have read in class. The games can also be easily adapted for students to study and quiz themselves about any of our various science or social studies units.

"In addition to the education benefits, I have seen some very strong social benefits as well. I feel that these games have provided a way for my students to work collaboratively with their classmates in ways I've not observed so much this school year. I have seen many of them share and work together to make decisions and solve problems through the creation of these games. I have also seen students work with classmates that they do not usually get to work with while in the normal classroom setting. It has been an experience that I feel has helped to bond my students together as a classroom community, and realize their creativity and thinking skill development."

Upon reading over Erin's observations the *Model for Academic and Social Cognition* mentioned at the start of this article comes into focus most profoundly. The idea of "social literacy" has been provided by sharing common social and societal realities, which form belief and value systems that, in this case, bring a classroom full of eight- and nine-year-olds to unity of purpose. Furthermore, "There is no competition," explains Ms. McCarthy, "but rather working together for learning. The result is that within a year's time the children will actually be teaching other children in the school when they use the IBR. Subsequently, school community is realized. Perhaps a sense of pride ensues . . . one that has children saying things like this, 'I think the IBR was very fun and I learned a lot of recycle stuff.' Or, 'I felt happy when doing the games' and 'I like doing this, because we shared.'"

School Four: Ann Hultmann Jakobsson: Sweden:

Ann Hultman Jakobsson from Edboskolan in Sweden writes, "When the students first got the package from the United States with student-made educational games, they were very excited. They wanted to start making their own games right away. After reading the book *Something from Nothing*, which the students also really appreciated, we repeated what we had learned during the year about sustainable development and ecosystems. We talked about what activities we had done to learn about these subjects, and then we talked about some English words for what we had learned.

"Because the students started to read English as a school subject this year and because the vocabulary in this subject is quite difficult even in their native language, the students started to search for information and write questions in Swedish. They chose the area for which they wanted to make a game, and then they wrote their own questions by reading about the area in books and/or on the Internet. To search for information on the Internet is something we have been practicing during this year, and, even if this is a challenge, the students definitely have been getting better at it.

"Even to write questions with multiple choice answers turned out to be a challenge and we had some good learning experiences while doing this. The students worked in groups and their next assignment was to translate the Swedish questions and answers into English. They used Google Translate for this, as they sat in groups and discussed the suggestions for the translation they got from this source. Follow-up was meeting with me for the right translation.

"The most popular games the students made were in groups and were the Flip-Chute, Pic-A-Dot and Electro-Board, all learning- style related activities. They wrote the final version of the questions. I found I have a very creative group of students, and they were really enthusiastic about making the educational games for the IBR. I have templates the students followed for these games on a CD that I got through and was made by Lena Boström, a professor near where I teach.

"Creatively, one group made a board game, and they also thought of making extra inventions on their game that weren't in the templates. They made it so that both the rules and the question cards stayed on the board at all times by an elastic band. Every day at least one or two students came and asked if we were going to work on the IBR project.

Even students that usually do not get inspired by school work came up to me and asked if we could 'play.'

"There have been a lot of challenges, especially since they had to read and write in a foreign language. Despite that, the students have been working eagerly, they have been very creative, and they have had fun with looking forward to exchanging their IBR with classes in the USA. Everyone has participated and done something, and they are very proud about this and how it broadened their English vocabulary. The students have learned a lot about sustainable development and ecosystems. What they haven't learned yet I´m sure they will learn while trying out their friends' games.

"Another thing that is very obvious is that, once the students had made their first game they easily made the second and third game. This is proof that they learned the process by taking part of it and then being imaginative and creating on their own.

I can also see that a couple of students were not benefited by working with the instructional games. These are students who mostly wanted to write answers in a book and who have a hard time focusing on the subject. My guess is that they will be helped by *playing the games*, and that it is the *making of the games* that did not suit them. Some groups are already done with their games, and they have started to make another game on a different subject. They are making games about the historic times, the years between Before the Common Era and 1,000 years after it for review of what we have learned this year, and these educational games, for an IBR, are definitely something we will keep on doing."

3. CONCLUSIONS

Comments by Beth McGovern and Heidi Heilmann from School Two:

Perhaps the best way to address the conclusion of this project, other than showing the Attitudinal Chart at the end of this article, would be to share the comments from Beth McGovern and Heidi Heilmann, when they related:

> "This IBR collaboration was a great learning experience for us as teachers, but was especially wonderful for our classes. They were thrilled to be involved in this unique collaboration between a veteran college professor, their teachers, and themselves. Collaboration is the operative!
> "We spent time together, creating interactive educational materials for a unit on Environmental/Ecology awareness. The activities were exciting and fun! Our students were very creative, truly enjoying their improvisational performances as one activity involved Dr. Schiering inviting them to 'act out' their creative writing stories about the life of a recycled item. Most importantly, aside from the cognitive development and social interaction, we observed students who were quiet in class

becoming 100 percent engaged! One child, in particular, who is struggling with English as a second language, really blossomed. We all learned that the interactive educational games could certainly be integrated and carried-over into all curriculum areas and meet our new Common Core learning standards."

The chart that follows, Pizzo's "Semantic Differential Scale" (1981), shows attitudes regarding learning when using interactive instructional resources/educational games such as those in the IBR.

Pizzo's Semantic Differential Scale

Helpful	46	24	3	1	0	Not Helpful
Clear-minded	40	17	12	2	3	Confused
Energetic	43	15	11	4	1	Tired
Calm	46	12	11	2	3	Nervous
Strong	46	17	9	0	1	Weak
Relaxed	39	12	13	6	3	Tense
Wonderful	55	14	3	1	1	Terrible
Steady	42	21	5	1	3	Shaky
Confident	43	19	6	1	5	Uncertain
Good	58	13	1	2	0	Bad
Peaceful	33	26	6	2	17	Frustrating
Sharp/Exciting	45	20	6	2	1	Dull/Boring
Successful	59	11	3	0	1	Unsuccessful

Figure 20.1.

SUMMATION OF CHAPTER

The study you have just read was synthesized and published in *Brain World* magazine in the summer of 2014. It's also on the Internet just as it appears here, as the study was presented in Billund, Denmark, at the Learning Style Conference sponsored by the LEGO Corporation. And, it was presented at the International Multi-Conference on Society, Cybernetics, and Informatics (IMSCI) in Orlando, Florida, in the summer of 2013. The study was part of the book you've just completed reading.

In summation, I can tell you this book has been a goal fulfilled. That goal was to bring to a wider audience than my classes, whether at the elementary, middle, or college levels, or for those interested in learning and/or teaching the ideas concerning the IM and IBR. These are a method and a strategy that bring theory into practice. Their use enables positive effects and affects, respectively, to learners and teachers alike. You are asked to give the IM and IBR a try. . . . they're not just fun, but a way to learn that will last forever in one's memory.

JOURNAL AND/OR DISCUSSION QUESTIONS

1. What were four of the topics of this chapter?
2. Who was involved in the study and where were the places it occurred?
3. What was the most meaningful teacher comment for you in this chapter?
4. What were some of the projects the students experienced before making their IBRs?
5. What were some of the pages the students created?
6. What are some thoughts you have about the IM and IBR?

Afterword

Who Are We?

How do you define me, and how do I define you?
"I am/you are . . . a conglomeration of matter that thinks and feels."
Simplistically, that is what some would say.
But, I believe that I am more than that, and so are you.

I am, perhaps like you, as individualistic as they come.

I am centered within a group that does and does not define me.
While there are similarities in size, shape, and color—
There are differences in thoughts, ideas, opinions, judgments, and feelings.
To know "who" we are is to embrace each with reciprocity and equal passion.
"We know few, we acquaint with many," is what I suppose.

Who are we? We are the "Cognitive Collective," and have "Creative Cognition."

For the most part, we are in a place where "doing" is appreciated
Personally, I write, teach, and draw to be among the doing . . . just as you do your "things," and we get defined that way.
However, knowing who I am or you are—is realizing the "being" of you and me.

I think when someone asks, "*Who are we*?" that the answer is:

We're the ones that have managed to *create* a linkage across an indiscriminate time continuum.
We are those who are in the act of being. It's nothing more or less than that. . . . but, perhaps different from one another . . . and that's a good thing, I imagine.

Why?

Because when we come together we may join those thoughts and feelings spoken of earlier . . . and in so doing, *create a community*, where we are . . . You, Me, and Us. (M. Schiering)

Bibliography

Abbott, J. (1994). *Learning makes sense: Recreating education for a changing future*. London: Education 2000.

Abedi, J., & O'Neil, H. F. (1996). Reliability and validity of a state metacognitive inventory: Potential for alternative assessment. *Journal of Educational Research, 89*(4), 234–245.

After-Schiff, M., & Schiering, M. (1953; 1967; 1976). *Advice from my mom: Conversations on ways to behave*. Presentations in Rochester, NY and Columbus, OH.

Allport, G. W. (1937). *Personality: A psychological interpretation*. New York: Rinehart and Winston.

Angelou, M. (2007, June). Quote in *Village Voice*. Clemmons, NC: PK and Co.

Balt, A. (2013, September 20). *Soulful life tips for Renaissance people*. [Web log message]. Retrieved from http://www.andreabalt.com/about/andrea/.

Bavelier, D., & Davidson, R. J. (2013, February). Brain training: Games to do you good. *Nature, 494*(7438), 425–5. England. Nature Publishing Group: Macmillan Journals.

Bernard, N., Gelbart, J., Connor, C., DiBlasio, N., Romano, A., Shea, J., Mannion, K., & Garay-Cruz, J. (2013). Reaction to EDU.506A. In *Create and inspire: A series of letters to the professor*. New York: Molloy College.

Bodrova, E., & Leong, D. (2003). The importance of being playful. *Educational Leadership, 60*(7), 50–53. Virginia: Educational Leadership/ASCD.

Bogner, D. (1990a). *John Dewey's theory of adult education and adult development* (PhD dissertation). University of Kansas.

———. (1990b). John Dewey, 1945. In *Self realization as the moral ideal* (EW, 4: p. 50). (PhD dissertation). University of Kansas.

———. (2007). The process of memorization and stimuli regarding feelings. In *A model for academic and social cognition*, 11–12; 21. Lanham, MD: Rowman and Littlefield.

———. (2008). *Conversations and unpublished narrative on a synthesis of Dewey's learning theory and personal reflections on teaching and learning*. (Unpublished). New York: Molloy College.

———. (2011). Conversations narrative on effective learners and teachers: Thinking and feelings. In *Teaching and learning: A model for academic and social cognition*. Lanham, MD: Rowman and Littlefield.

Botte, J. (2014, Spring). *Fifth graders make IBRs on body systems: An analysis of the IM and IBR*. (Unpublished). New York: PS 188.

Bowen, J. A. (2014, Spring). The teaching naked cycle: Technology is a tool, but psychology is the new pedagogy. *Liberal Education, 100*(2). Wisconsin: AAC&U.

Brandt, R. (1999). Educators need to know about the human brain. *Phi Delta Kappan, 81*(3), 235–238.

Bunting, D. (2012). Creative cognition. *Brain World: Humanity's new frontier magazine, 3* (4). Arizona: IBREA Foundation.

Carhart, O. K. (2014, Summer). *Thoughts on the process of creativity: A personal accounting*. Oregon.

Cerruto, A. (2014). *Using the IM & IBR: A Psychologist's perspective: Learning-through-play*. New York: Rockville Centre.

Cerruto, A., & Moroney, R. (2012). *APPy together: A Molloy College and Parochial School hands-on computer project*. New York: Molloy College Syllabus.

Cerruto, A., & Benton, T. (2013). *Conversations on using the IBR*. Queens, NY: Lexington School for the Deaf.

Csikszentmihalyi, M. (1996a). *Creativity: Flow and the psychology of discovery and invention*. New York: HarperCollins.
———. (1996b). *Creativity: The work and lives of 91 eminent people*. New York: HarperCollins.
———. (1998). *Finding flow: The psychology of discovery and invention*. New York: Harper Perennial.
———. (2009). *Flow: The psychology of optimal experience* (1st edition, July 1, 2008). E-book. New York: Harper Perennial Modern Classics.
Damasio, A. R. (1994). *Descartes' error*. New York: Grosset/Putnam.
Delialioglu, O. (2012). *Journal of Educational Technology and Society, 10*(2), 133–146.
Dewey, J. (1893/1972). Self-realization as the moral ideal. In *John Dewey: The early works, 1882–1898*. (Vol. 4). Carbondale, IL: Southern Illinois Press. In Bogner, (PhD dissertation). University of Kansas.
———. (1937). From absolutism to experimentalism. In *Contemporary American Philosophy*, 13–27. New York: Macmillan.
Doidge, N. (2007). *The brain that changes itself: Stories of personal triumph from the frontiers of brain science*. New York: Penguin Books.
Dunn, R. (1995). *Characteristics of special needs learners: Introductory course for learning styles*. St. John's University. New York: St. John's University Press.
———. (1996). (unpublished) *At home conversations addressing gifted learners*. New York.
Dunn, R., & Dunn, K. (1978). *Teaching students through their learning styles: A practical approach*. Englewood Cliffs, NJ: Prentice Hall.
———. (1992). *Teaching elementary students through their individual learning styles*. Boston: Allyn and Bacon.
F. M. & A. (2013, Summer). *Thoughts on the process of creativity: Siblings personal accounting*. (Unpublished). North Carolina.
Ferrantello, A. (2013, Fall). *Thoughts on the process of creativity: A personal accounting*. (Unpublished). Westchester, New York.
Fleckner, M. (2014, Spring). *Thoughts on the process of creativity: A personal accounting*. Virginia.
Frost, Robert, (1916). The road not taken. In *Mountain interval*. New York: Henry Holt and Company.
Galvin, R. (1997). Creativity requires commitment. In *Creativity: Flow and the psychology of discovery and intention*. New York: Harper Perennial.
Garcia, M. (2012). Creative cognition. *Brain World: Humanity's new frontier magazine, 3* (4). Arizona: IBREA Foundation.
Gazzaniga, M. S. (1998). *The mind's past*. CA: University of California Press.
Gilman, P. (1993). *Something from nothing*. New York: Scholastic Inc.
Giouroukakis, V. (2014). *Conversations on "Is everyone creative?"* (Unpublished). Rockville Centre, NY: Molloy College.
Gladwell, M. (2014, September). Late Bloomers. In *Reader's Digest* excerpted from *What the dog saw and other adventures* (2009), 295–313. New York: Little Brown and Co.
Glatthorn, A. (1995). *Developing the classroom curriculum: Developing a quality curriculum*. Alexandria, VA: ASCD.
Goleman, D., Kaufman, P., & Ray, M. (1992). *The creative spirit: Companion to the PBS television series*. Mass market paperback. New York: Dutton-Penguin.
Gray, P. (2014, January). Is the American school system damaging our kids? *Readers Digest Magazine, 18*(37). Retrieved from http://www.rd.com/advice/parenting/american-school-system-damaging-kids/2/.
Hargadon, A. (2003). *How breakthroughs happen: The surprising truth about how companies innovate*. Boston, MA: Harvard Business Review Press.
Haugsbakk, G., & Nordkvelle, Y. (2007, March). The rhetoric of ICT and the new language of learning: A critical analysis of the use of ICT in the curricular field. *European Educational Research Journal, 6*(1), 1–12.
Hegarty, J. (2014). *Hegarty on creativity: There are no rules*. New York: Thames and Hudson.

Hultman Jakobsson, A. (2013). *International exchange of IBR pejoratives*. Trångsund, Sweden.

Keefe, J. W. (Ed.). (1979). Learning styles: An overview. In *Student learning styles: Diagnosing and prescribing programs* (1–17). Reston, VA: National Association of Secondary School Principals.

Keefe, J. W., & Languis, M. (1983). Description of the learning style profile. In J. W. Keefe and J. S. Monk (Eds.), *NASSP Bulletin* (43–53). Reston, VA: National Association of Secondary School Principals.

Kline, T. (2011). *The creative self*. New York: Ars Omnia Press.

Kneller, G. (1965). *The art and science of creativity*. New York: Holt, Rinehart and Winston.

Land, G. (1998). *Breakpoint and beyond: Mastering the future today* . Arizona: Leadership 2000 Inc.

Li, M. (1993, January). *Empowering learners through metacognitive thinking, instruction, and design*. Proceedings of selected research and development presentations at the Convention of the Association for Educational Communications and Technology. Sponsored by the Research and Theory Division, New Orleans, LA. (ERIC Document Reproduction Services No. ED362180).

Lockwood, A. (2010, Spring). The interactive tri-fold board word family house: IM in a pre-school and reflections about the interactive book report method and book. Based on 2010 EDU.506A: *Integrated ELA and reading*. New York: Molloy College.

———. (2014, Summer). *Thoughts on the process of creativity: A personal accounting*. New York: PS 9 Ryer Avenue Elementary School.

Lord, Bette Bao. (2003). *In the year of the boar and Jackie Robinson*. New York: HarperCollins.

Maisel, Eric. (1995). *Fearless Creating: A step-by-step guide to starting and completing your work of art*. New York: Tarcher.

Marino, A. (2000). The IBR and ownership. (Unpublished). New York.

———. (2013). *The common core and the IM: Personal perspective from research*. New York: Oceanside School District.

———. (2000; 2014). *What's an IBR and its connection to learning standards?* EDU.506A: *Integrated ELA and reading for the diverse learner*. New York: Molloy College.

———. (2014, Fall). *The IM and IBR regarding learning standards*. Based on 2000 EDU. 506A: Integrated ELA and reading. New York: Molloy College.

———. (2014). *Graphic organizer design: Reciprocal process*. New York: Molloy College

Mason, P. (2012). College professor's narrative on the IM. *From college teacher candidates to special needs classroom: Pen pals*. Course syllabus EDU.572. New York: Molloy College.

May, R. (1975). *Courage to create*. New York: W. W. Norton & Company.

McCarthy, E. (2013). *Conversations on using the IBR*. New York: Thiells Elementary School.

McGovern, E., & Heilmann, H. (2013). *Conversations on using the IBR in a fifth-grade interdisciplinary classroom*. Floral Park, NY: Our Lady of Victory School.

Million, J. (2015). *Conversations on mindfulness: Thinking is talking inside one's head*. (Unpublished). Ohio.

Moroney, R. (2013). *Conversation on creativity: Process and product*. (Unpublished). Long Island, NY.

Naiman, L. (2012). *Creativity at work: What is creativity?* [Web log message]. Retrieved from http://www.creativityatwork.com/2014/02/17/what-is-creativity/.

NYSED Common Core website, https://www.engageny.org/common-core-curriculum.

O'Connor-Petruso, S. A., Schiering, M., Hayes, B., & Serrano, B. (2004). Pedagogical and parental influences in mathematics achievement by gender from select European countries from the TIMSS-R study. *Proceedings of the IRC-2004 TIMSS, 2*, 69–84. Nicosia, Cyprus: Paper presented at the International Research Conference.

Olsen, D. G. (1995). "Less" can be "more" in the promotion of thinking. *Social Education, 59*(3), 130–138. Maryland: National Council for the Social Studies (NCSS).

Pink, D. (2000). *A whole new mind*. New York: Riverhead Books.

Pizzo, J. (1981). Semantic differential scale. *Dissertation Abstracts International, 42*, 2475A.

Robinson, K. (2006, February). *How schools kill creativity*. TEDTalks filmed at Monterey, CA: TED 2006 Conference.

Roizman, T. (2010). *The brain functions involved in cognitive functions*. Livestrong.com. Retrieved from http://www.livestrong.com/article/177861-the-brain-functions-involved-in-cognitive-functions/.

Romano, A. (2013). *Thoughts on my being creative: A reflection paper*. Integrated ELA and reading for the diverse learner. New York: Molloy College.

———. (2014). *The don'ts for having a creative classroom environment*. (Unpublished). Rockville Centre, NY: Molloy College.

Rosenberg, D. (2013). *Resume of my IBR: An internet digest*. Retrieved from http://daniellerosenberg.weebly.com/interactive-book-report.html.

Russo, M. (2014). *Mindfulness and creativity: A summative view*. New York: Molloy College.

Sapienza, L. (2004–2014). *Reflections on the IBR and bringing it to my teaching assignments*. (Unpublished). New York: PS 153 Maspeth Elementary School.

———. (2014). *Thoughts on the process of creativity*. Rockville Centre, NY: Molloy College.

Sasken, H. (2014). *Neuroscience and creativity*. (Unpublished). New York: Lincoln Hospital Pathology Dept.

———. (2014). *Creative cognition, neuroplasticity, and the IBR: A scientist's perspective*. (Unpublished). New York: Lincoln Hospital Pathology Dept.

Schiering, M. (1974). *A comparison of teacher made educational games and traditional reading methods in visual perception, visual discrimination, reading achievements and reading attitudes among slow primary students*. (Published master's thesis). New Rochelle, NY: College of New Rochelle.

———. (1976). *One classroom/life rule: No put downs . . . Only lift ups!* Poetry by Schiering. (Self-published). Stony Point, NY: Farley Middle School.

———. (1995; 1998). *The interactive book report and our interactive earth day book*. Stony Point, NY: Stony Point Elementary School.

———. (1996). *Ecosystems, now there's a niche for you*. Queens, NY: St. John's University Press.

Schiering, M. R. (2014). *Reflections on the creative process: A composer's viewpoint*. (Unpublished). New York.

———. (2015). Qualities of a leader. In LinkedIn *"Princess bride" leadership lessons*. Retrieved from https://www.linkedin.com/pulse/20141014115549-3569415--princess-bride-leadership-lessons.

Schiering, M. S. (1999). *Reciprocal thinking phases: Cognition and metacognition*. (Doctoral dissertation). New York: St. John's University.

———. (2000–present). Course syllabi for *Integrated ELA and reading* (EDU.506A) and *Interdisciplinary methods for the diverse learner in the inclusion classroom* (EDU.504). Rockville Centre, NY: Molloy College.

———. (2000). Reciprocal thinking identification chart. In Molloy College course syllabi (ed.). *Integrated reading and language arts for the diverse learner in the inclusion classroom* (EDU.506A). Curriculum. Course. Rockville Centre, NY: Molloy College.

———. (2002) Pedagogy: A matter of sharing one's experiential past for today's Learning. *Academic Exchange Quarterly , 6*(1), 27–31.

———. (2003a). *Rubric for the interactive book report: Nancy*. New York: Molloy College.

———. (2003b). The cognitive collective paradigm: The "how" and "who" of teaching and learning. In Raynor and Armstrong et al. (eds.), *Bridging theory and practice*. ELSIN 8th International European Learning Styles Conference. Hull, England: ELSIN.

———. (2009, Winter). Character development and the brain. *Brain World: Humanity's new frontier magazine*, 2(1), 28–29, 68–69. New York: IBREA Foundation.

———. (2010, Autumn). The mind always grows. *Brain World: Humanity's new frontier magazine, 1(2)*, 32–33. New York: IBREA Foundation

———. (2012). Creative cognition. *Brain World: Humanity's new frontier magazine, 3*, 40–43. New York: IBREA Foundation.

———. (2013, July). *The interactive book report: Playing the pages*. Orlando, FL: 7th International multi-conference on society, cybernetics and informatics (IMSCI).

———. (2014, Summer). The brain on ecosystems and sustainability. *Brain World: Humanity's new frontier magazine*, 5(4), 56–59. Arizona: IBREA Foundation.

Schiering, M. S. A. (1999). *The effects of learning-style instructional resources on fifth-grade suburban-student's metacognition, achievement, attitudes, and ability to teach themselves.* (EdD dissertation, 190). (Order No. 9948389). New York: St. John's University. Retrieved from http://phdtree.org/pdf/25228004-the-effects-of-learning-style-instructional-resources-on-fifth-grade-suburban-students-metacognition-achievement-attitudes-and-ability-to-tea/.

Schiering, M., & Bogner, D. (2007). *Conversations on the definitions of thoughts, ideas, opinions, judgments and feelings*. (Unpublished). Rockville Centre, NY: Molloy College.

Schiering, M., Bogner, D., & Buli-Holmberg, J. (2011). *Teaching and learning: A model for academic and social cognition*. Lanham, MD: Rowman and Littlefield.

Schiering, M., & Byrne, J. (2013). *Conversations on the linear process of creativity*. (Unpublished). Denver, CO.

Schiering, M., & Marino. A. (2014). *The content and design of the Reciprocal Creative Cognition Process*. (Unpublished). Rockville Centre, New York.

Schiering, M., & Taylor. R. (1998). In R. Dunn (ed.), *Practical approaches to individualizing staff development for adults: Chapter 14*. Westport, CT: Praeger Publications.

Schiering, R. M. (2014, Fall). *Thoughts on artistic creativity: A personal accounting*. (Unpublished). New York.

Schon, D. (1997). *Reflective practice and professional development*. ERIC Digest. Retrieved from http://eric.ed.gov/.

Scott, G., Leritz, L. E., & Mumford, M. D. (2004). The effectiveness of creativity training: A quantitative review. *Creativity Research Journal, 16*(4), 31–38. Oklahoma: Lawrence Erlbaum Associates.

Schwartz, J., & Begley, S. (2003). *The mind and the brain: Neuroplasticity and the power of mental force*. New York: Regan Books/Harper Collins.

Skalaban, J. (2014, Summer). *Thoughts on the process of creativity: A personal accounting*. (Unpublished). North Carolina.

Staiger, D. (2012, November 13). *Casual Fridays: (Creativity)*. Retrieved from www.thepeoplebrand.com Casual Fridays—the Blog home of Dustin Staiger on the Peoplebrand.com/blog.

Staiger, D. (2012, November 13). Maximizing team creativity and results. [Web log message]. Retrieved from http://thepeoplebrand.com/blog/category/creativity/page/2/.

Storer, D. (2000–2015). *Creativity is our birthright*. Blog: Retrieved from, www.creativityportal.com/bc/cca/creativity-is-your-birthright.html.

Thompson, C. (2007). *What a great idea 2.0*. New York: Sterling.

Tobias, S., & Everson, H. T. (1995, April). *Development and validation of an objective measure of metacognition appropriate for group administration*. Paper presented at a symposium on "Issues in Metacognitive Research and Assessment," at the annual convention of the American Educational Research Association, San Francisco, CA.

Tomlinson, C. A. (2000). *Differentiation of instruction in the elementary grades*. ERIC Digest. Retrieved from http://files.eric.ed.gov/fulltext/ED443572.pdf.

Toscano, D. (2014, Spring). *Reflections about creativity and the interactive book report method and book*. Based on 2013 EDU.506A: *Integrated Reading and ELA*. Rockville Centre, NY: Molloy College.

———. (2014a). *Creativity in the classroom for the student learner*. Long Island, NY.

———. (2014b, Fall). *Creativity in the classroom for the teacher*. Rockville Centre, NY: Molloy College.

Vygotsky, L. (1980). *Mind in society: The development of higher psychological processes*. Cambridge, MA: Harvard University Press.

Yamada, Kobi. (2014). *What do you do with an idea?* Seattle, WA: Compendium Inc.

About the Author

Reverend Dr. Marjorie Schiering has devoted her career as an educator to developing learner's creative cognition. Opening individuals to new ideas, modifying their former ones, and emphasizing creativity to exploring one's thinking and feelings has been a mainstay in her teaching. A firm believer in interactive and engaging instructional techniques, she incorporated the Interactive Method (IM) decades ago when beginning her professional endeavors in an inner-city school in Columbus, Ohio. Taking these ideas to North Carolina in the latter part of the 1960s, she then moved to New York and began teaching using educational gaming strategies. It was a few decades later that she invented the Interactive Book Report (IBR) to enhance and have a concrete application of the IM.

She received her bachelor's degree in childhood education from Ohio State University and earned her master's degree in reading from the College of New Rochelle, New York. She wholeheartedly supports the concept of teaching students the way they learn. Her doctoral work was concentrated on developing and identifying what one is thinking with beginning awareness, critical and creative thinking, and metacognition in a social and academic context. Primarily this was done with the use of interactive-instructional resources/educational gaming for developing learners' sense of self-efficacy.

Dr. Schiering has presented extensively and been published on the aforementioned topics as well as aspects of children's literature, character development, brain-based education, and in 2003, she designed a model for academic and social cognition. She is internationally recognized for her innovative approaches to teaching and learning about one's creativity, critical thinking, motivating teachers and students, inspiring learning, and creating a safe classroom where there's a true sense of community. Dr. Schiering is an ordained interfaith minister since 2008 and has volunteered as a chaplain at Westchester Medical Center in Valhalla, New York. She is on the Board of Directors and Advisory Board of the International Brain Education Association (IBREA).

Made in the USA
Middletown, DE
29 August 2018